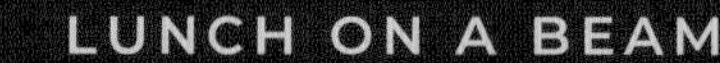
LUNCH ON A BEAM

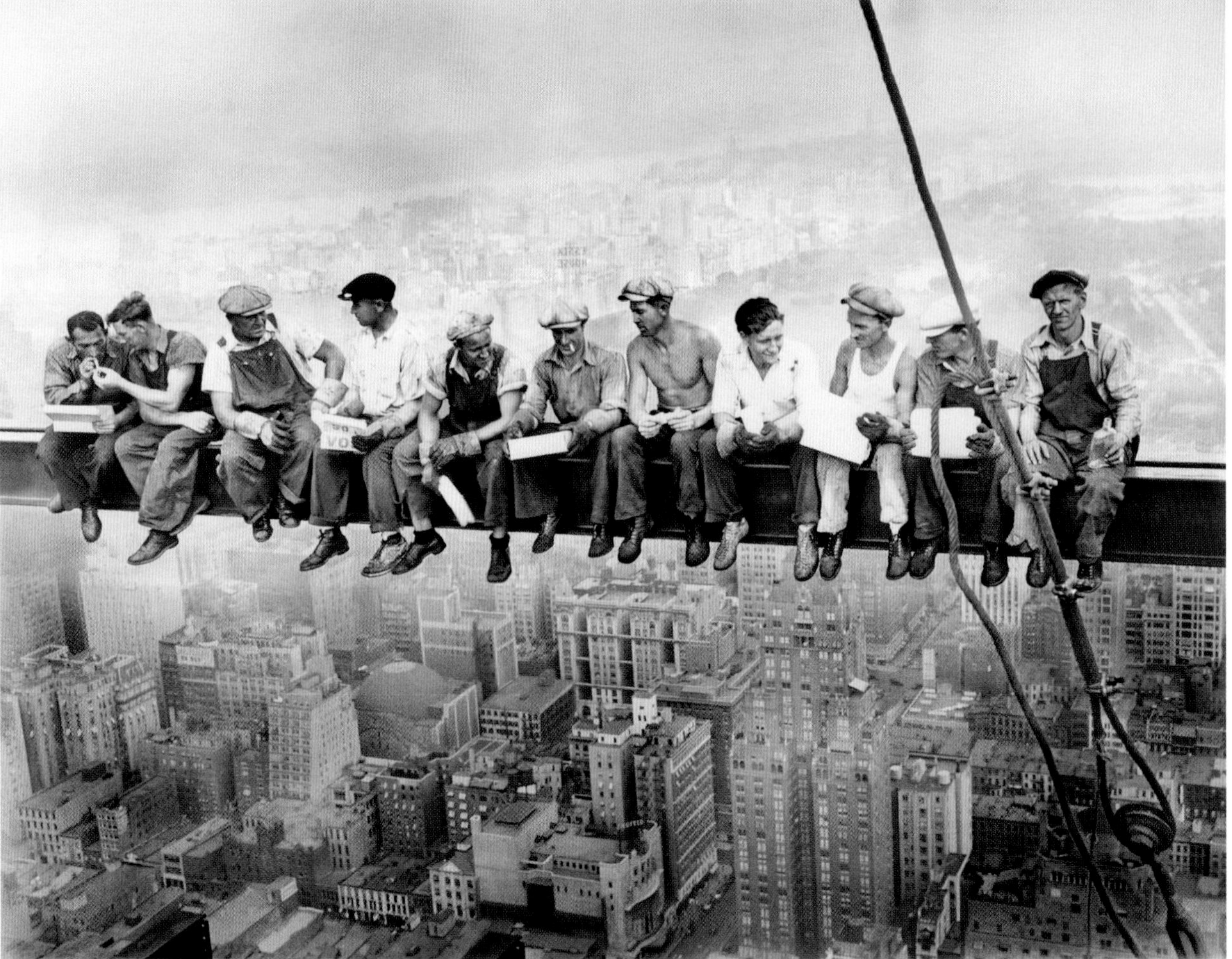

LUNCH ON A BEAM

THE MAKING OF AN AMERICAN PHOTOGRAPH

CHRISTINE ROUSSEL

BRANDEIS UNIVERSITY PRESS

WALTHAM, MASSACHUSETTS

Brandeis University Press
© 2026 by Christine Roussel
All rights reserved
Manufactured in China
Designed and composed in Mercury by Alex Camlin

For permission to reproduce any of the material in this book, contact
Brandeis University Press, 415 South Street, Waltham MA 02453, or visit
brandeisuniversitypress.com

Library of Congress Cataloging-in-Publication Data
available at https://catalog.loc.gov/
cloth   ISBN 978-1-68458-304-1
ebook   ISBN 978-1-68458-305-8

5 4 3 2 1

*For Dianne, my funny, beautiful,
brilliant daughter who started this adventure
with me and finished it in my heart.*

"The ideal article…would be one in which every reader could find his own name. The ideal illustration would be a group photography of all the readers, so that each reader could have the fun of finding himself in the picture."

—Merle Crowell

CONTENTS

One afternoon in 1977, after lunch and a couple of glasses of wine in his private dining room on 54th Street, Nelson Rockefeller invited me to join him on a tour of Rockefeller Center. We opened forbidden doors, explored hidden tunnels, and poked our heads into every corner imaginable. He led me to the eleventh floor of the R.C.A. Building to show me the Gardens of the Nations. finding the door locked, we stood on a desk, and I followed the Vice President of the United States out a window.

It was an exciting moment in what has been, I am fortunate to say, an exciting career. It all started with an itch to keep busy. When I put my third child into kindergarten, I discovered I had time to fill. I felt I *must* find something to do. My education was in fine art, I had trained in Paris under the Russian-French sculptor Ossip Zadkine, and I lived then, as now, two blocks from New York's Metropolitan Museum of Art. So that is where I started.

I told the Met's personnel lady that I'd like to work part time, but I could not work holidays, summer vacations, or when the kids were sick. I didn't expect her response:

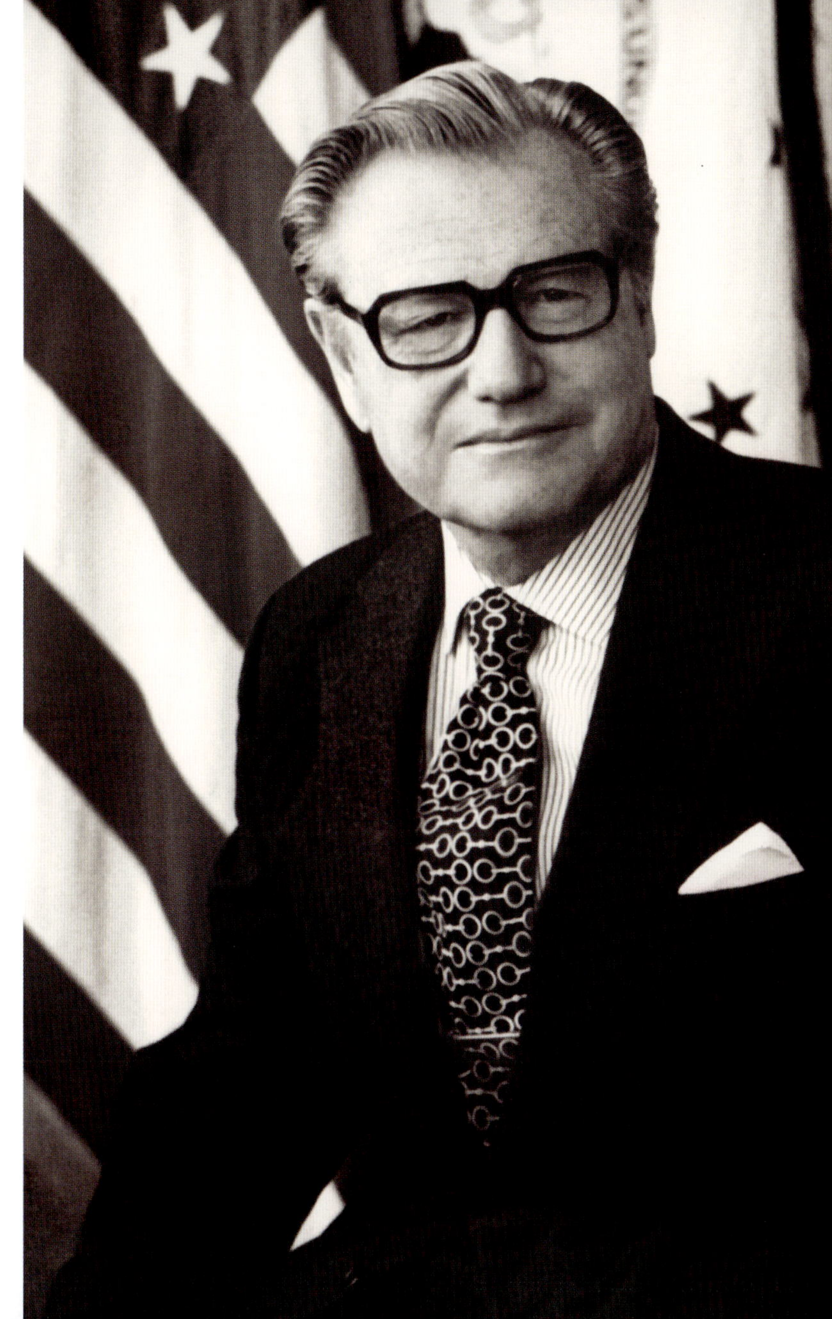

0.1 Vice-president Nelson Rockefeller. (White House Photo)

"I have just the job for you." She said that the Met had recently created a mold-making and reproduction studio. "We could use your skills there." It was perfect. I went to the studio most weekday mornings.

The studio had been conceived in response to Met director Tom Hoving's mandate that the museum expand its gift shop merchandise to increase unattached funds. Benefactors often earmark their gifts for a specific interest, and they get to put their name on the object or gallery such as Medieval, Far East, or European Paintings. It was harder to raise money for housekeeping, utilities, and guards. Who wants to put their name on a mop?

This was also the time when Tom Hoving's father, Walter Hoving, was chairman of Tiffany & Co. The elder Hoving was arrogant and handsome, and he imposed his uncompromising views about society on Tiffany merchandise. He refused to sell diamond rings for men, silver plate, or plastic. His lofty standards—and knack for promoting them—propelled Tiffany from a somewhat fusty legacy brand into a global juggernaut. Tom had worked at Tiffany during school vacations, and the experience had a profound effect. Tom's wheelhouse was the intersection of art, commerce, and public relations.

In 1974, US President Richard Nixon and Egyptian President Anwar El-Sadat signed a bilateral agreement encouraging better relations between the countries. Tucked into the agreement was a clause devoted to culture. The United States would help the Egyptians reconstruct Cairo's opera house, while Egypt would send the "Treasures of Tutankhamun" to the United States. The Met was to run the exhibit as The National Gallery in Washington, DC, was not equipped to handle it. Tom rejoiced and seized the opportunity to enlarge the gift shop merchandise based on the Tutankhamun exhibit. The Tut collection had all the elements of a blockbuster: a young boy-king who died mysteriously, a tomb hidden for centuries, a stunning gold mask, beautiful goddesses, and thousands of treasures never before exhibited outside of Egypt. And Tom had an unusually large budget to make it happen.

Tom sent a team including me to Cairo. After several joyful months of hard work in the Cairo Museum and the Valley of the Kings, we had selected the objects and had drafted a merchandise program that would be expanded by the museum's publications department. I met Anwar El-Sadat. Not physically handsome or imposing, he nonetheless radiated graciousness. Later, while visiting the Met in New York, he suffered an excruciating toothache. Tom arranged an emergency dental visit at Rockefeller Center.

The Tut exhibit opened at The National Gallery in Washington, DC, in 1976 to long lines of people hoping to get in to see the treasures—and buy something at the gift shop. It was an unbelievable success. It smashed all exhibit records as it traveled around the country. And the merchandise reaped wild amounts of income that would help run the museums that held the exhibit. Gleefully rolling in the success of this venture, Tom forged ahead with new exhibits: "Lands of the Scythians," "The Splendor of Dresden," "Treasures of Ireland," and the opening of the permanent exhibit "The Temple of Dendur." By this time, I was Tom's special assistant for international exhibits. I traveled constantly for the museum to develop programs for these exhibitions while balancing my family life.

Then 1977 came and brought more change in my life. Tom quit over a squabble with the museum trustees. He called me and said, "Quit! You're dead meat here—too closely associated with the revolution! Come work with me."

Instead, I started my own business, at first helping museum trustees with their private collections. Raising three children in New York, I decided to expand my world—and my income. Museums do not pay well. Among my first clients was Nelson Rockefeller, who would take me on another whirlwind tour through the intersection of art and commerce. We started a business based on his collection of thirty thousand art objects. It was called "The Rockefeller Collection," and within a year it opened its first store near Tiffany & Co.

This was a heady time. Helicopter trips, days at his estate Pocantico Hills, buying art, introductions to world leaders, and the boyish enthusiasm of Nelson Rockefeller, as he shared his world and his unabashed love of art and Rockefeller Center.

. . .

Which brings us back to the eleventh floor of the R.C.A. Building at Rockefeller Center, following Nelson out the window, and into the Garden of the Nations.

The garden was huge—a half-acre wrapped around three sides of the R.C.A. tower like a living apron. A brook bubbled through a rock garden, past walls, trees, and split-rail fences. Rockefeller exulted in this private world above the city.

As a tour guide, he reveled in his knowledge of the Center, not only its art and architecture but also its elevators, "fastest in the world," air conditioning, and truck garage. Entering it, we followed a winding cobblestone roadway down to the multitude of loading docks deep below the buildings, which "keeps deliveries and trash off the streets." Nelson was as proud of these innovations as he was of the towers soaring above.

I learned that day that Rockefeller Center held more to explore than just its buildings. It is one of the most diverse and exciting urban centers in New York and, odds on, the

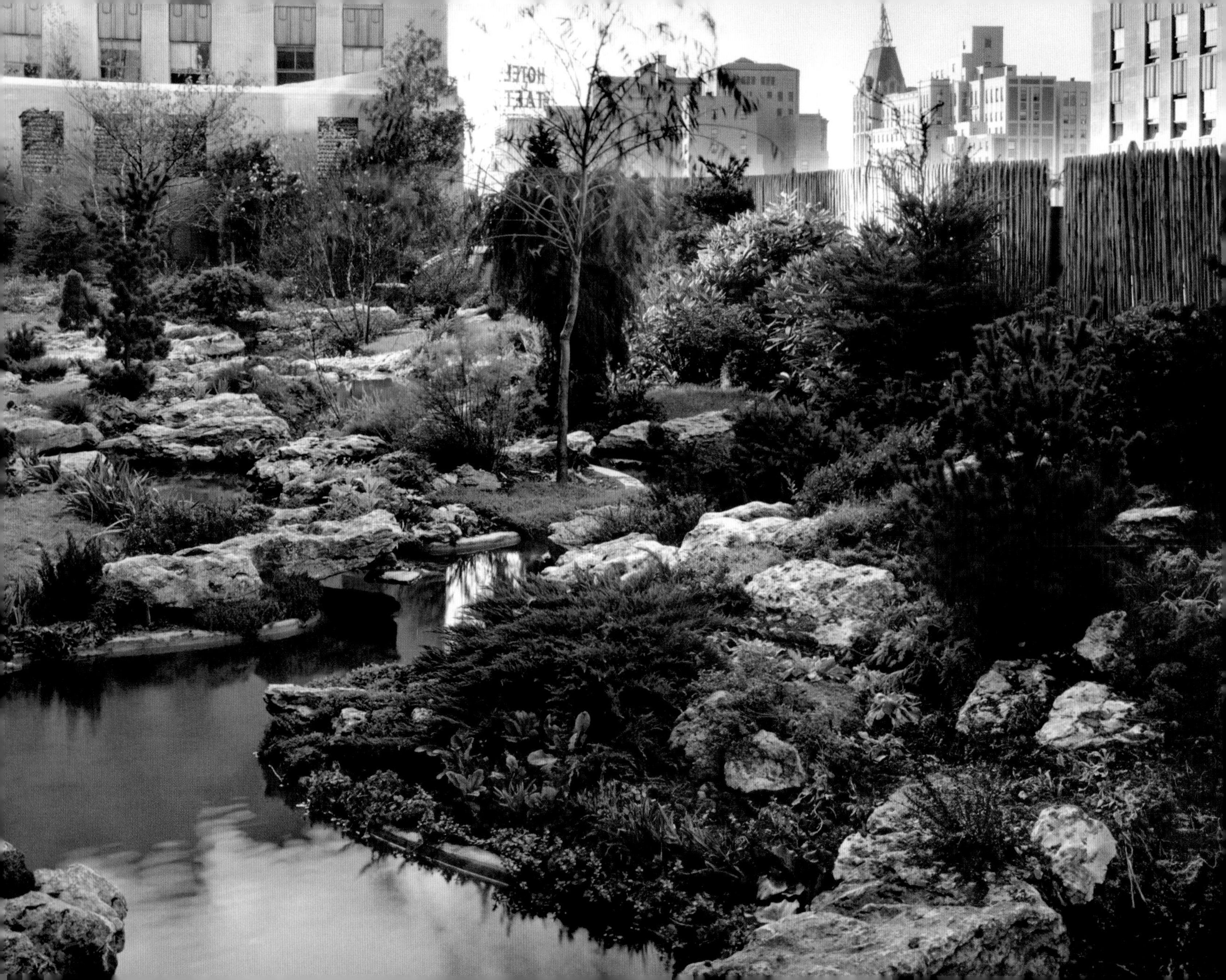

best ever developed. It teems with history. It distills one man's vision of the finest that New York can offer: culture, commerce, and spectacle, confident and cosmopolitan, the engine at the center of the world. Its story tells of both great troubles and great perseverance. A triumph of art and commerce, Rockefeller Center is more than a showplace or a workplace. It's a symbol. A symbol of progress, determination, hope in the face of despair, and American greatness. Nowhere is that more vivid than in "Lunch on a Beam."

Over time, I became intrigued with how the art and commerce of Rockefeller Center fueled each other. I became curious about the men who built it—especially the ironworkers known to the world for lunching on a beam floating above the city.

I had no idea that forty-five years later, I would be the Rockefeller Center archivist and write a book about that iconic photograph.

The names of the eleven men in "Lunch on a Beam" have remained a mystery for ninety years. There have been numerous claims to their identity. Some of these claims are convincing. Others have little but faith. As the archivist of Rockefeller Center, I set out to solve this mystery. My access to the resources at the Archives has provided a unique opportunity to research this book. It has also taken more than seven years, dozens of interviews, and a few lucky discoveries to finally put names to the faces.

The photograph is ubiquitous. It hangs in college dorms and union halls, corner pubs and corner offices. But despite—or because of—such fame, the true story of "Lunch on a Beam" has been shrouded by layers of legend, half-truth, and conjecture. This book peels back those layers to understand "Lunch on a Beam" not only as a historical record, but also as a work of art, a work of commerce, and a work of strategic, impassioned propaganda. At a moment of historical crisis, "Lunch on a Beam" told Americans a story about themselves—fearless, resilient, united—that resonates today.

We look at "Lunch on a Beam" and see ourselves.

ACKNOWLEDGMENTS

Photographs from the Rockefeller Center Archive (RCA photos) are used with permission of Rockefeller Group International, Inc. These photos are preserved on black-and-white negatives, 4 by 5-inch glass plates, and/or 8 by 10-inch prints. The photographer was not usually credited, but any credits are included in the captions. Index numbers were added by the Rockefeller Center's Publicity Department sometime after 1932 and are not always present or strictly chronological. Photos from the Rockefeller Archive Center (RAC) are included with permission, all from the collection John D. Rockefeller Jr. Papers, JDR Jr. Family Photographs, Series 1005, Homes—Seal Harbor 1914–1953. (The Rockefeller Archive Center in Sleepy Hollow, New York, and the Rockefeller Center Archive in New York City are separate entities.)

Family photos are used with permission.

This book would not have been possible without the people who preserved the treasury of photographs, documents, books, and ephemera that make up the Rockefeller Center Archive.

Thank you to Dwayne Doherty of Rockefeller Group, who told me, "It's a story that's waited nearly a century to be told. If not now, when? If not you, who?"; to my agent, Jane Dystel, whose clear-eyed advice guided an idea into a book; to Sue Ramin at Brandeis University Press, who saw its potential; to Ashley Burns, Ally Findley, Jim Schley, and the production team, who saw everything else and improved it; to Tami Ebbets, Thomas Kelley Jr., and William Leftwich Jr., whose patience and generosity helped me understand their fathers, the photographers Charles Ebbets, Thomas Kelley, and William Leftwich; to the men and women of the Kahnawake community, including Lynn Beauvais, Lisa Montour, Sandi Goodleaf, Reaghan Tarbell, Scott Berwick, Amanda Diabo, Chris Jocks, and especially the late Bill Sears, a unique voice and proud ironworker who enriched this book as he enriched many lives; to all the other people who shared family stories and photos, including Steven Elling, Brian

McClain, Christina Silla, Darlene Pearson Castillo, Scott Janowitz, Gene Breheny, Ruth Pedersen Smith, Quinn Newton, Glenn LaPietra, George and Carol Urbanneck; to EB Kelly, an early reader and steady hand at the helm of Rockefeller Center; to Anil Khachane, Jordan Sandridge, and William Shen, who are a pleasure to work with; to Jim Rasenberger, who let me pick his brain and whose book, *High Steel,* is essential reading to understand iron-workers in New York; to Carol Krinsky, a brilliant his-torian of architecture and incisive early reader; to Dan Okrent, whose friendship and advice is my great for-tune; to Devorah Romanek, curator extraordinaire; to Ken Johnson and Clint Saunders, for their expert eyes; to Éamonn and Seán Ó Cualáin, filmmakers who shared my curiosity; to Harold Flynn and Carol Ann Lake, who extended my search to Nova Scotia; to Barbara Pitynska, whose strength and friendship is immeasurable; to Bobby Spinna, who made order from my chaos; to Robert Walsh of Local 40, an early reader and invaluable source; to Tom Hoving, who gave me the opportunity of a lifetime; and to Nelson Rockefeller, who did it again.

And thank you, with all my heart, to my family, for their love, support, and belief in me and this book. You are simply the best: Arnold, Elizabeth, Marc-Christian, Helen, Jean-Luc, Harry, Annabelle, and Olivia. My brilliant nephew Alan Leo played a special role in the creation of this book, and I am eternally grateful.

A note about Dick Parsons, who died in 2024: An early reader and friend since the days we both worked for Nelson, Dick encouraged me to explore the ineq-uities just outside the frame, which led to the chapter "Not Pictured."

Abbreviations are noted in the text, but two coincidences bear explanation: first, The Radio Corporation of America is abbreviated R.C.A., and its namesake building at 30 Rockefeller Plaza was the R.C.A. Building. The Rockefeller Center Archive is abbreviated RCA, and photographs from the archive are identified as "RCA photo," with an index number (if provided by the archive) and the photographer's name, if known. The Rockefeller Center Archive, which occupies a small office suite in Rockefeller Center, is distinct from the vast Rockefeller Archive Center in Sleepy Hollow, New York.

LUNCH ON A BEAM

THE MAKING OF AN AMERICAN PHOTOGRAPH

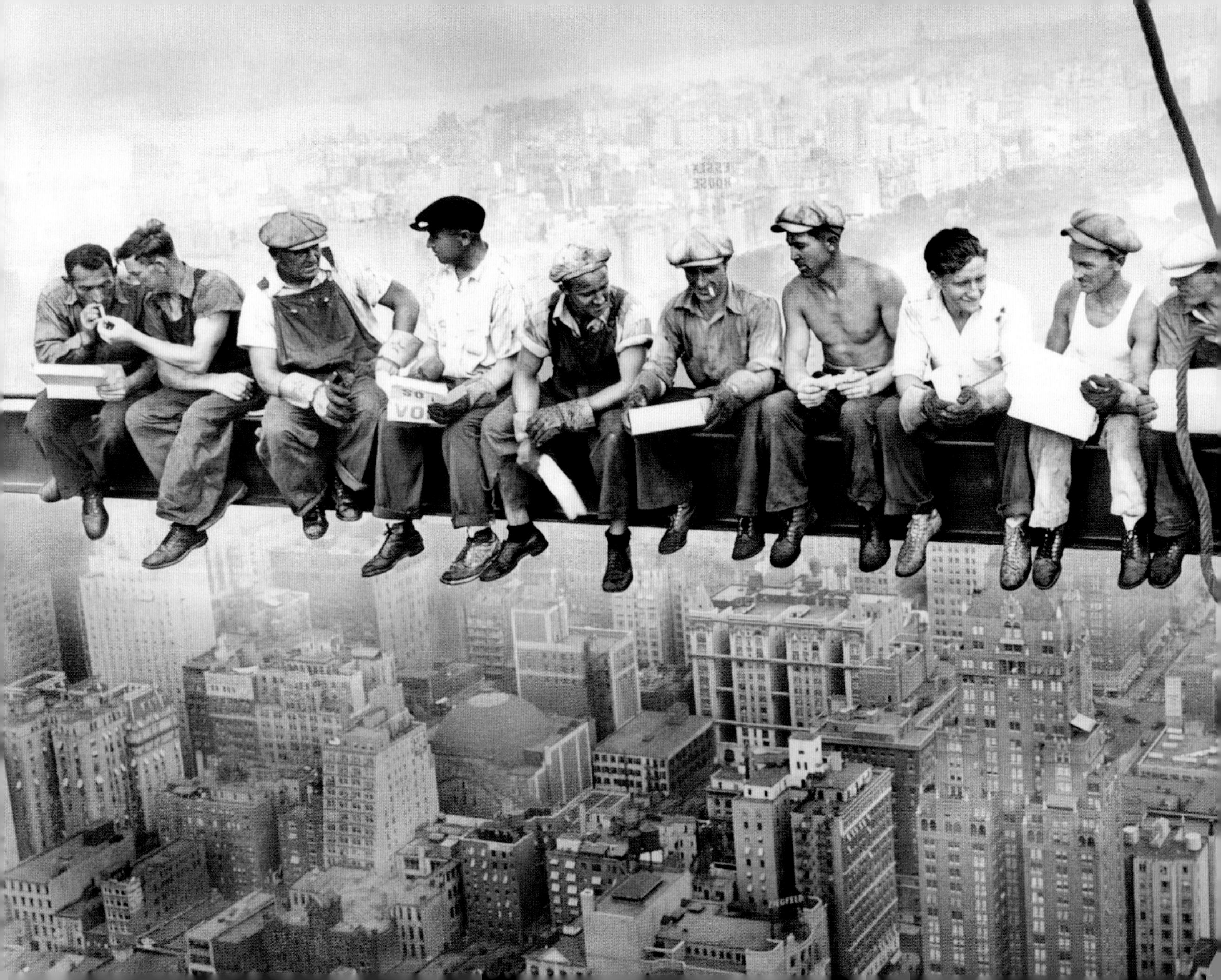

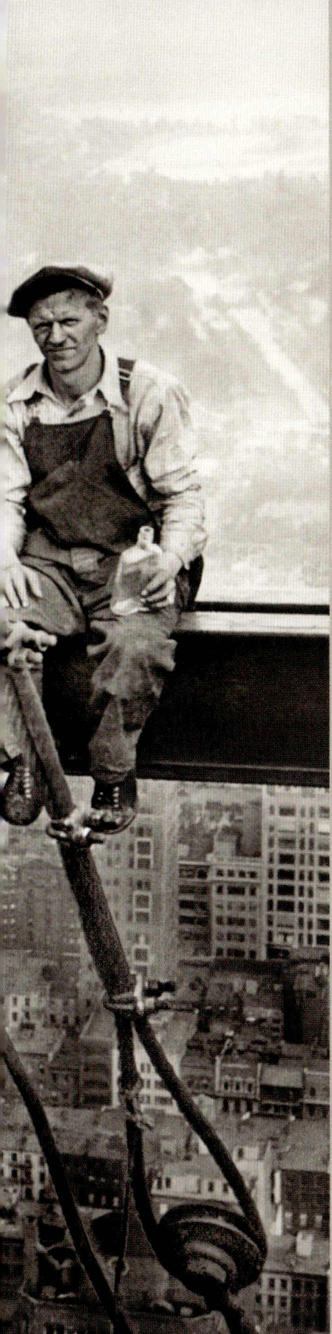

THEY WERE BETTER OFF THAN MOST

1.1 Lunch on a Beam. (Rockefeller Group photo 110)

ON SEPTEMBER 20, 1932, eleven ironworkers sat shoulder-to-shoulder on an I-beam, chatting over cigarettes and sandwiches. These few ironworkers made an ordinary lunch break extraordinary as the beam appeared unattached, floating 840 feet above New York City, transcending gravity.

Those eleven men have been renowned and unknown since the image was published on October 2, 1932, in the Sunday supplement of the *New York Herald Tribune*. The caption read "Builders of the City Enjoy Luncheon. Steel workers during the noon hour on a girder of the R.C.A. Building eight hundred feet above Rockefeller Center. The last steel for the structure has been raised."

Today, the photo is known as "Lunch on a Beam" or "Men on a Beam" and is among the most recognized and reproduced documentary photographs ever. This fleeting moment in 1932 became universally iconic, symbolizing strength and unity in the face of adversity and fear.

The *Herald Tribune* did not identify the men. They were simply eleven typical ironworkers. Their names were not essential. The image conveyed a universal message: the ordinary man can be extraordinary.

Times have changed, and people ask me, as the archivist of Rockefeller Center, who they were and what compelled them to risk their lives sitting on a beam high above the city streets. I hoped by researching and following the few clues that remain, I could answer their questions and complete the picture with the names of these anonymous men who, nearly a century ago, helped build Rockefeller Center, girder by girder.

Rockefeller Center Archive's collection of photos and documents from the 1930s was the essential source for the men's names. In the 1930s, the Publicity Department hired photographers on a day-to-day basis to document the construction of the Center, but did not annotate most of the images with workers' names. This meant my search would continue through union halls, libraries, museums, private archives, public appeals, the internet, magazines, newspapers, and interviews with ironworkers and descendants of ironworkers.

Those interviews shed new light on some names and their lives in the 1930s in New York. Many ironworker families shared their stories; some said they "knew" their man was sitting on that beam. Their beliefs may stem from the fame of the image. It may be family lore. It might be true.

After the passage of nine decades, proof was hard to come by. I interviewed many ironworker families and compared family documents and photos with other records. Sometimes, I found, memories fade. Records are lost. Generations die out. Family stories are forgotten or embellished.

What stood out is: Desire is a strong motivator for conviction.

Nevertheless, these interviews were invaluable. Family members related poignant accounts of life in the Roaring Twenties. They described new challenges and opportunities for their families—especially in New York City. America was speeding toward prosperity and social change. For the first time, more Americans lived in cities than rural areas, creating a building boom and jobs for the unprecedented number of immigrants arriving in New York.

This era brought about social change, technological wonder, and engineering advances to a burgeoning middle class. Telephones, movies, radios, cars, washing machines, and refrigerators were just becoming part of mainstream American life. Cities were cultural melting pots, and economic growth seemed limitless. Steel suspension bridges reached across great rivers, and structural steel skyscrapers like the Empire State Building and the Chrysler Building soared into New York's sky.

And then the crash.

On Thursday, October 24, 1929, the stock market began its collapse, sending America and the rest of the industrialized world spiraling downward into the Great Depression.[1] Half of all banks failed, unemployment rose to 25 percent, and many became homeless, plummeting people into unparalleled misery. Families were upended; immigrants' American dreams went up in smoke.

"Those were bleak times," said Michael Breheny, one of the scores of descendants of New York ironworkers who shared their family stories with me. Many of them told me that the decade it took to construct Rockefeller Center saved their families from devastation during the Great Depression. "At least they were putting bread on the table," Breheny said. "They were better off than most."[2]

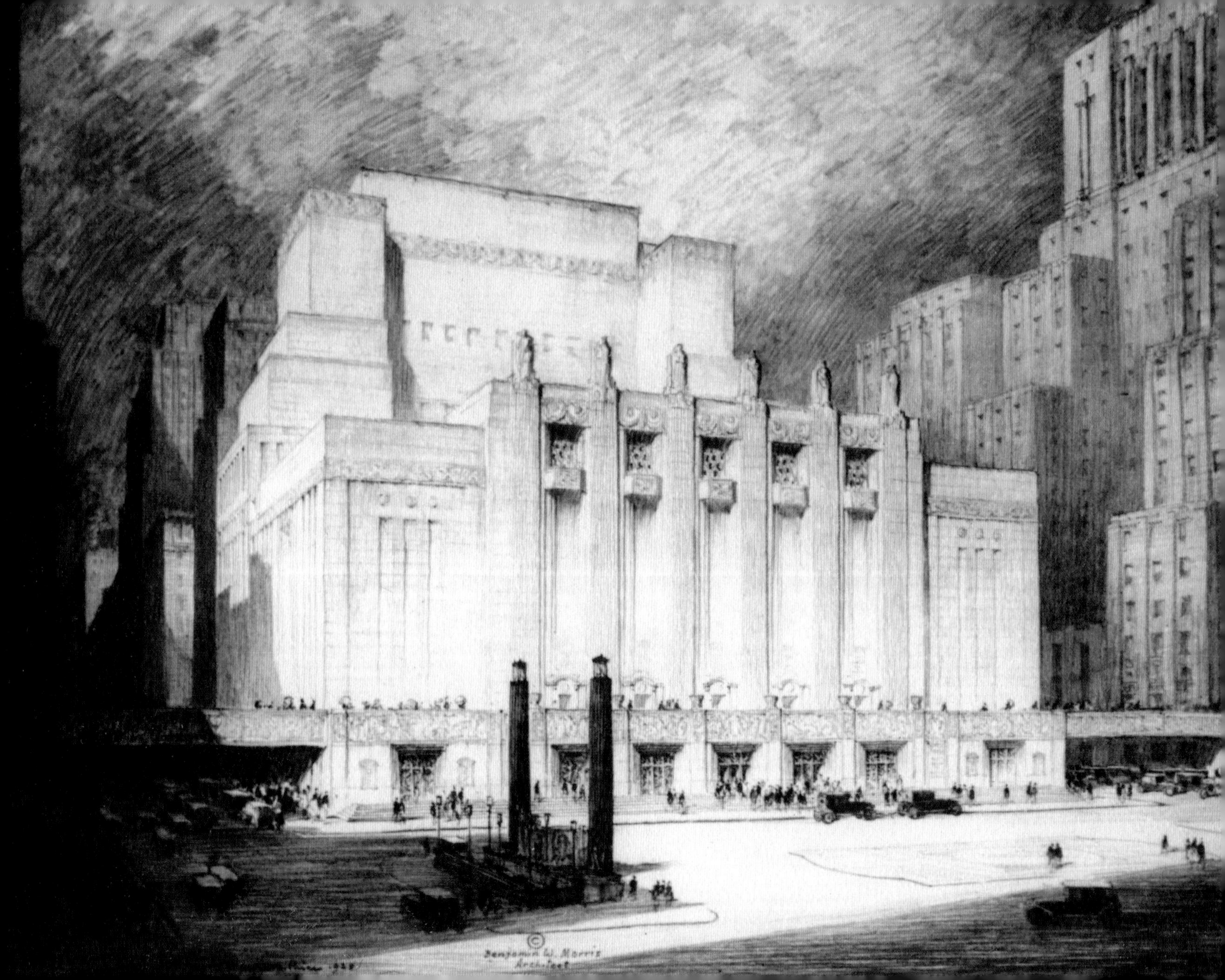

Benjamin W. Morris
Architect

2

THE GENESIS OF ROCKEFELLER CENTER

2.1 Rendering of the E. B. Morris Opera House. (Rockefeller Group photo)

JOHN D. ROCKEFELLER JR. was the heir to America's greatest fortune, and he gave most of it away. His philanthropic causes included health, education, and culture. However, he may be best remembered for a construction venture: the creation of Rockefeller Center, the first private urban complex in New York City.

He hadn't planned to build it alone.

In 1928, John D. Rockefeller Jr., known within the family as Junior, or Mr. Junior to most subordinates, joined a syndicate of wealthy New Yorkers led by Otto Kahn, president and chairman of the Metropolitan Opera, who intended to create a cultural center anchored by an opera house and supported by adjoining commercial buildings.

The cream of New York society had built the original opera house on West Thirty-Ninth Street and Broadway in 1885. By 1928, the area had seen better days. "Not only was the Opera house too small, but it was badly planned. It was possible to sit in a seat for which one paid a handsome price without benefit of the view of the stage."[1] What's more, the neighborhood had evolved into a commercial district. While the theater had excellent acoustics and an elegant, gilded interior, the exterior was famously ugly for its industrial facade; it was nicknamed "The Yellow Brick Brewery." The Opera Company was the property of its original box holders, New York's

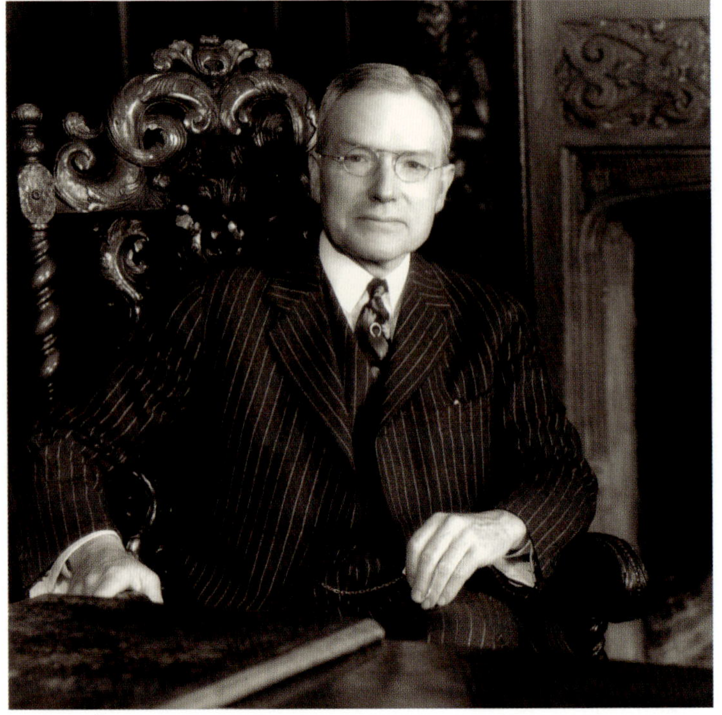

2.2 John D. Rockefeller, Jr. (Rockefeller Group photo)

prominent Gilded Age families, including the Astor, Vanderbilt, and Whitney. They retained the coveted boxes in the Diamond Horseshoe year after year, preventing new millionaires from buying the best seats. This was a challenge to these titans of industry who thought a move could solve that situation.[2]

   2.3 The Upper Estate, looking northwest from Sixth Ave and 51 Street in 1931. (Rockefeller Group photo 541A)

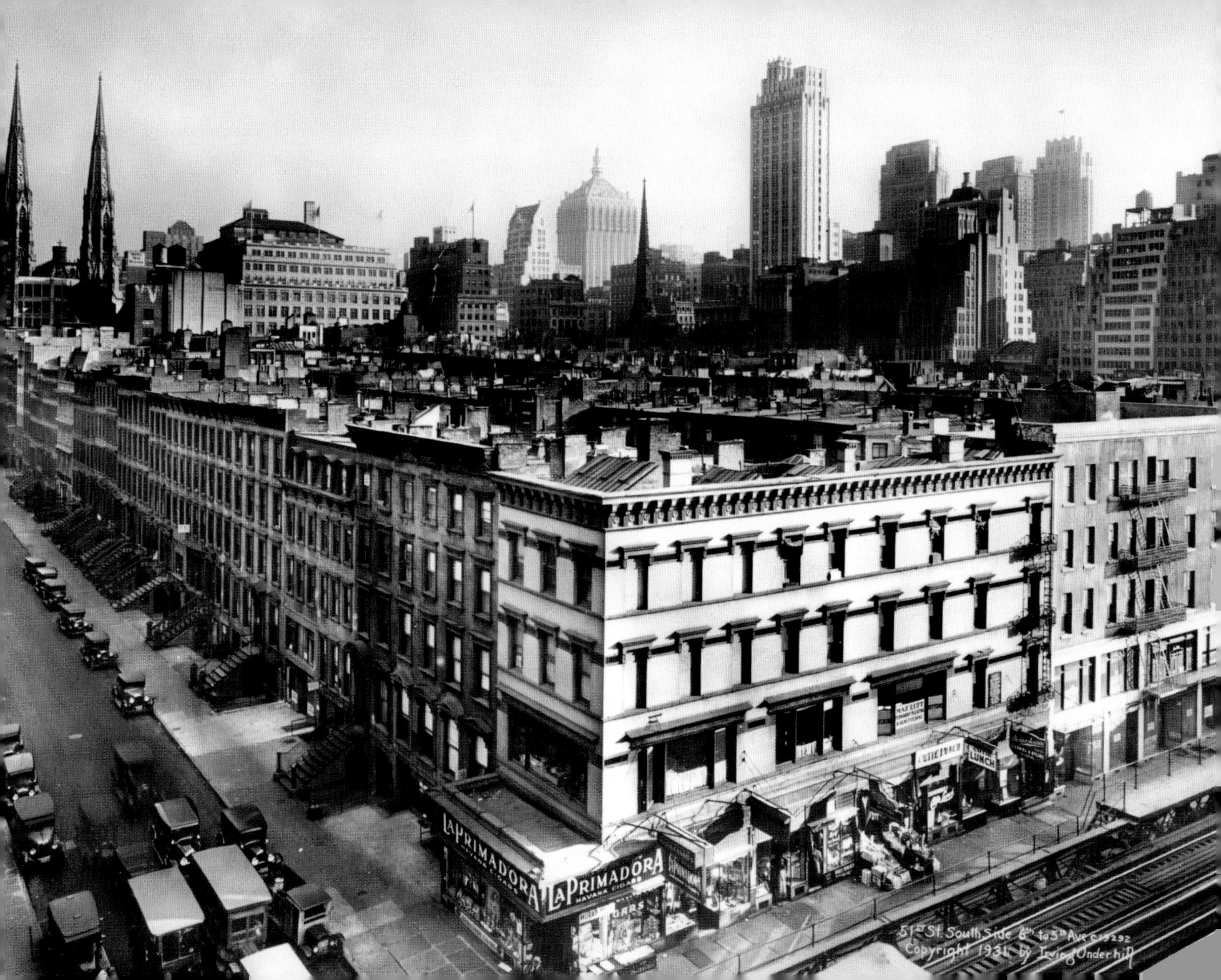

LA PRIMADORA
LA PRIMADORA
HAVANA CIGARS
LUNCH
51st St. South Side 6th to 5th Ave C-5292
Copyright 1931 by Irving Underhill

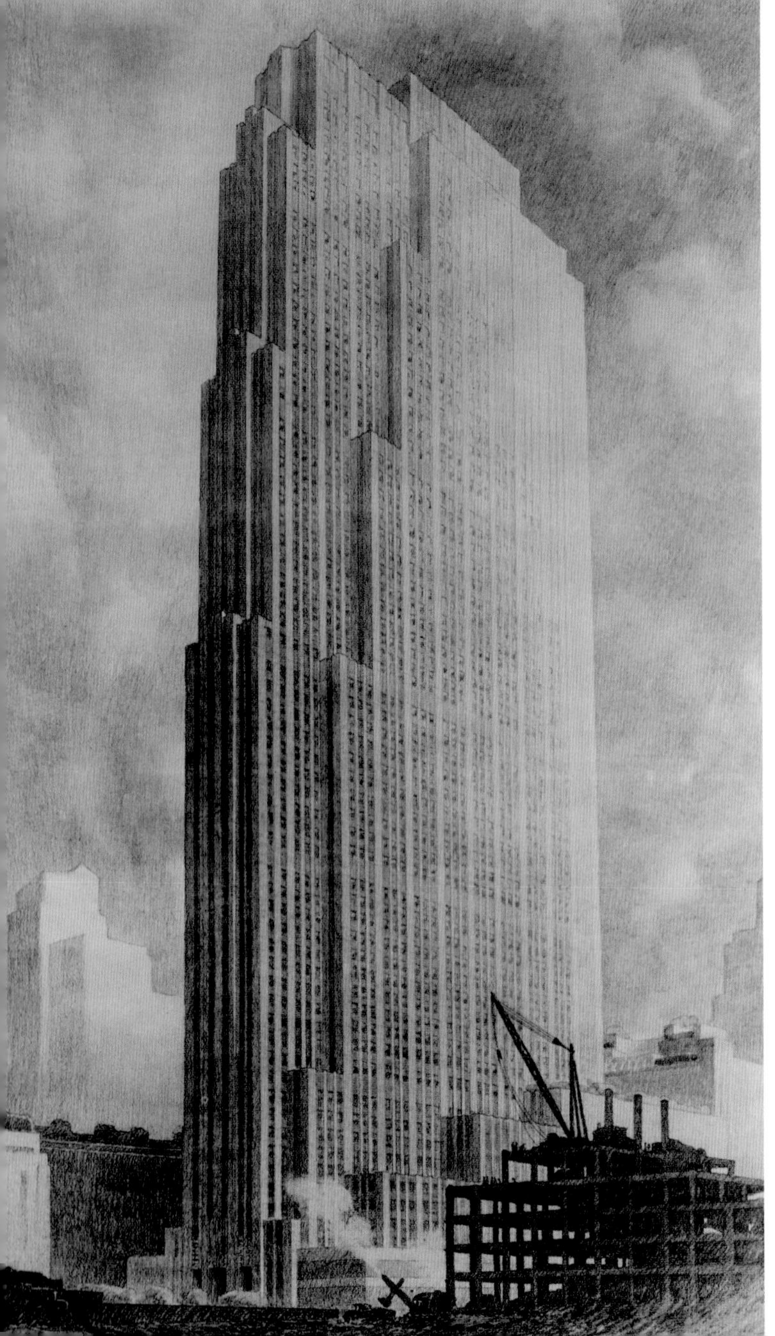

After examining numerous options for a new opera house, the syndicate settled on the area between Forty-Eighth and Fifty-First Streets from Fifth to Sixth Avenues. Columbia University owned the tract and referred to it as the "Upper Estate." Unused by the school for decades, this property had become a sprawling slum with the Sixth Avenue elevated train rattling nearby.

Columbia had decided it wanted an area more suitable for a university, as this one was too expensive to maintain or improve. It was so seedy that the university was in an awkward position as a landlord. The need to rehabilitate the area was evident. About five thousand low-rent tenants were housed in dreary, run-down brownstones and boarding houses, surrounded by small shops, numerous speakeasies, dance halls, brothels, and a gambling joint run by the notorious underworld boss Arnold Rothstein, better known as "The Brain." The nearby elevated train contributed to noise, dirt, and gloom.

By 1928, the university determined it would not develop the land, and needed money to add to its new campus in Morningside Heights. Junior signed a twenty-four-year lease for the land of the Upper Estate. He agreed to pay $3,800,000 annually to Columbia University. He would collect barely $300,000 in rent from the five thousand tenants. Junior intended to tear down the tenements building

2.4 Rendering by John Wenrich of a proposed design in 1931. (Rockefeller Group photo)

by building to make way for the new opera center. At this time, "Rockefeller Center" was not under consideration.

To Junior and the other barons of industry—including Kahn, William K. Vanderbilt, R. Fulton Cutting, and J. P. Morgan—the site seemed ideal. They envisioned building the world's most valuable shopping center to support the opera and be a civic virtue. They would call this vast new urban center of culture and commerce "Metropolitan Square." To manage the project, the group named Colonel Arthur Woods, Junior's trusted adviser who also led the development of Colonial Williamsburg.[3]

Junior acquired other properties on Forty-Eighth Street, including the Dutch Reformed Church and privately held homes near Fifth Avenue, to create a nearly perfect twelve-acre rectangle. Purchases were made in stealth to avoid tipping sellers that their buyer, the wealthiest man in the world, was purchasing property. Junior's agents used front companies. "Underel" reflected the property's proximity to the elevated train.

What could go wrong?

The syndicate's plans moved along smoothly until October 24, 1929, Black Thursday, when the Stock Market crashed, beginning ten years of the Great Depression.[4]

Within weeks, Junior's partners in Metropolitan Square retreated with what was left of their money. Newspapers reported that "the project for locating the new opera house . . . has been abandoned."[5]

Junior was nonplussed and a little embarrassed as he had spearheaded financing the project. "There were only two courses open to me," he later wrote. "One was to abandon the entire development. The other is to go forward with it in the definite knowledge that I myself would have to build it and finance it alone, without the immense impetus that the new opera house would have given, and with no escape from the fact that under the changed conditions it would be necessary to improve all the land in order to lease it, thus involving immense capital outlays never contemplated. I chose the latter course."[6]

The Center would consume Junior for a decade and cost more than a hundred million dollars during the Great Depression.[7] He stuck it out as only he could.

Junior relied on the shrewd real estate developer John R. Todd to assemble a team. Todd, the Princeton-educated son of a Presbyterian minister, had pursued a law career before turning to real estate with his brother, James, and a college friend, Hugh Robertson. Together they founded

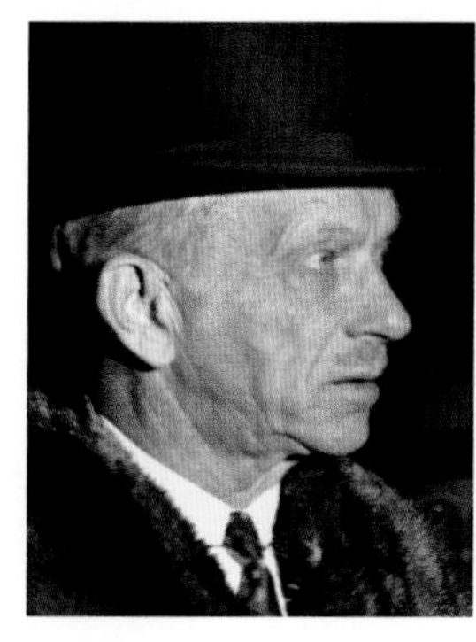

2.5 John Todd. (Rockefeller Group photo)

Todd, Robertson and Todd Engineering Corporation. At the time, in 1929, the firm was already at work on Colonial Williamsburg, another Rockefeller endeavor.

Until Rockefeller Center, the restoration of Colonial Williamsburg had been Junior's consuming project. His principal aide, Col. Arthur Woods, and his legal and real estate advisors, Mr. Thomas M. Debevoise[8] and Mr. Charles O. Heydt, accompanied him to Williamsburg in 1928 to assess the feasibility of reconstructing the capital of the Virginia Colony as it stood in the eighteenth century. At the end of that visit, Junior provided fifty-six million dollars to do so, and to fund related projects to educate visitors about the era. Hundreds of nineteenth- and twentieth-century buildings were removed from the restored area, and many former buildings and gardens were reconstructed on their original sites.[9]

For Todd, securing Junior's next big project was a *coup d'audace*. In the late summer of 1929, he wooed Junior at the Rockefeller family's Maine estate, the Eyrie, in Seal Harbor on Mount Desert Island. The island was a retreat for America's wealthiest families: not only the Rockefellers but also Astors, Carnegies, Fords, Morgans, and Vanderbilts.

Junior's 107-room "cottage" was impressive even to Todd, a Princeton man, well traveled and familiar with New York's elite. Todd, in turn, impressed Junior with his acuity and confidence as Junior's handsome black horses pulled their carriage through the fifty-seven miles of private trails below towering pines and above the rocky coast. For three days and two nights, Todd regaled Junior with stories of extraordinary horses (he had led the National Horse Show Association) and his successful complex construction projects. He was a forceful speaker and seduced Junior thoroughly. His timing, confidence, and poise secured the deal.

Despite Junior's many philanthropic endeavors, he kept a tight rein on his business expenditures. Yet, in three short days, Todd had wrangled operating control over the entire Opera project as the principal builder and managing agent. On October 1, 1929, a contract was signed. He got a quarter-million-dollar annual fee, a one-third share of the profits, and a five-million-dollar investment in another of his projects. But Junior made the final decisions, knowing how to delegate without relinquishing control.

Todd's leap over the usual chain of command irritated many of Junior's advisers. But not Charles O. Heydt, a real-estate man who had begun his career with the Rockefellers as a young stenographer in 1897—the same year Junior graduated college and joined the family firm. In his early years with the Rockefellers, C. O. established

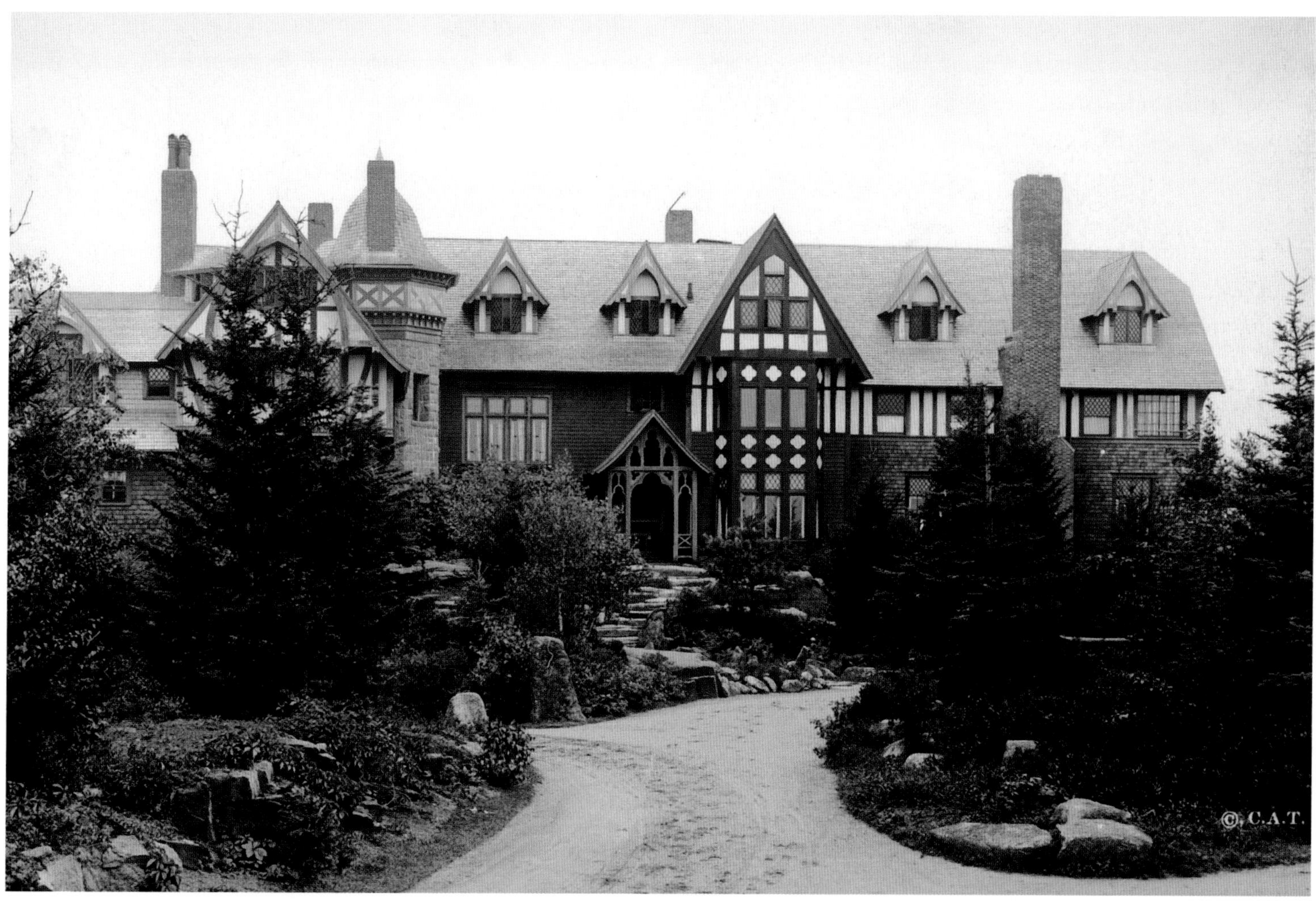

2.6 The Eyrie, the Rockefeller family retreat in Seal Harbor on Mt. Desert Island, Maine. Photo courtesy of the Rockefeller Archive Center.

himself as a trusted factotum of Rockefeller Sr. and served as confidential secretary to Senior and his wife. By 1905, Heydt had become Junior's personal secretary. As Junior's confidant, Heydt enjoyed a special relationship with the family, but always remembered his role as an employee.

As the opera plan's financial prospects soured, Heydt shrewdly guided Junior through the minefield of negotiations, and supported the withdrawal of the opera company.

Heydt believed in Todd and accompanied him to the pivotal meeting with Junior on Mount Desert Island. He assured Junior that Todd was a "hard-headed business man"[10] who "has never made a failure of any of his undertakings."[11] Heydt then used his power of persuasion to win most of the other advisers over to Todd. The rest had no choice. Junior had decided.

Todd "was a blunt and arrogant (if brilliant) egomaniac," wrote Daniel Okrent in his dazzling history of Rockefeller Center.[12] Life, Todd said, consisted of four things: "selling, romance, dog fights, and horse trades."[13] With that in mind, Todd built with ruthless practicality for nearly a decade. His firm was in charge of everything: design, construction, promotion, and management. Todd himself controlled every aspect of the venture. Junior liked it that way, as he was inclined to push responsibilities on others; success was his bottom line.

By September 1929, before any contracts had been signed, Todd was determined to discard the idea of an opera house. Todd foresaw in it a financial burden, not a moneymaker, as it would be closed for more than half the year. Benjamin Wistar Morris, the Opera group's architect, had a poor relationship with Todd. He left graciously with a five-thousand-dollar kill fee in his pocket, and Todd lined up a new team, enlisting a diverse group of distinguished architects from several firms. They included Harvey Corbett, Raymond Hood, Wallace Harrison, and two architects from Todd's firm, Andrew Reinhard and Henry Hofmeister, as well as a bevy of younger architects and draftsmen. Together, they would operate as the "Associated Architects."

They were a mixed lot in experience, personality, and vision. Hood and Corbett consulted on architectural style and the grouping of buildings across the twelve-acre site. Reinhard and Hofmeister designed the floor plans for the complex; as the rental, or tenant, architects, they were known as the most pragmatic of the group. These five men—Hood, Corbett, Harrison, Reinhard, and Hofmeister—were generally considered the principal architects.

Raymond Hood, a graduate of the École des Beaux-Arts and considered the most brilliant and creative on the team, was the lead architect until he died at fifty-four in

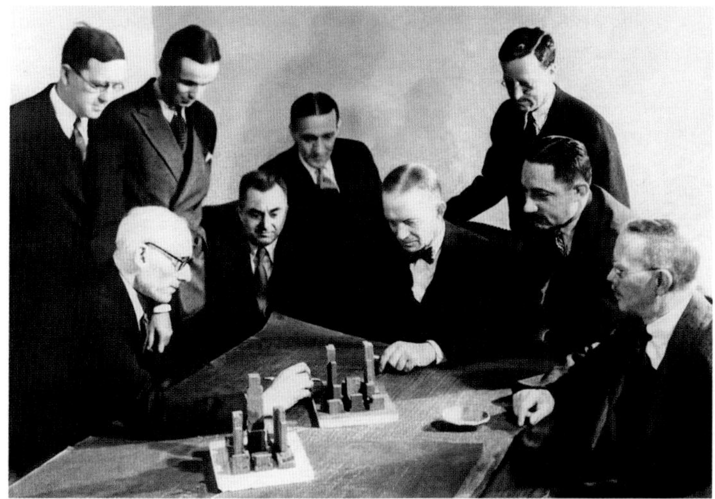

2.7 Developers and architects: seated, from left, Harvey Wiley Corbett, Raymond M. Hood, John R. Todd, L. Andrew Reinhard, James M. Todd; standing, Joseph O. Brown, Webster B. Todd, Henry Hofmeister, and Hugh S. Robertson. (Rockefeller Group photo)

1934. André Fouilhoux and Wally Harrison then became the principal architects. Harrison was connected to the Rockefellers by marriage—his wife's brother married Junior's daughter, Abigail.[14] A formidable architect whose projects spanned many decades, Harrison would continue to work with the Rockefellers, his tall, angular frame striding the Center until he died in 1981.[15]

The architects were lucky to be working and knew it, agreeing to compromises that would not have been acceptable before the Depression. "They had little or no contact with John D. Rockefeller, Jr.," Alan Balfour, the architectural historian, wrote. "They dealt with Todd, Robertson, Todd. And from the beginning, John Todd had shown little interest in aesthetic speculation."[16] Todd's attitude toward most architects was contempt, and he drove a hard bargain: While the industry standard for architects was 6 percent of construction costs, Todd insisted on just 4 percent—plus "some extras."[17] Opportunities for creating an enterprise of this importance are rarely presented to any architect. The architects grumbled, but the Great Depression was no time to bicker.[18] By 1934, six out of seven American architects were unemployed.

Todd held all the cards.

In a memorandum, Todd, who had no strong or even admirable architectural convictions, but many opinions, admonished them: "This square will be based on [a] commercial center as beautiful as possible and consistent with the maximum income that could be developed."[19] The Opera was forgotten.

The architects Hood and Corbett suggested many plans, some that were eccentric by the standards of any time. This entailed the construction of a massive pyramid spanning all three blocks; this was later downsized to a small retail pyramid, which evolved into a three-story oval retail bank building. This oval-shaped retail building was to dominate the center space on Fifth Avenue and serve as a center for banking. "It was at this very building that the critics hurled their sharpest and mightiest thunderbolts,"[20] wrote Winston Weisman, the architectural historian. The press called it "the oil can." The architects denied that the criticism had any influence and insisted the oil can was scrapped only because the bank plan fell apart.[21]

The architects worked feverishly to satisfy Todd's demands. Renderers Hugh Ferris and John Wenrich translated each new idea into beautiful drawings. Both men were renowned. Ferris was known for dramatic, atmospheric drawings, characterized by striking, even impossible, perspectives and contrasts. The effect was otherworldly. John Wenrich did most of the renderings for the Center's architects. His drawings in pencil and watercolor are a brilliant mix of mood and information. The renderings breathed life into the architects' imaginative ideas.

Sculptor Rene Chambellan, who had worked with Hood for the Chicago Tribune Tower, modeled the proposed buildings in clay. Hood liked malleable clay models, which could quickly be reconfigured. Later, Chambellan would sculpt the leaping bronze fish in the Channel Gardens. Dozens of renderings and clay models were proposed and discarded before the project was presented to the public.

Slowly the architects' plans were evolving. A new plan was released in January 1930, and revisions continued until March 1931, when the current site design was unveiled. Architecture-by-committee could have led to mediocrity but didn't, thanks to the team's most influential architect, Raymond Hood.

"That the R.C.A. Building was not just another skyscraper is proven by comparison with the other towers on the island," Weisman wrote. "Their shape, best exemplified by the Empire State Building . . . is that of a column with a square floor plan, tapering to a point at the top. How different is the slab-like form of the R.C.A. Building." To explain the R.C.A. Building's long, narrow footprint, Weisman quoted Hood.

In the central tower building, we have worked out a scheme which is likely to have an important bearing on all future commercial office buildings. Grouped in the center are the elevators and the service facilities, and surrounding them on each floor, we have sketched the twenty-seven feet of lighted space that experience has proven is the maximum to be allowed to provide adequate light and air to all parts of the building. This method of designing office space accounts for the slab-like shape. . . . The taller the building, the greater must be the facilities. Ergo, the longer the building becomes.[22]

Weisman speculates that given the length of the plot, the R.C.A. (Radio Corporation of America) Building could have gone up to four hundred and fifty stories. Why stop at sixty-six? Above that, construction costs would have exceeded expected rental returns.[23]

Hood entered the project with a reputation for dramatic skyscrapers. In 1922, he and a partner, John Mead Howells, beat out several of the world's leading architects, including Walter Gropius and Eliel Saarinen, to win publisher Robert McCormick's contest to design "the most beautiful building in the world" as headquarters for the *Chicago Tribune.*

> Todd admired Hood for his ideas, once conceding that Raymond Hood would always come to meetings all fired up with ideas, perhaps twenty, of which nineteen would be all wet, but there was always a good one.[24]

Hood's ideas were evolving. The 1925 Gothic style of his Tribune Tower gave way to modernism in his design for the 1930 Daily News Building. It was among the first large buildings in NYC to fuse a modern design within the aesthetic

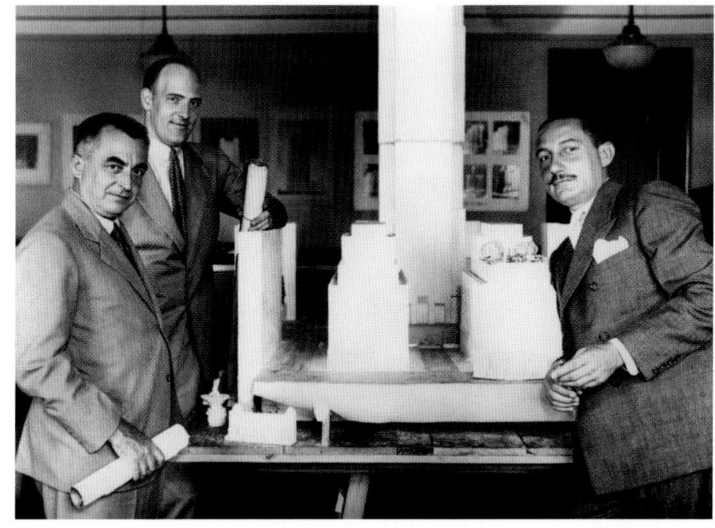

2.8 Architects Hood, Harrison, and Reinhard with the final plaster model. (Rockefeller Group photo 156)

movement of Art Deco; modern architecture reflected the function of the building rather than its ornamentation. Hood applied these ideas to the architecture of Rockefeller Center.

Hood established the Center's basic plan with three essential elements: light, air, and transportation. He believed that the most effective urban design was the axial plan, promoted by his alma mater, the École des Beaux-Arts. The axial plan arranged streets or walkways flanked by harmonious structures to lead to a clearly defined focal point: in this case, the R.C.A. Building.

The plan proved to be brilliant.

After the architects presented Todd and Junior with dozens of models and renderings, the final model was unveiled to the press on March 5, 1931. The complex's design had many detractors, which Junior had the fortitude to ignore.

He told Harrison that during the Ludlow strike (see chapter 3) he had learned that "I should avoid reading about the things that would be too painful to read."[25]

In some cases, the reviews were brutal. "Radio City is ugly," snarled the *New York Herald Tribune*. It was jeered at by influential architectural critics like Lewis Mumford, who declared that it followed "the canons of Cloudcuckooland." He wrote that "the whole effect of the Center is mediocrity—seen through a magnifying glass" and "every touch of ornament is bad with an almost juvenile badness."[26]

Even Emily Post, the doyenne of etiquette, was moved to the brink of discourtesy: "As one to whom architecture is the highest of the arts,[27] I cannot refrain from expressing my disappointment in the architects' plans for Radio City," she wrote to the editor of the *New York Herald Tribune*. "I feel that Mr. Rockefeller should in some way be apprised of the protests that one hears on every hand—protests from every class and from every walk of life—protests against what is coming to be known as the 'architectural crime of the century.'"[28]

Eventually, Rockefeller Center won over even Mumford, who pronounced it "a serene eyeful" and "the most exciting mass of buildings in the city."

Time has improved its reputation further still. "Rockefeller Center was not designed by a genius working alone but by a committee of architects working as a consortium," wrote the *New York Times* architectural critic Paul Goldberger on the occasion of the Center's fiftieth anniversary in 1982. "It is one of the only times in history that a committee has created a truly great work of art."[29]

Todd organized his firm into various departments on separate floors of the Graybar Building, which he owned. These departments included architecture, finance, legal, renting, and publicity. This judicious separation made it easy for Todd to monitor each division's progress. The groups reported to him or his younger partner, Hugh Robertson.

A subsidiary corporation oversaw construction. Todd's son Webster and Joseph O. Brown separated from Todd, Robertson and Todd to form Todd and Brown. The new business, which shared offices with its (literal) parent company in the Graybar Building, would negotiate contracts and tend to the complexities of getting the buildings constructed

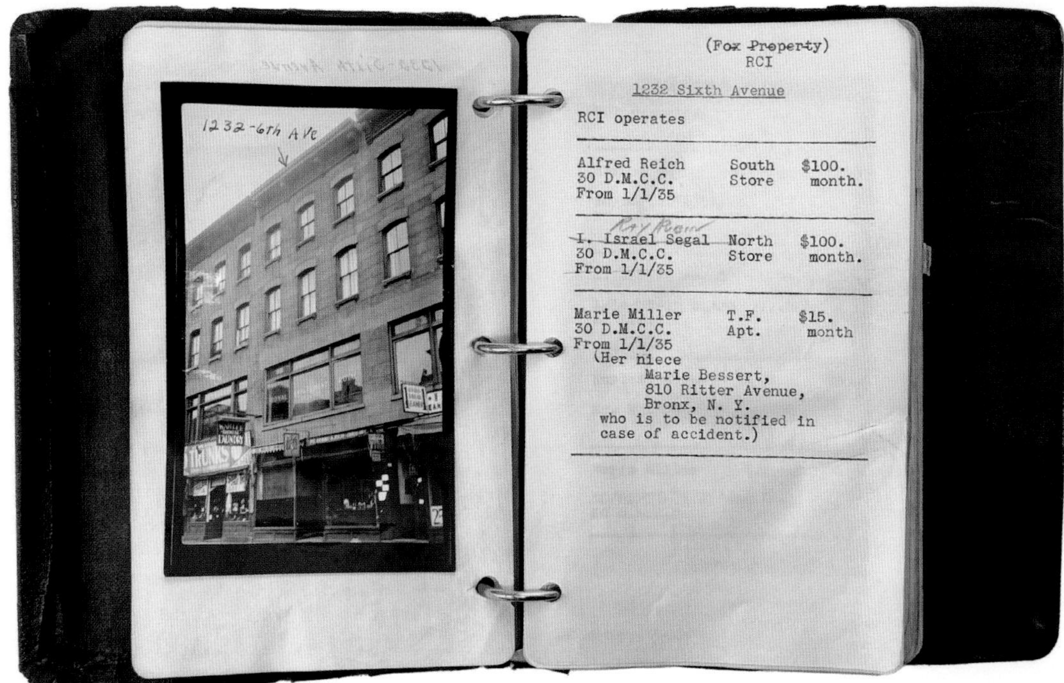

2.9 Agent's book. (CR photo)

and functioning. Todd and Brown were two sides of a coin: Web Todd was the good guy with a mild, agreeable disposition. Joseph Brown was the hard-nosed, tough guy who seemed to enjoy making contractors sweat.[30]

Over the next decade, Todd and Brown oversaw the construction of fourteen buildings, requiring the destruction of 225 brownstones and the relocation of five thousand tenants. "A number of separate and unrelated purchasing agents set out to acquire the properties piecemeal."[31] They were assigned to each block to track the location and availability of every apartment or store. Each building was photographed, and the owners were identified. The agents carefully noted tenants' names, duration of leases, and rents in small black loose-leaf binders. As leases ended, tenants had to relocate themselves immediately.

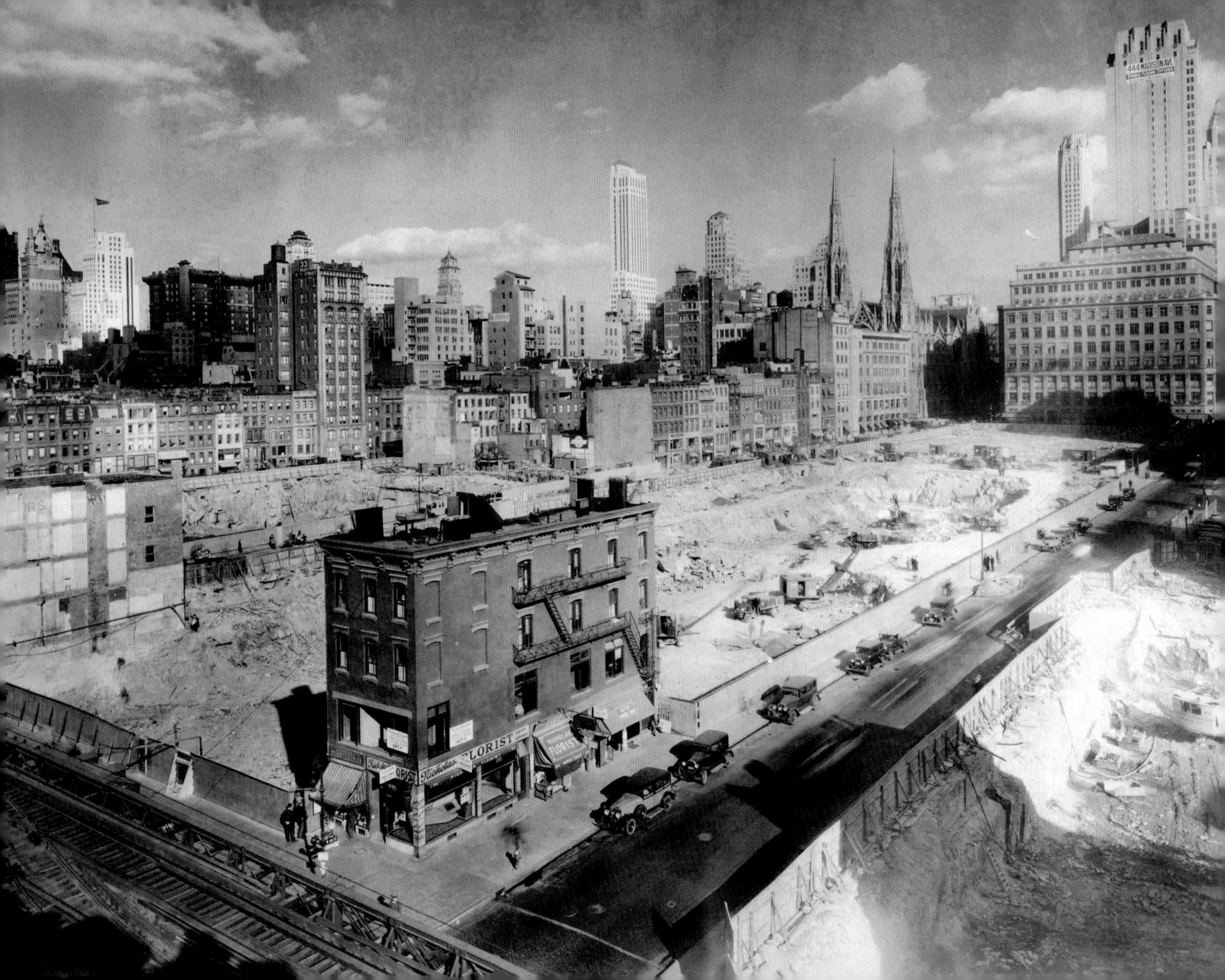
444 MADISON AVE
FLORIST
FLORIST
Nicholas
33 STREET

Displacement was well planned and well organized. Bargaining with and unrelenting grinding down of the hold-outs was done brownstone by brownstone. It was vital to obtain the land quickly, assemble the site, and begin construction. Delays would mean a loss of future profits. I imagine the thought dismayed Junior.

Today, only two holdouts remain, nineteenth-century walk-ups on either side of 30 Rockefeller Plaza on Sixth Avenue. To the north, on the corner of Fiftieth, was a grocer. To the south, on the corner of Forty-Ninth Street, was a florist and a speakeasy, whose proprietors—the Hurley brothers—refused to give up their lease. They held out for decades, declaring, "I've seen sonofabitchin' Rockefellers come and sonofabitchin' Rockefellers go and no sonofabitchin' Rockefeller's gonna tear down my bar."[32] And no Rockefeller did, even after acquiring the property in 1975.[33]

In the spring of 1930, the Albert A. Volk Company began demolishing the old buildings, and unemployed men flocked to the site trolling for work. It was the only place construction work might be available. By this time, publicly financed projects like the George Washington Bridge were nearing completion, and private sector construction had shuddered to a halt. It would be five lean years until President Franklin D. Roosevelt asked Congress to appropriate 4.8 billion dollars for New Deal Programs to put the unemployed back to work.

2.10 The last two holdouts (far left and center) at the site cleared for the R.C.A. Building, January 20, 1932. (Rockefeller Group photo)

It is payday, Thursday, December 24, 1931, as a bedraggled band of demolition workers shuffle toward the pay clerk standing beside an upended crate to hand each man his pay. Just six months into the job, workers with the George Atwell Foundation Corporation celebrated Christmas by erecting a twenty-foot-high balsam fir in the rubble on Fifth Avenue between Forty-Ninth and Fiftieth Street.

This photo never reached the fame of "Lunch on a Beam," but it has become a poignant symbol: a cluster of dirty, tired workers gathers near a fir tree in a dirt lot awaiting payday on Christmas Eve. The men's names were

2.11 The first Rockefeller Center Christmas tree. A brochure directed viewers to "note the contented expression of the formerly unemployed." (Rockefeller Group photo 466 by Maurey Garber)

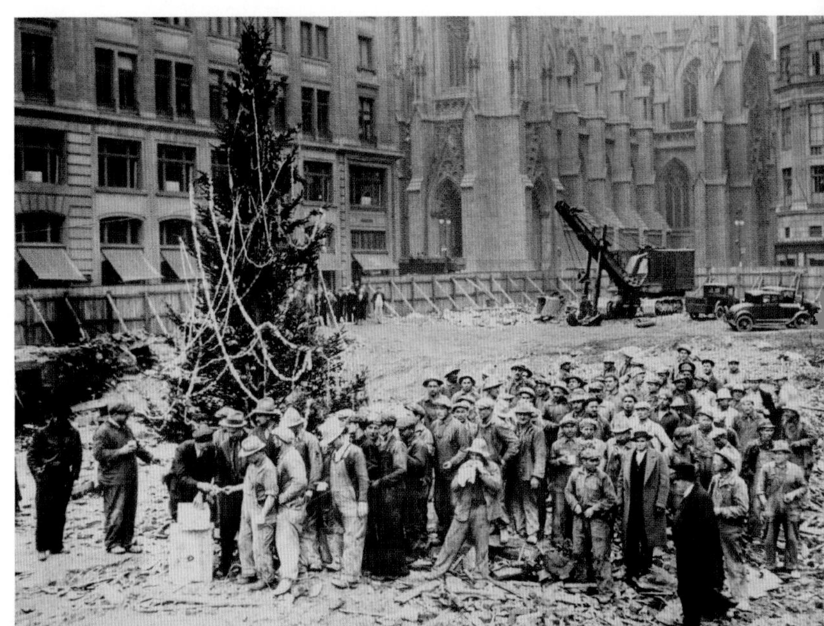

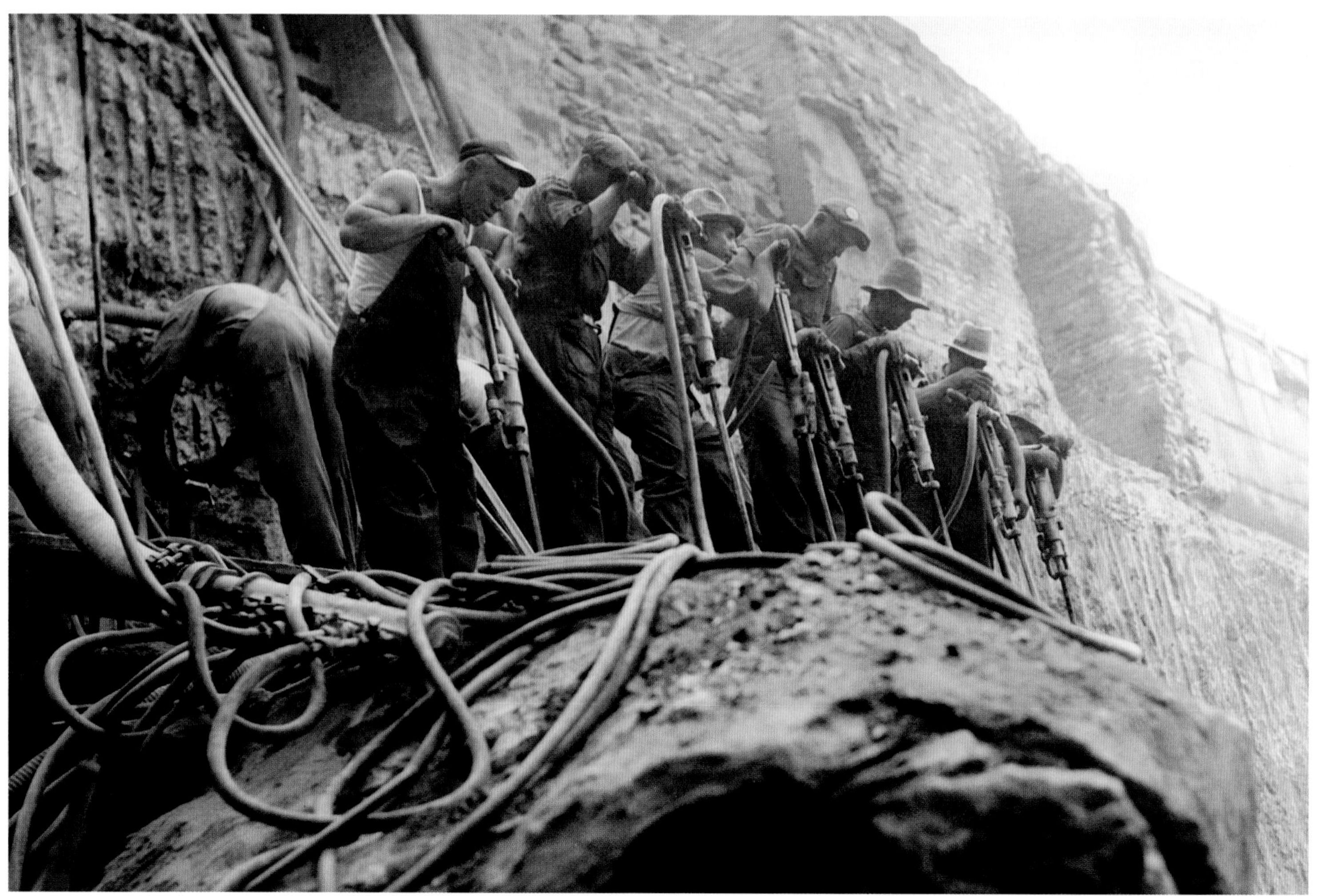

2.12 August 2, 1932: Excavators drill into bedrock to lay the foundation of Rockefeller Center. (Rockefeller Group photo 51)

not recorded by the photographer or any public relations department. Over time a few families have slowly begun to patch together the story of the first Christmas tree. Their search parallels the quest to acknowledge the men in "Lunch on a Beam"; both recognize the unsung many who created Rockefeller Center.

Steven Elling told me the employee who provided the tree was his grandfather, Cesidio Perruzza, who brought it from his property in New Jersey.[34] Others say the workers bought it on a street corner. Perruzza, the blasting foreman, told his children that the workers decorated the tree with garlands of popcorn and cranberries, as well as foil, tin cans, and blasting caps from the worksite. Elling, a New York artist who has doggedly researched that first Christmas tree, said his grandfather was one of at least three men in the photo from the village of San Donato Val di Comino, in central Italy. Perruzza settled near Prospect Park, a Brooklyn neighborhood then dotted with ethnic Italian enclaves.

The builders' publicity machine pounced on the photograph. An Atwell Company brochure urged readers to "note the contented expression of the formerly unemployed." Rockefeller's PR men would sell the same story, with a great deal more finesse. Two years and six buildings later, the project's irrepressible director of public relations, Merle Crowell, would embellish this idea with an annual tree lighting spectacle, now a hallmark of Christmas in Rockefeller Center and New York City, sealing the image of these scruffy workers with their balsam fir as an icon of fortitude.

For Junior and Todd, the upside of the Depression was a glut of workers, building materials, and desperate contractors. In New York, a city of about seven million, three-quarters of a million workers were unemployed. 64 percent of the city's construction workers were unemployed. Half gave up their union membership.[35]

Many families were barely surviving.

Steady, reliable work was hard—nearly impossible—to find. "The jobs available in 1931 were small and very scarce," recalled Harold McClain, an ironworker in the 1930s. "Some weeks, the job worked two days, and some of it was three; to stretch the work over a longer period and keep men off the street."[36] While his brother Jerome was one of the fortunate men hired on, Harold counted himself among the idle "sidewalk supervisors."

The "Sidewalk Superintendents' Club" was formalized several years later, after Junior paused near the truck entrance to look at construction and a guard told him, "Move on, buddy." Soon, a covered viewing platform was set up on the east side of the construction pit so the public could view the construction. It was so successful that membership cards were issued.

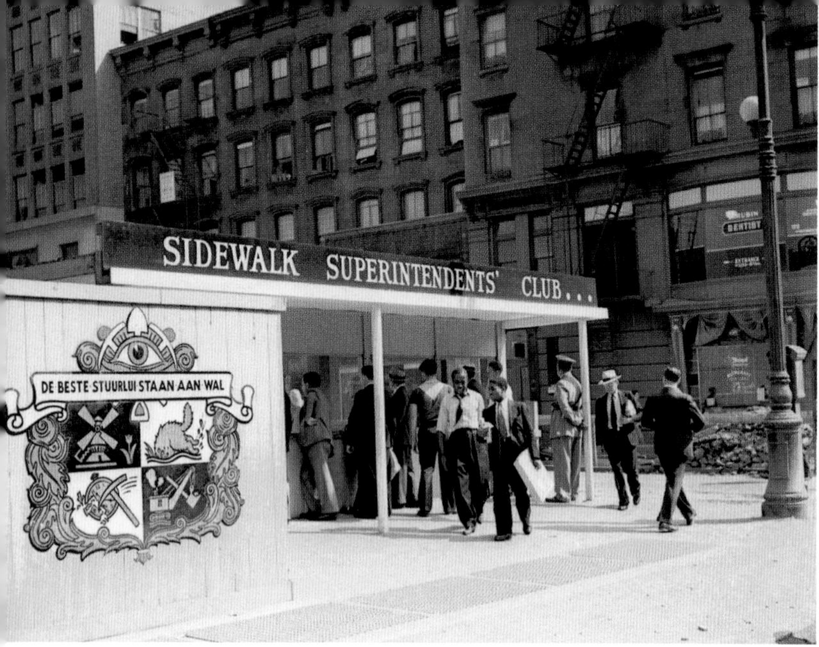

2.13 The Sidewalk Superintendent's Club. (Rockefeller Group photo 772B)

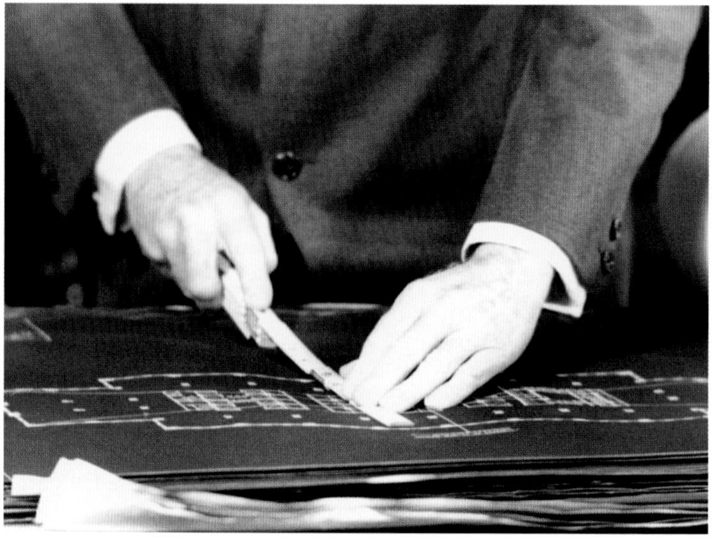

2.14 John D. Rockefeller Jr. poses with his folding ruler. (Rockefeller Group photo)

Junior had always been interested in construction and restoration. His friend and biographer Raymond Fosdick described him as "living knee-deep in blueprints."[37] His projects could be found at Versailles and the Reims Cathedral in France, the Cloisters in New York, and Colonial Williamsburg in Virginia. Rockefeller Center became the capstone of all his building projects. Tellingly, he kept a four-foot folding ruler in his back pocket and seemed to relish verifying designs. It was his happy place.

Rockefeller's project brought dependable construction jobs that would last until the end of the decade and contracts for contractors and suppliers desperate for business. The bidding process was ferocious and highly controlled by Joseph Brown of Todd and Brown. With his inflexible one-time-bidding scheme, he could wring every drop of blood out of major corporations. There was no second chance.

The entire development would showcase modern design and technology, both to attract tenants and to point the world toward Rockefeller's vision of enlightened capitalism. High-speed elevators could travel upward at 1,200 feet per minute by 1931 and 1,400 per minute by the time the R.C.A. Building opened. The elevator doors also featured the first "electric eye" safety mechanism. Cooled air circulated through the theaters, underground areas, the French and English Buildings, and the western section of the R.C.A. Building.

One early name for Rockefeller Center, "Radio City," reflected the importance of the National Broadcasting Company's early commitment to the development, as "the coming together of Metropolitan Square and the Radio Corporation of America"—two fledgling corporations—"was an event of almost divine fortune."[38]

Architect Raymond Hood had designed studios for the National Broadcasting Company at 711 Fifth Avenue and proposed that Rockefeller's project would be the perfect fit for NBC's parent company, the Radio Corporation of America. With its two networks, and its Radio Keith Orpheum (R.K.O.) movie and theater operations, R.C.A. was looking for modern facilities and prime office space. R.C.A.'s president, David Sarnoff, agreed to pay more than 4.25 million dollars a year in rent. The contract supplied not only its largest tenant with multiple broadcasting studios and stages on sixteen floors in the central building, but also "a tenant that was a leader in mass communication and glamorous new technology."[39]

In March 1931, newspapers across the country seized any good economic news. "The Rockefeller enterprise, to be finished in three years, will employ eight to ten thousand men at good wages,"[40] gushed the *Taylorville Breeze* in Illinois. The contract for 120,000 tons of steel "is enough to build a fleet of 12 modern warships," fawned the *Youngstown Vindicator*. "The order will require the service of about 10,000 men, at various times, from miners who dig the iron ore to the structural workers who erect the steel girders."[41]

"We are now passing the signposts of prosperity," pontificated the financial editor of the *Boston Post*. "But many of us fail to heed them."[42]

By January 1932, work was underway on the first three buildings: the thirty-one-story R.K.O. (Radio Keith Orpheum) Building, the ten-story Radio City Music Hall, and the flagship skyscraper, the sixty-nine-story[43] R.C.A. Building, better known today as 30 Rock.

The first building completed was the R.K.O., in October 1932. There was little fanfare, which the developers were holding back for Radio City Music Hall's grand opening, just two months away.

Radio City Music Hall celebrated its grand opening on New Year's Eve, 1932. The event gave no indication that

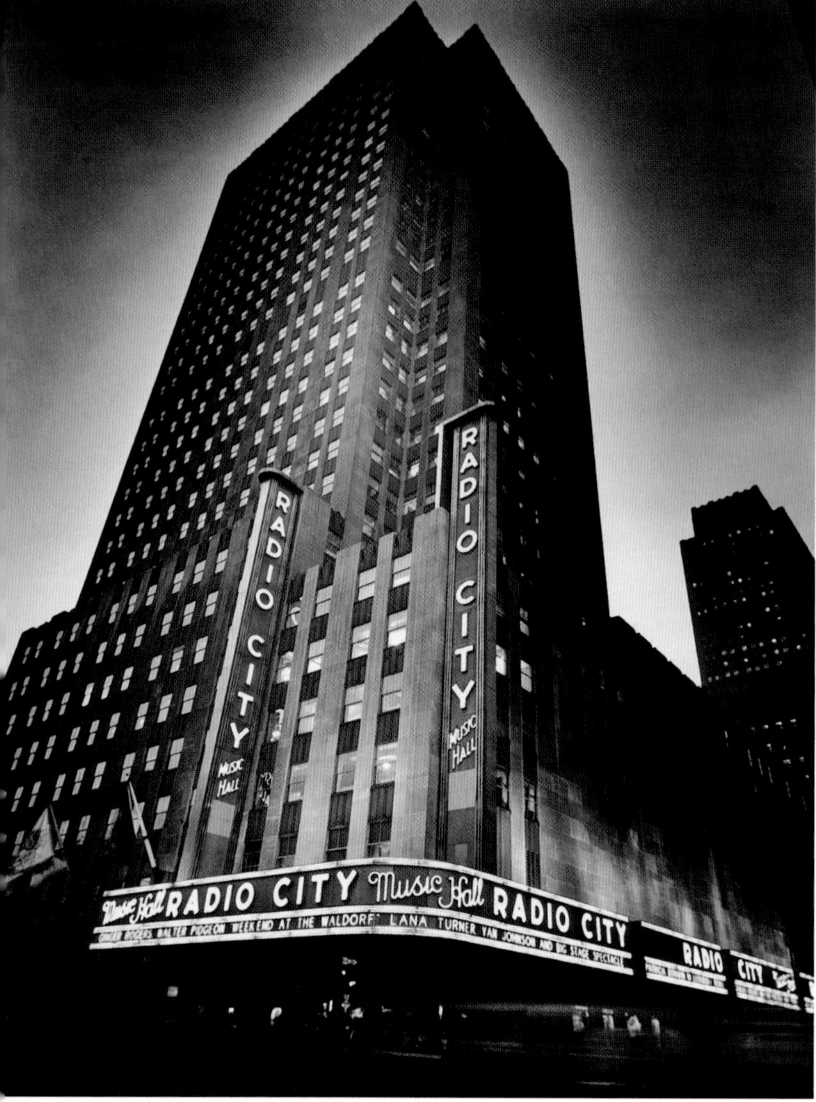

2.15 Radio City Music Hall. (Rockefeller Group photo 1201)

the country was in the midst of the Great Depression, that the global economy had shrunk more than 10 percent, and that millions were struggling to find work and put bread on the table. As I researched this book, I kept reflecting on the devastation affecting so many and how this supercilious show of wealth looked from the breadlines. The six thousand invitees included socialites adorned in furs and gowns, celebrities, and politicians wearing silk toppers—all arriving in limousines. The seventeen-act opening night production ranged from Dancing Curtains and The flying Wallendas to six scenes from *Carmen*.

The reviews were painful, criticizing everything from the size of the theater to the decor to the performers. The acts were too long, too pretentious, too erratic, and after six excruciating hours—boring.

The powerful columnist and critic of the *New York Herald Tribune*, Walter Lippmann, did not hold back. "The man behind the concept," he wrote, "had built a pedestal to sustain a peanut."[44] Although opening night was an abject failure, the state-of-the-art theater would soon become a glittering triumph with movies and Rockettes as star attractions. The opera house was forgotten, vaudeville replaced Valkyries, and comedy replaced *Carmen*.

By July 1933, Rockefeller buildings were growing rapidly, averaging one building completed yearly. Publicists boasted that the venture directly employed forty thousand people, from architects to laborers, and provided work for thousands of other people working in various trades worldwide.

Hood, the architect, convinced Todd and Junior that a large-scale program of decorative embellishment was essential to the design of the Center to provide "consistency and vitality."[45] He envisioned carved reliefs, decorative panels, murals, and monumental sculptures installed throughout the Center. Junior was very supportive and initially set aside 150,000 dollars for this program. As buildings were erected, that sum increased tenfold.

Raymond Hood also proposed plazas with fountains, gardens, verdant rooftops, and terraces. He believed that the city should be pleasant from every angle, even to a worker looking down from a nearby office, and it would also increase the revenue from renters. Hood approached Todd, disingenuously inquiring how much rental value might be gained if the Center's towers overlooked an open space like Bryant Park. When Todd replied "Around an additional dollar per square foot," Hood exclaimed: "A dollar, Mr. Todd! . . . Do you know there will be about seven acres of roof over the lower parts of Radio City? A lot of office space will look out over those roofs. At a dollar more per square foot extra you could afford to landscape those roofs like the hanging gardens of Babylon."[46]

Early blueprints show narrow bridges spanning the streets and connecting terraces within the expanding complex. Hood's grand plans were never fully realized, but he had a supporter in Junior, who thought the gardens would attract sightseers "because they are 140 feet up in the air."[47]

In 1935, Hood, with the help of the Welsh horticulturalist Ralph Hancock, designed a roof garden for the low roof of the eleventh floor NBC Building. The garden was named "The Gardens of the Nations," reflecting Junior's international vision. Three quarters of an acre, the garden held small vignettes of native plantings from thirteen countries, including Holland, France, and Japan. There was an American rock garden with a meandering stream, a "modern" garden, a bird sanctuary, and a children's garden which, during World War II, became a victory garden.

It was to be a commercial enterprise, with an entry fee of one dollar (later reduced to forty cents) and a Horticultural Hall and shop. But the enterprise never turned a profit, and the gardens drifted into neglect. Today it is closed to the public but remains an oasis for birds and the occasional NBC interview.

Visitors entering the Center from Fifth Avenue travel a two-hundred-foot sloping promenade. They descend gently past six granite pools, each with cast-bronze fountainheads of Tritons or Nereids astride sea creatures, sculpted

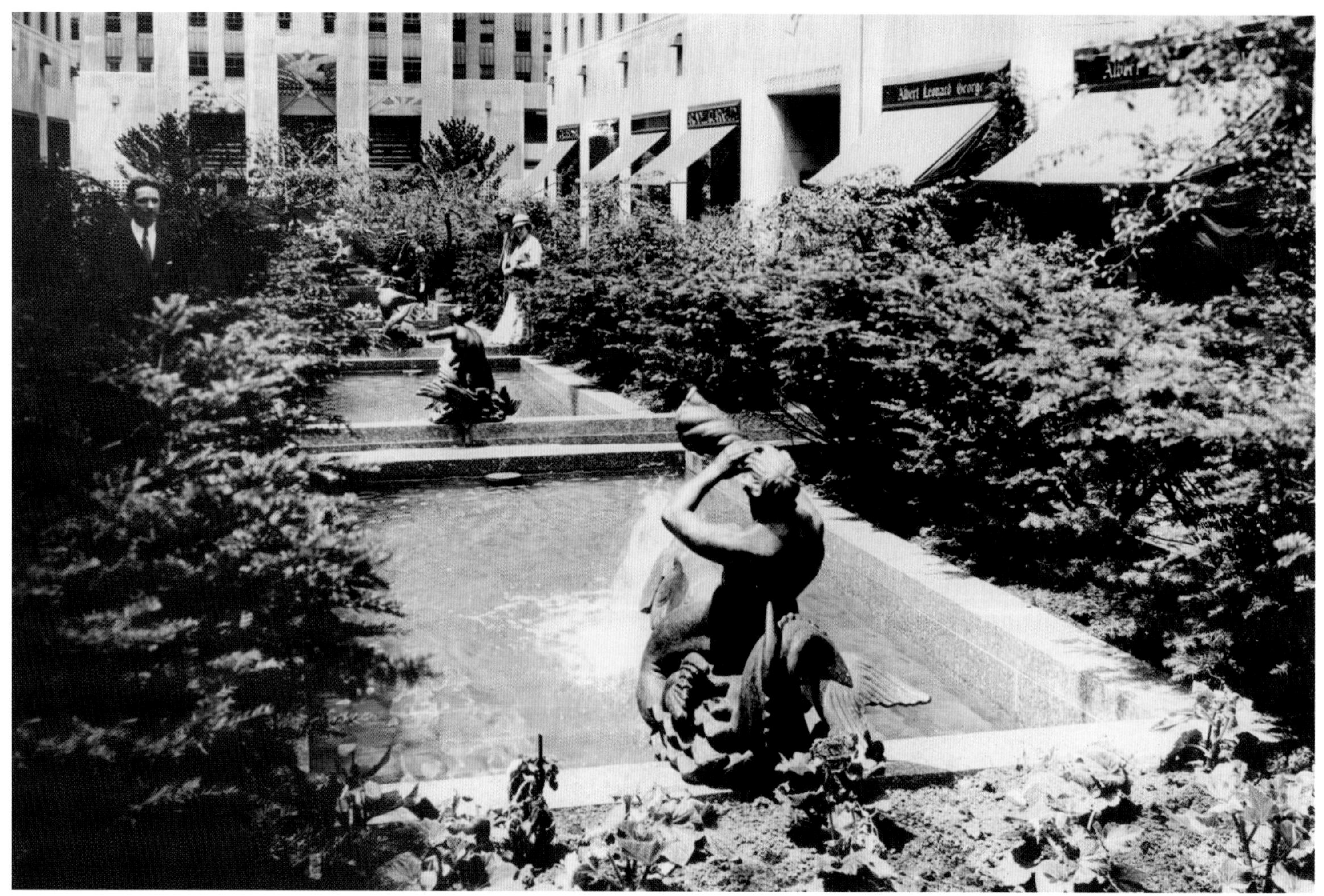

2.16 The Channel Gardens between the British and French buildings. (Rockefeller Group photo 506)

by Rene Chambellan. Because the courtyard separates the French and English buildings, it would be dubbed "the Channel gardens." The gardens lead the visitor to the Lower Plaza, the central axis of the Center. Here, the architectural historian Weisman observed that from that point "arteries for pedestrian traffic must be numerous, intercommunicating, and lead in all directions"[48] to shops, shows, exhibitions, and restaurants, and the office worker to his job.

In 2021, Rockefeller Center returned to Hood's original idea and unveiled Radio Park, a meandering garden with a great sloping lawn atop Radio City Music Hall. The twenty-four-thousand-square-foot area was originally built as an exercise and rest area for Radio City Music Hall's dancers. Today it is open to the tenants of Rockefeller Center.

By December 1933, the newly formed public relations department had reimagined the excavators' plucky Christmas tree as a showcase of modern technology and communications. The gardens were adorned with seasonal holiday plants, and a Christmas holiday program in the Lower Plaza featured several choirs and the Gloria Trumpeters. The first official Rockefeller Christmas tree was "set on the sidewalk, at street level, just above the west wall of the Sunken Plaza and directly in front of the entrance to the seventy-story R.C.A. Building."[49] Seven hundred twinkling blue and white lights adorned the fifty-foot Balsam pine. It was "illuminated by a huge incandescent Klieglight, a new development with a special reflector lens and shutter combination which will project a beam in the shape of a tree, just large enough to cast a brilliant light upon the Christmas tree."[50] NBC broadcast the event nationwide, setting the stage for decades of Rockefeller Center Christmas productions.

Eventually, the plazas, art, and gardens would integrate fourteen limestone-clad buildings of varying heights into a singular urban center. An underground concourse connected the buildings and the public to the subways. People were encouraged to come in, shop, eat, and appreciate the surroundings. The brainchild of Raymond Hood's concept of air, light, and transportation, combined with his alchemy of art, space, and landscaping, had a magical appeal. Rockefeller Center would become a city-within-a-city.

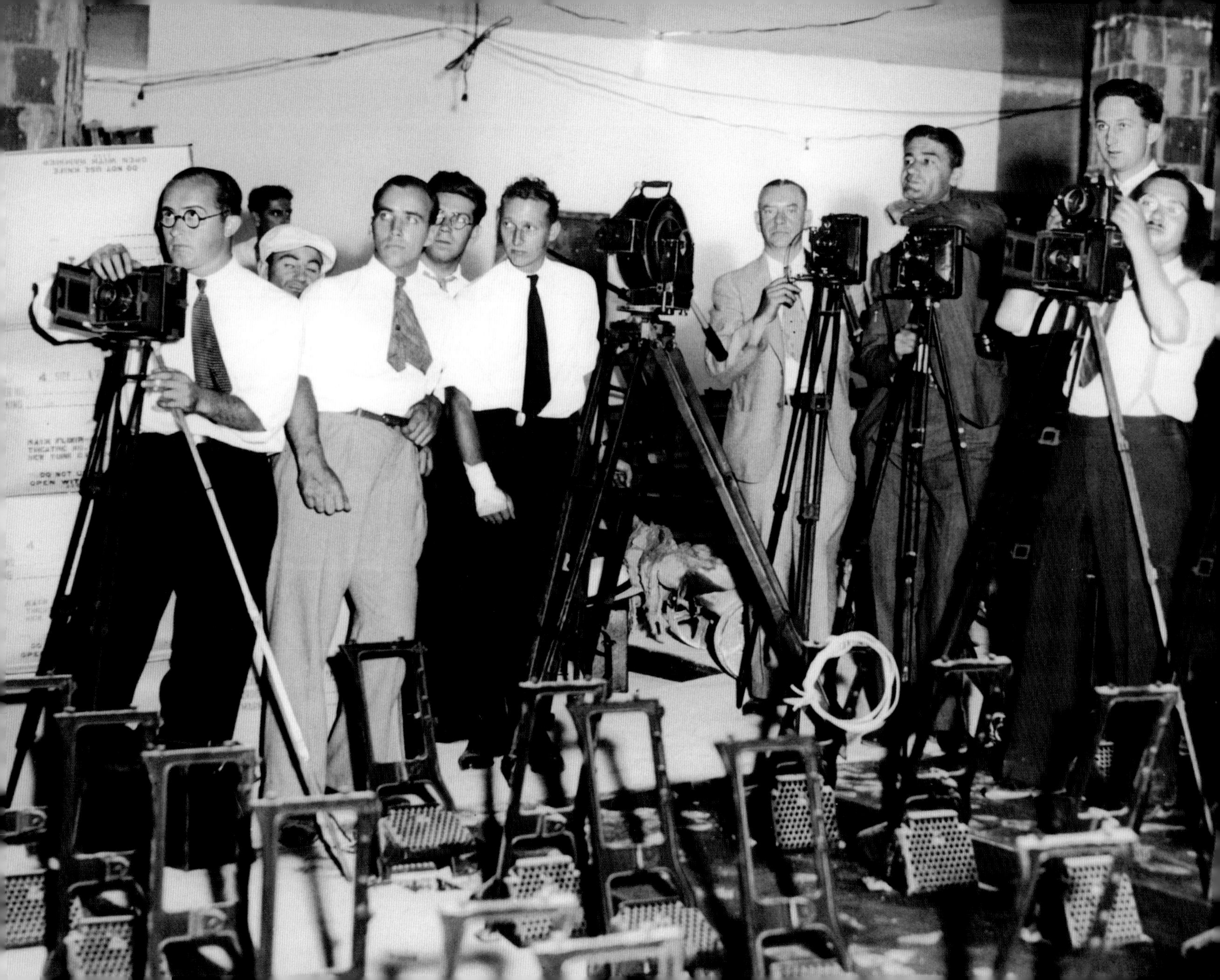

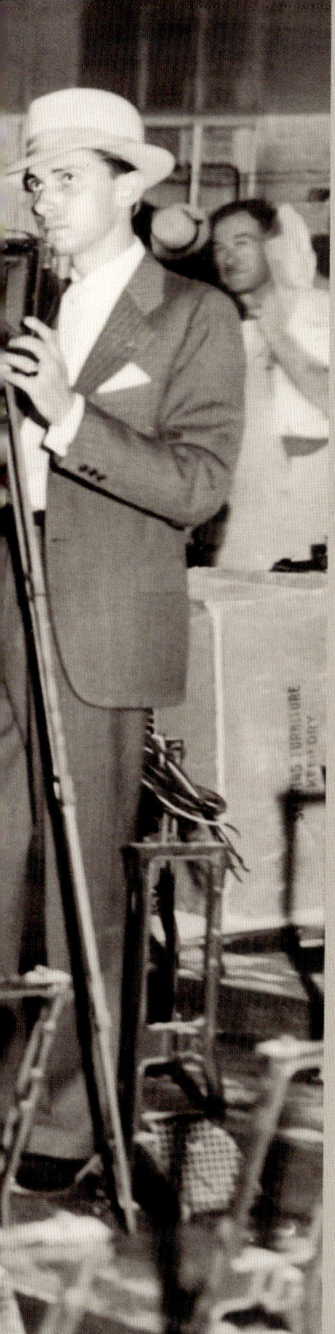

3
MAKING THE IMAGE

3.1 Journalists crowd into the unveiling of the world's largest chandelier. (Rockefeller Group photo 896)

N 1914, JOHN D. ROCKEFELLER JR. was the most hated man in America. One of his many companies, Colorado Fuel & Iron, had turned the machine guns of the state militia on striking miners and their families. As dawn broke on Easter Monday, the militia set fire to the tent camp, killing more than twenty people, including eleven children—the Ludlow Massacre. In an open letter to Junior, the progressive journalist Upton Sinclair wrote, "I intend to indict you for murder before the people of this country. The charges will be pressed, and I think the verdict will be 'Guilty.'"[1] Many Americans shared his view.

But then, over the next decade and a half, public opinion would shift dramatically. While many Americans would go to their grave hating Junior, many more would come to embrace a different vision of the man: philanthropist, patriot, builder. Sympathetic biographers suggested the Ludlow Massacre had a profound effect on Junior, sparking an evolution that was genuine, even profound. He was forty years old when he finally understood that his was the Rockefeller voice that mattered. His friend and biographer Raymond Fosdick represented this view:

Never before had the younger Rockefeller been so keenly and painfully aware of his isolation from the American public. Already his thinking on the subject of the strike was undergoing important changes. At first his knowledge of conditions in Colorado had been limited to the information provided by [CF&I officers] Bowers and Welborn. It is impossible to know at what point he began to question, not so much their veracity, as their point of view. What is significant, however, is that at some moment along the way he realized that the picture was not as simple as it had been painted for him by the two officers. He began to sense that something more than mob hysteria and union agitation lay behind the strike. Perhaps no one would ever untangle the complex maze of cause and effect which led up to the Ludlow tragedy, but that was no longer of paramount importance. What was important was to understand the basic resentment which had rankled in the hearts of so many miners on the day that they had finally abandoned their homes and work to go on strike. To know this would be to know how to avoid the repetition of such a conflict, and this was what primarily concerned JDR Jr.[2]

But whatever transformation happened within Junior, the rehabilitation of his public image was deliberate, strategic, and the work of professionals.

Ivy Ledbetter Lee, a family adviser and pioneer in public relations, set the mold for the image rehabilitation tour. Junior visited Ludlow, accompanied by Lee, Charles Heydt, and Mackenzie King,[3] a Canadian social reformer whose devoted Christian beliefs and socialist views softened Rockefeller's profile. King and Lee drafted articles, speeches, and testimony for Junior. "King and others wrote Junior's lines; staged his appearances before congressional committees, business associations, and public forums; and transformed him into an advocate of enlightened labor relations."[4]

Lee, himself a former business reporter, worked to counter the "Robber Baron" narrative of muckraking journalists. A pioneer of access journalism, he cultivated relationships with prominent newsmen and urged his elite clients to offer at least the appearance of transparency. Although he advised them to tell the truth, he spun facts strategically to explain away any contradiction and embellished them to hype dubious claims. Today, he is often called the father of public relations. Poet Carl Sandburg called him "Ivy Lee, paid liar."[5] Muckraker Upton Sinclair called him "Poison Ivy."[6]

After Ludlow, Lee became a key adviser to Junior. He rehabilitated the nascent philanthropist's public image and even served as a financial consultant. He played a key role in shaping Rockefeller's reputation as a thought leader in industrial relations, a clear-eyed capitalist whose interests aligned with the welfare of his workers. Lee was involved with the opera project from its conception, introduced Junior to it, and encouraged him to acquire the leasehold from Columbia.

But public relations was changing slowly, and then all at once.

The day was October 21, 1929. Three years before eleven ironworkers lunched atop a skyscraper, another group of builders sat shoulder to shoulder, sharing a different meal, at a different sort of dizzying height. Five hundred of America's most powerful men had gathered outside Detroit to celebrate the modern world—a world, it was no exaggeration to say, they had built. The occasion was Light's Golden Jubilee, marking fifty years since the invention of the incandescent bulb. The guests had seen civilization transform from a world of oil lamps and horse carts, steam engines and stonework, to one of dazzling light, telephones, movies, radios, cars, air travel, and skyscrapers. Many of the assembled that day had ushered that change.

Here were titans of finance: Charles M. Schwab, Otto Kahn, Andrew Mellon. Of the automobile: Ransom Olds, Charles Nash, Walter Chrysler, Harvey Firestone. Of flight: Orville Wright, first in flight (after Wilbur, who had died in 1912). Here was movie mogul Will Hays (bestower of the Hays code) and star Will Rogers, who observed that "whenever Charley Schwab and Otto Kahn are not sufficient prominent to be seated at the head table, you have been to some banquet."[7] They squeezed into fifteen long tables in an exact replica of Philadelphia's Independence Hall, built by the evening's host, Henry Ford.

Ford sat at the front of the hall between his wife and the guest of honor, Thomas Edison. In all the world, only two scientists were arguably as famous: Marie Curie, seated a few chairs over, and Albert Einstein, who participated from Berlin via the first live transatlantic radio broadcast. They were joined, with spouses, by America's barons of electricity: the heads of General Electric, Westinghouse, R.C.A., and major power companies. "Sufficient prominent" to round out the head table were George Eastman, who brought photography to every home, Herbert Hoover, president of the United States—and John D. Rockefeller Jr.

The climax of the evening was a dramatic recreation of the eureka moment, fifty years prior, when Thomas Edison had lit his first successful incandescent bulb. Edison, now eighty-two, Ford, and a small entourage made their way from Independence Hall to the inventor's laboratory, which Ford had relocated, plank and nail, from Menlo Park, New Jersey, to his new Ford Museum (restoration of historical sites being an enthusiasm he shared with Junior).

Graham McNamee narrated the evening's events in a live nationwide broadcast on NBC. As Edison puttered alongside his original assistant Francis Jehl, the pioneering radio announcer brought a sportscaster's energy to the action before him.

"But here is Mr. Edison again. While he was at the powerhouse, Mr. Jehl sealed up the old lamp, and it is now ready. Will it light? Or will it flicker and die, as so many previous lamps had died?"

"Oh, you could hear a pin drop in this long room."

"Now the group is once more about the old vacuum pump. Mr. Edison has the two wires in his hand. Now he is reaching up to the old lamp. Now he is making the connection. It lights!"

"Now Mr. Edison is smiling. He is shaking hands with the president, and with Mr. Ford."

"And now the light is springing up on all sides, the modern light of 1929."[8]

The Jubilee was not only a celebration of invention, technology, and industry, but also—even foremost—a triumph of the new science of public opinion. The event's mastermind was Edward Bernays, a pioneer of public relations who had honed his ideas as a World War I propagandist for the US War Department. The nephew of Sigmund Freud, Bernays saw public relations as a profession, equal in precision and rigor to law or medicine. Bernays advised Ford and General Electric on every aspect of the Jubilee and worked for a year leading up to it to forge its place in the public imagination.

Where Lee sought to shape how the press covered the news, Bernays realized he could create it. To overcome taboos against women smoking, he organized a group of young debutantes to march, cigarettes in hand, in New York's 1929 Easter parade. His "Torches of Freedom" campaign never mentioned his client, American Tobacco, but nevertheless sales surged. Likewise, Bernays explicitly designed Light's Golden Jubilee to increase sales for its sponsors—lighting manufacturers and utilities—without promoting them directly, while also establishing his client, Henry Ford, as Edison's heir to the claim of America's foremost inventor. Bernays established local Jubilee committees and events across the country, lobbied successfully for a commemorative US postal stamp, and even drafted the congratulatory remarks of world leaders, from Prince Edward Albert of Wales to Benito Mussolini of Italy.[9]

At the event itself, Bernays had wide latitude over the guest list. "Ford authorized me to invite representatives of the wire services, the photographic services and the weekly newsreels, as well as representatives of fifteen of the most important newspapers in the country and an additional number of outstanding journalists." That list included the Hearst columnist Arthur Brisbane; the powerful publishers Adolph Ochs, William Randolph Hearst, Frank S. Gannett, Cyrus Curtis, and Robert McCormick; and three editors: Ogden Reid of the *New York Herald Tribune*, George Horace Lorimer of the *Saturday Evening Post*, and Merle Crowell of *The American* magazine.

Among the newsmen invited, Crowell stood out. Tall, broad, and gregarious, with a shock of red hair, strong jaw, and piercing blue eyes, he made a striking first impression. The son of a Maine farmer, Crowell came to New York in 1907 after graduating from Colby College with hopes of becoming a writer. He cut his teeth as a reporter at the *New York Sun*, where he started a lifelong friendship with Bernays, who was also launching himself, first as a journalist and then as a press agent for the city's theater industry.

Crowell's big break followed a brush with the Rockefeller organization in 1915. A year after the Ludlow massacre, another violent labor conflict gripped the Standard Oil refinery in Bayonne, New Jersey. Crowell was covering the standoff when the local sheriff, Eugene Kinkead, ordered his officers to arrest the plant's private security force, which had violently suppressed the strike.

For seventy-two hours, Kinkead worked with the strikers and plant management to negotiate an end to the strike, before the sheriff collapsed from exhaustion.

After filing his daily reports with the *Sun,* Crowell pitched a profile of the sheriff to *The American* magazine. The pitch caught the attention of the magazine's new editor, John M. Siddall, who not only bought the article but also hired Crowell as an associate editor and staff writer. *The American* was commercially successful—its circulation approached two million—but also had a reputation for puffery—*Time* magazine called it "a pedestrian, commercially-minded, 'success story' magazine." Its specialty was the "business romance"—heroic, Horatio Alger-style profiles of men making their way in the world. And Crowell embraced the assignment, until the interruption of World War I.

While service steered his friend Edward Bernays toward the science of propaganda, the crucible of war forged Crowell's path to middle management. As a college graduate, Crowell entered the Army in 1917 as a lieutenant. He was stationed in Newport News, a major port of embarkation for soldiers en route to the trenches of Europe. He was promoted to captain and made the base's personnel adjutant. His mission: to ensure that no doughboy board a ship without his papers, and no paper board without its doughboy.[10] After two years of efficient stateside service, he was discharged as a major.

In 1919, Crowell returned to *The American* and quickly emerged as Siddall's protégé. He described the philosophy he learned from his mentor: "Every human being likes to see himself in reading matter—just as he likes to see himself in a mirror," Crowell wrote in 1925. "The ideal article for any publication (so far as 'reader interest' is concerned) would be one in which every reader could find his own name. The ideal illustration would be a group photography of all the readers, so that each reader could have the fun of finding himself in the picture.

"Newspapers are read widely because the individual reader sees himself constantly in the paper. I do not mean that he sees his own name. I mean that he reads about things happening to individuals which might happen to him, and he keeps comparing himself with what he reads."[11]

In March of 1923, Siddall was diagnosed with stomach cancer. Told it was incurable, he chose to forgo palliative care and instead continued to helm *The American.* He died four months later, hailed as a hero. "John M. Siddall, Doomed, Worked On" was the headline of his front-page *New York Times* obituary.[12] Crowell, his hand-picked successor, vowed to continue "Sid's" vision for the magazine.

And he largely did. Each month delivered a reliable mix of success stories and genial advice to *The American*'s two million readers. But a subtle shift was underway. Fewer of the "business romances" were self-made men; more were organization men, rising through the corporate ranks. It was during this time that Crowell coined perhaps his only aphorism still quoted today: "It's the men behind who make the man ahead."[13]

Crowell saw himself as an avatar of his own philosophy. An organization man, he had worked his way up to journalism's pinnacle of success. His Yankee accent and imposing frame burnished his backstory, which had included a seasonal job, during college, at a Maine lumber camp. In 1926, *Vanity Fair* listed him among "the foremost contemporary builders of public opinion and taste in every department of American life and thought."[14] A profile in *Author & Journalist* described his perch: "On the thirteenth floor of 250 Park Avenue, New York, we find the editor at a large mahogany desk in an office which commands the editorial rooms of the Crowell Publishing Company."[15] (Merle was not related to his eponymous employer.)

The profile ran the same month that Crowell found himself rubbing elbows with the world's most powerful men and their image makers at Light's Golden Jubilee. For Crowell, like many others at the banquet, Monday, October 21, 1929, would be his apogee, followed by a sudden and precipitous fall. Three days later came Black Thursday, the stock market crash, and the dawn of the Great Depression.

In less than a month, Crowell had lost his editor's chair. He announced he had resigned for health reasons (rheumatism), but his sudden departure suggests his (again, unrelated) bosses at Crowell Publishing were responding to the crash with urgency, even panic. In one of his first acts, Crowell's successor, Sumner Blossom, sent a memo to staff: "Horatio Alger doesn't work here anymore."[16]

Crowell found himself unemployed, if not on the bread line. He sold articles to other magazines and announced a lecture tour (which seemingly fizzled). But his obligations were mounting. His second marriage ended in 1930. (His first, to suffragist and fellow reporter May Stanley Finch, had ended a decade earlier.) When he married again on New Year's Day, 1931, to the writer Dorothy Walworth, they both entered the marriage with children to support. The call from Rockefeller Center that summer was a lifeline.

Crowell joined a publicity operation in flux. Junior still relied on Lee to promote the project—and even name it. Lee proposed "Rockefeller Center," arguing that it would attract the "right kind of tenants." When Junior equivocated, Todd stepped in and told him, "It's your money."[17] The change was announced on April 27, 1932: Metropolitan

Square Corporation was now Rockefeller Center, Inc.[18] But that decision would be the high-water mark of Lee's influence on Rockefeller Center. With the project underway, Lee's role shrank. Junior eased him aside and cut his compensation. By the fall of 1931, *Variety* was reporting that "the question of whether and how Ivy Lee, the publicist for the Rockefellers, will be involved in Radio City, is answered by the statement that Lee will confine himself to personal publicity for the Rockefellers and act as consultant in a general way on the development." Increasingly, the voice of Rockefeller Center (or at least its pen) was Merle Crowell.[19]

Crowell's daunting task: drum up interest in more than five million square feet of office and retail space, which didn't yet exist, during the darkest years of the Great Depression.

His solution: Hype the construction and hype it relentlessly.

Crowell issued his first press release on July 25, 1931. "Excavation work for the largest building project of all time will be in full swing tomorrow. Already steam shovels are gouging the recently razed surface of the three blocks from Forty-Eighth to Fifty-First Streets between Fifth and Sixth Avenues, scene of the mammoth midtown construction project controlled by Metropolitan Square Corporation and sponsored and financed by John D. Rockefeller Jr." He went on for three pages extolling the arrival of an excavation team and produced massive amounts of questionable statistics and calculations. Crowell blitzed newspapers and magazines worldwide with releases glamorizing construction and trumpeting the future city-within-a-city.

The announcement heralded "the largest building project ever undertaken by private capital. . . . between two and three hundred men will be on the job of creating Manhattan's model of the Grand Canyon." It name-checked NBC, R.C.A., excavators Gahagan-Canavan and George Atwell & Co., foundation contractor Clarence Smith & Co., and, of course, John D. Rockefeller Jr. At the very end, Crowell remembered to mention the developers. The architects, he almost forgot—their two lines in small type are pasted to the bottom of the release.

Todd was piqued. To remind the publicity man of his importance, he sent a testy memo on August 11, 1931, addressed to "Mr. Crowell," underlined with no salutation.

Mr. Crowell

The loan from the Metropolitan Life Insurance Company on Rockefeller Centre will be recorded in a few days. As it may attract attention it is proper that the public understand Mr. Rockefeller's and our respective relationships to the development.

That relationship, he explained, was that he was in charge.

> Rockefeller acquired the property as an Opera Site before we were in it. Then he turned it over to us—Todd, Robertson, Todd Engineering Corporation and Todd & Brown, Inc.—for us to handle, including the financing, the same way we have handled other smaller matters.

Todd concluded by reminding Crowell of his place in the pecking order: "Please give out nothing without our written approval first had. Use Mr. Ross of Ivy Lee's office as necessary in Mr. Lee's absence."[20]

It was a humiliation for Crowell, who so recently commanded one of the nation's largest magazines. But he recovered from that rocky start, and would run Rockefeller Center's Public Relations Department until 1944, when he left to join *Reader's Digest*. Soon his releases appeared weekly, even daily, and were always sensational. Anything—a pile of bricks, a load of limestone—became newsworthy in his hands. Cleverly, he did not buy much advertising space; he enticed newspapers and magazines to promote the future center by providing extravagant descriptions and powerful photos.

Crowell compared the building of Rockefeller Center to the Great Pyramids and the Great Wall of China. And well he might. Beyond its enormous social and financial impact, the Center had another echo of the pyramids—a potentate's hope for an unknowable future.

By Crowell's fourth press release on August 22, 1931, he hyped Rockefeller Center's planned lower terraces and set-backs as "a modern and much magnified Hanging Gardens of Babylon. Seven acres of intensive landscaping will be devoted to waterfalls, fountains, reflecting pools, trees, shrubbery, formal flower beds, multi-colored tile walks, grass plots, and statuary."[21] But he was just getting started.

Over his first year, Crowell issued about six press releases a month. His seventy-seventh heralded the rise of Rockefeller Center's tallest skyscraper: "The steelwork of the R.C.A. Building now towers thirty-seven stories above the busy streets below. Approximately 47,000 tons of structural steel have been erected at this site by the firm of Post & McCord, Inc. This comprises almost three-quarters of the total tonnage. More than 400 steelworkers are now busy on this site."[22]

But the pressure was increasing. By the last two weeks of August 1932, he was cranking out releases at a pace of nearly one a day.

> Aug. 18: "Robert Garrison, the distinguished American sculptor, has been awarded a contract for the sculptural treatment of the main entrance to the RKO Building on the Radio City side of Rockefeller Center."

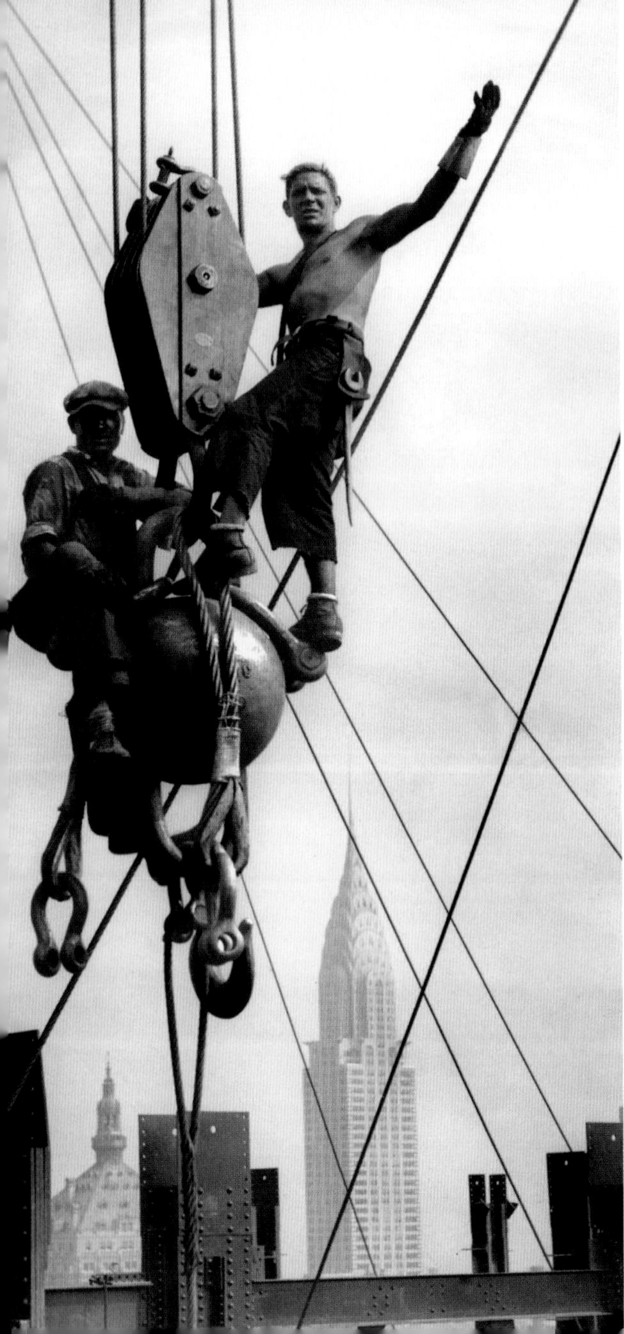

3.2 Two ironworkers ride the hoist ball. (Rockefeller Group photo by Charles Daughtery)

AUG. 21: "Further plans for novel exhibits in La Maison Francaise, the projected French building on the Fifth Avenue front of Rockefeller Center, were announced yesterday."

AUG. 22: "The installation of the world's largest chandelier, twenty-five feet in diameter, which will be used in the International Music Hall on the Radio City side of Rockefeller Center, will start today."

AUG. 26: "A plaster model, probably the largest of its type ever built, has been erected on the orchestra floor of the International Music Hall, Rockefeller Center's 6,000-seat theater."

AUG. 28: "John R. Todd, head of the builders and managers of Rockefeller Center, and Raymond Hood, one of the architects prominently identified with the big mid-city building project, will sail on the French liner *Paris*, on Friday, September 2, to contact a notable group of English, Italian, French and Spanish artists relative to their execution of murals in the Great Hall of the 70-story R.C.A. Building."

AUG. 29: "Twenty-two building mechanics will put aside their tools of trade at 11:45 o'clock this forenoon and foregather with their fellow workmen on the main floor of the nearly completed RKO Sound Theater on the Radio City side of Rockefeller Center. Here, they will receive certificates of Superior Craftsmanship and gold buttons as recognition of the unusual meritorious manner in which they have exercised their skill in the building of the big Motion Picture House."

Sept. 1: "Demolition is again underway at Rockefeller Center. Thirty-seven of the old buildings, in the easterly portion of the block between 50th and 51st Streets, are resounding today to the crash of falling partitions, uprooted floors, and the forcible removal of all salvageable materials."

In those dog days of summer, as his bosses prepared to steam to Europe, Crowell's output totaled nearly five thousand words. The descriptions included beautiful, colossal, deluxe (twice), famous (twice), great, huge, important (thrice), imposing (twice), infinite, largest, magnificent, notable, palatial, significant, and unique.

Construction had never been so dazzling.

And nothing dazzled like jaw-dropping photos of daredevil ironworkers.

Not everyone at the Center liked Crowell's logorrhea. But with the support of Junior, and increasingly Nelson, Crowell continued to produce bulletins in his bombastic style, which the press, longing for good news, welcomed. He would eventually see the tables turn on John Todd, who had once tormented him over a perceived slight.

When a 1936 *New Yorker* profile suggested that Todd was the real mastermind of Rockefeller Center, and Junior merely a pliant sack of money, an outraged Nelson ordered that all future press inquiries be directed to himself or Merle Crowell.[23]

Crowell would go on to stage celebrity visits, art shows, fashion shows, ice skating shows, flower shows, dog shows, literal horse and pony shows—anything to get Rockefeller Center in the news. Ceremonies honoring the achievements of construction workers presented the Rockefellers as enlightened employers and a model of industrial relations. These events also gave Nelson, then in his twenties, an early platform in front of the media and a reputation as an unlikely friend of labor that would follow him to the governor's office and, eventually, the White House.[24]

Newspapers across the beleaguered country eagerly featured articles and images about the Center without questioning the embellishments. Crowell's relentless coverage, his reams of press releases, and the squads of photographers he sent to the ever-growing construction site gave us the wealth of historical images and documents preserved today in Rockefeller Center Archives. These dispatches are his legacy.

With construction still underway in August 1934, Crowell pioneered a corporate magazine. *Rockefeller*

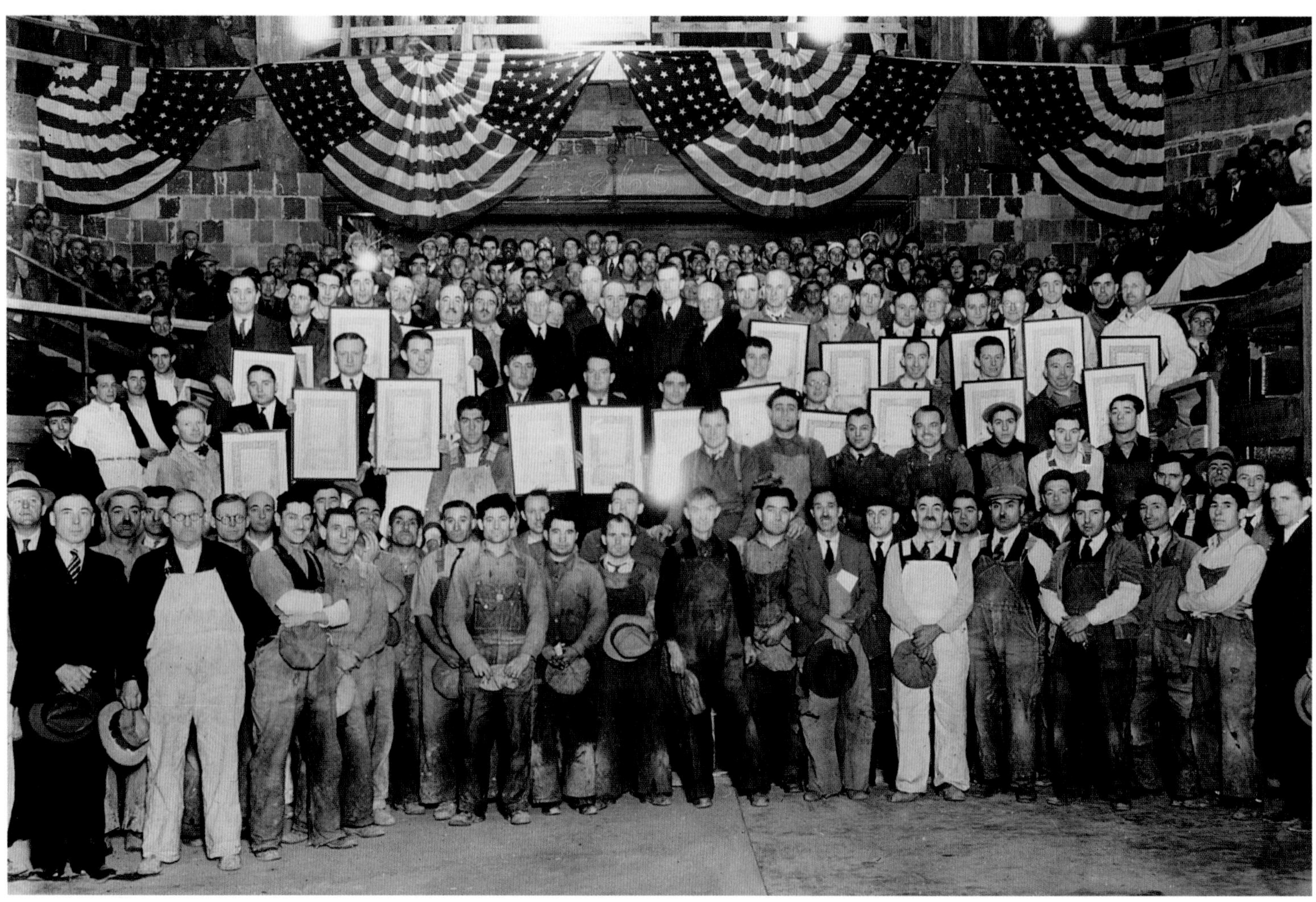

3.3 A ceremony honored Best Craftsmen on Feb. 1, 1932. (Rockefeller Group photo)

Center Weekly debuted with a sweeping cover shot of the R.C.A. Building. The Rockefeller Group distributed the magazine to tenants and its own executives. The cover price was ten cents, though newsstand sales were negligible. Its stated purpose was to highlight events, woo tenants, and boost employee morale, though it seemed to exist because Merle Crowell, two years into his publicity job, still wanted to run a magazine. He penned a column for the magazine titled "In Here," a reincarnation of the editor's notes he wrote for *The American.*

As Rockefeller Center filled, and the desperate hunt for tenants eased, the magazine reduced its publication schedule from weekly to monthly and ceased altogether in December 1942, replaced at times by newsletters. Crowell left Rockefeller Center in 1944—for a magazine, naturally. He would serve as a senior editor at *Reader's Digest* until his death, from a heart attack, in 1954. He would never regain his perch at the pinnacle of American media, but like his mentor John Siddall, he was a magazine editor to the end.

When Crowell supplied newspapers with ironworker photos, he was feeding a public primed by pulp fiction and Hollywood to romanticize the "cowboys of the sky."[25] In 1928, DeMille films produced *Skyscraper*, a farcical silent melodrama that extolled the heroic ironworker.[26] William

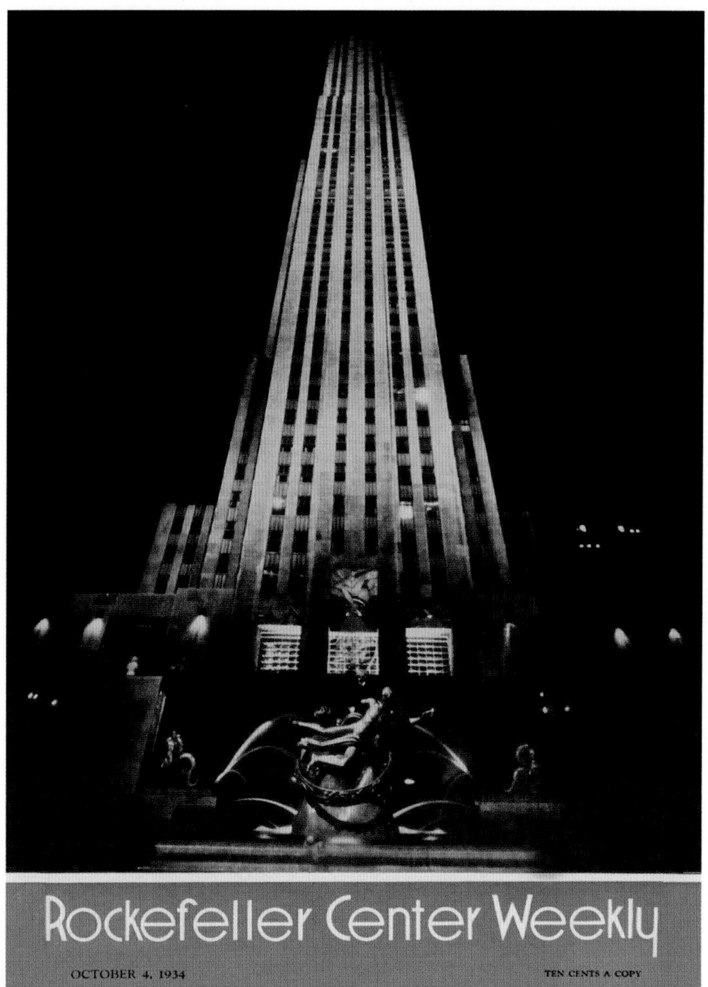

3.4 The first issue of *Rockefeller Center Weekly*. (Rockefeller Group photo)

Boyd starred as a riveter named Blondie working alongside his pal, Swede—"bang-em and slam-em roughneck riveters flirting with death far above the street." The thriller featured ironworkers leaping from girder to girder, culminating with a high-stepping chorus line. Critics panned it, but audiences soaked up the spectacle.

Two Seconds, a 1932 film noir, stars Edward G. Robinson and Vivienne Osborne as a New York ironworker and his conniving girlfriend. When she asks what he does for a living, he replies, "Oh, I'm a riveter."

"That's where you get those big muscles," she purrs. "How much do you earn?"

"$62.54," he says.

"You and Rockefeller!"

Photography and photojournalism made enormous strides in the first part of the twentieth century. Smaller handheld cameras and advances in film allowed photographers to take pictures anywhere, in rapid succession, without tripods or lights. The quintessential press camera was the Graflex Speed Graphic 4X5. Because of its weight, mobility, and image quality, it became the photographer's dependable companion for many years of tough assignments. The iconic Graflex Speed Graphic was carried into World War II and Vietnam.

These cameras created a new profession: the photojournalist, who documented both breaking news—sports, accidents, and murders—and features, like the construction of Rockefeller Center. Listening to police radios, a photographer could grab his camera and race to the scene, giving the profession an aura of drama. Photojournalists were frequently romanticized as a scrum of fedora-wearing, hard-hitting men hustling to get the shot. They were glamorized as tough guys breaking news in dangerous situations. Some of them actually were.

The new photography launched magazines such as *Life* and special sections of newspapers like the *Herald Tribune*'s *Sunday Magazine*, which began in 1927 and lasted through the 1950s. This period was a golden age of photojournalism. The *Daily News* carried the slogan "*New York's Picture Newspaper*." Photo features allowed newspapers to report events with catchy captions that gave the reader the gist of the story without lengthy text. It was a perfect formula for promotion, and "Lunch on a Beam" certainly did that.

As the seventy-story R.C.A. Building neared completion in 1932, the world's largest office building[27] needed tenants. The recently completed Empire State Building was nearing bankruptcy with a vacancy rate of 77 percent. (New Yorkers had nicknamed it the "Empty State Building.")

Crowell's employers had to fill 2,200,000 square feet of empty office and retail space. Crowell regularly contacted news agencies, which dispatched freelance photographers, known as "stringers." In the course of a few weeks, he engaged a platoon of photographers "to climb skeleton stairways to the sixtieth story and mount ladders ten more stories to the top."[28]

Those efforts culminated at 3 p.m. on Monday, September 26, 1932, when ironworkers riveted the final beam in a "topping out" ceremony.

Topping-out ceremonies remain an important rite among ironworkers. On major jobs, the honor of completing the topmost attachment goes to the senior gang, or to another crew singled out for recognition. Other trades mark their own construction milestones. Two months after the ironworkers' topping-out ceremony, masons worked into place the last piece of the R.C.A. Building's limestone facade. Once again, Rockefeller Center's publicity team was there. A photo from the masons' ceremony identifies the man riding the last block of limestone as James Grindrod, a stone derrickman.

"Lunch on a Beam" was among a number of photographs taken the week preceding September 26 by three intrepid photographers working with Rockefeller Center's public relations department and photo agencies, including

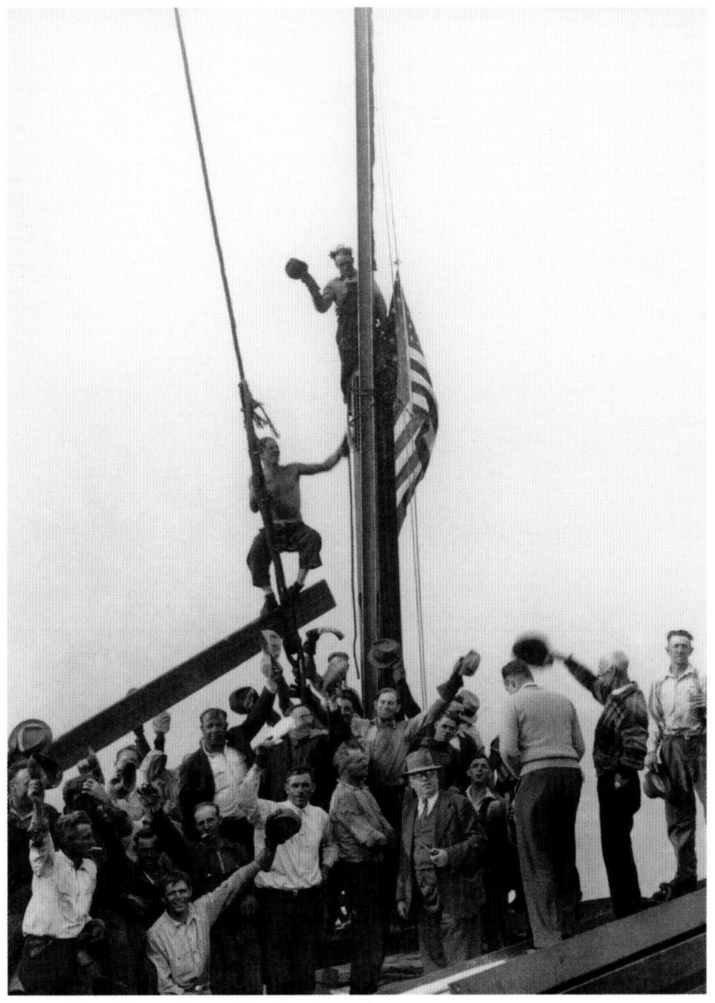

3.5 The topping-out ceremony, Sept. 26, 1932. (Rockefeller Group photo 137)

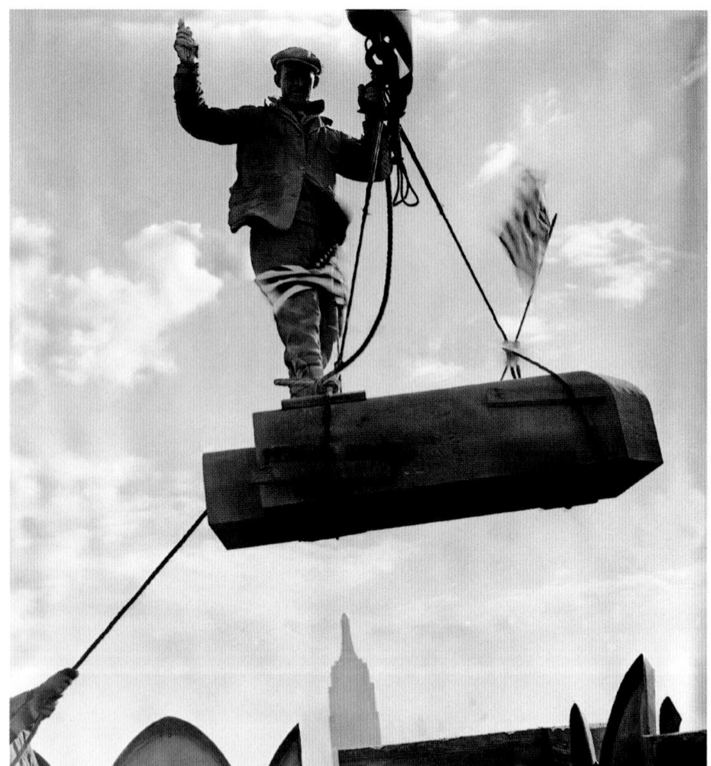

3.6 Stone derrickman James Grindrod completes the limestone facade on Dec. 7, 1932. (Rockefeller Group photo 268)

Acme-Newspictures, Hamilton Wright, and Newspictures Inc., that sold or freely distributed news photos to magazines and newspapers. Whether Crowell choreographed the photo shoot is unknown, but it bore all the hallmarks

of the man. His office even released photographs of the photographers—made either with a timer or the help of a second photographer. "Taking risks to get pictures is an everyday affair with the crack news photographers in New York," read each release. "Here is [Crowell would name the photographer] perched on a six-inch beam, 69 stories above the ground at ROCKEFELLER CENTER, shooting pictures for the newspapers."

Until now, the photographer who took that iconic picture has remained as much a mystery as the names of the workers in the image. The original work orders for that photo assignment have never been found in Rockefeller Center Archives, the now-defunct photography agencies, or the photographers' studios. Most of the images cannot be attributed to an individual. Still, we know who some of the photographers were, because pictures taken that day include mind-blowing shots of the photographers themselves.

Since 1932, three photographers from that day have been identified in the archives of Rockefeller Center: Charles Ebbets, Thomas Kelley, and William Leftwich. Until now, no claim has been made, nor has evidence been produced that either William Leftwich or Thomas Kelley took the iconic image, "Lunch on a Beam." Only Ebbets's family has claimed he took the famous picture. Their evidence includes a

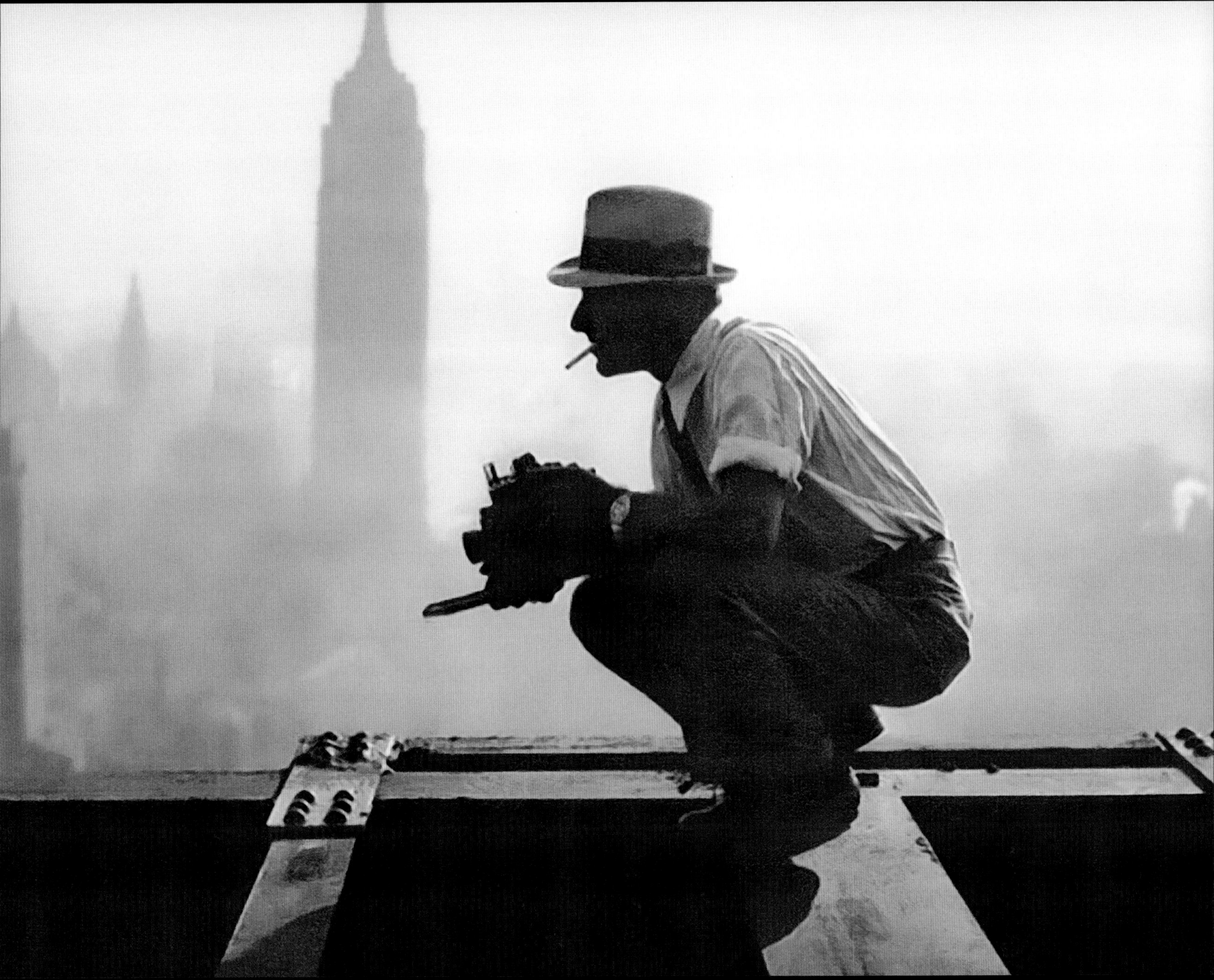

handwritten note from Charlie's wife, Joyce, attesting to his creation of "Lunch on a Beam."

Ebbets was present at the R.C.A. Building that day, as documented in a photo of him crouching atop the steel skeleton with a camera in hand. Ebbets would often photograph himself on the job, he told an interviewer in a 1938 article for *Popular Photography* magazine. "In order to obviate any opportunity for critics to claim that he fakes his pictures, Charlie Ebbets carries an automatic timer in his equipment and makes a picture of himself in every setting," the article reported. "Thus he is the most photographed camera operator ever. The timer is set for one minute, which affords the photographer ample opportunity to pose in the picture after he has focused and set the camera."[29]

His daughter, Tami Ebbets, confirmed that the photo is a self-portrait and said that files, negatives, and contemporary accounts indicate that her father took self-portraits on many job sites to record his presence. Even though no photographs of Rockefeller Center credit Ebbets directly, they do credit the agencies he worked with. "Charlie frequently worked for news agencies like Hamilton-Wright and Acme-Newspictures, which rarely gave him photo credits,"[30] Tami Ebbets told me.

However, there were exceptions where he billed directly. October and November invoices on Ebbets's letterhead (CHAS. C. EBBETS PHOTOGRAPHER 3903 Chrysler Building 405 Lexington Avenue New York City), to Rockefeller Center 420 Lexington Avenue, NYC. This suggests that in the fall of 1932 he was a freelance photographer working directly with the Center. The Ebbets family also produced a November 29, 1932, letter of recommendation from Merle Crowell, Director of Public Relations for Rockefeller Center: "To Whom It May Concern: Mr. Charles C. Ebbets has been the official photographer for the Rockefeller Center development during the last two months."

It is plausible that Ebbets shot the photo "Lunch on a Beam."

When Charlie left New York in November 1932, he returned to Miami, where he lived until his death in 1978. He was renowned as an adventurer, wrestler, parachute jumper, wing walker, pilot, automobile racer, and a World War II Army Air Corps photographer. He promoted Miami, trekked the Everglade swamps, and crossed the sands of Egypt, producing a body of work found in almost every picture publication of the time.

Another photo depicts eighteen-year-old Thomas Kelley audaciously straddling a narrow I-beam while adjusting the focus of his camera seventy stories above the city. He wears trendy spectator shoes, suspenders, and a white belt, the getup of a man who wants to be noticed—or at least keep his pants up. Kelley appears undaunted by the extreme height as he casually hooks the heel of his shoe on the flange of the I-beam. The view is south, as the Empire State Building looms in the background. Lesser buildings recede into the far haze of lower Manhattan.

In the 1940s, Kelley left New York and opened a photography studio in Hollywood. He became known for his portraits of movie stars, and famous for his iconic 1949 nude photos of Marilyn Monroe, later published in the first *Playboy* magazine, "Marilyn Monroe on Red Velvet."

After Kelley died in 1984, his son, Thomas Kelley Jr., continued the studio. Kelley Jr. told me that many of his father's New York photos are lost. But he said his father liked to tell stories about his famous photos. (One such story: His father met Marilyn Monroe at a party, near the beginning of her career. He gave her five dollars for a taxi home and later reached out three times to propose shooting her in the nude. She declined twice but finally agreed, and posed for Kelley only with his wife in attendance.) Tellingly, Kelley never claimed credit for the famous photo of the ironworkers, Kelley Jr. said. "My father never mentioned 'Lunch on a Beam.'"[31]

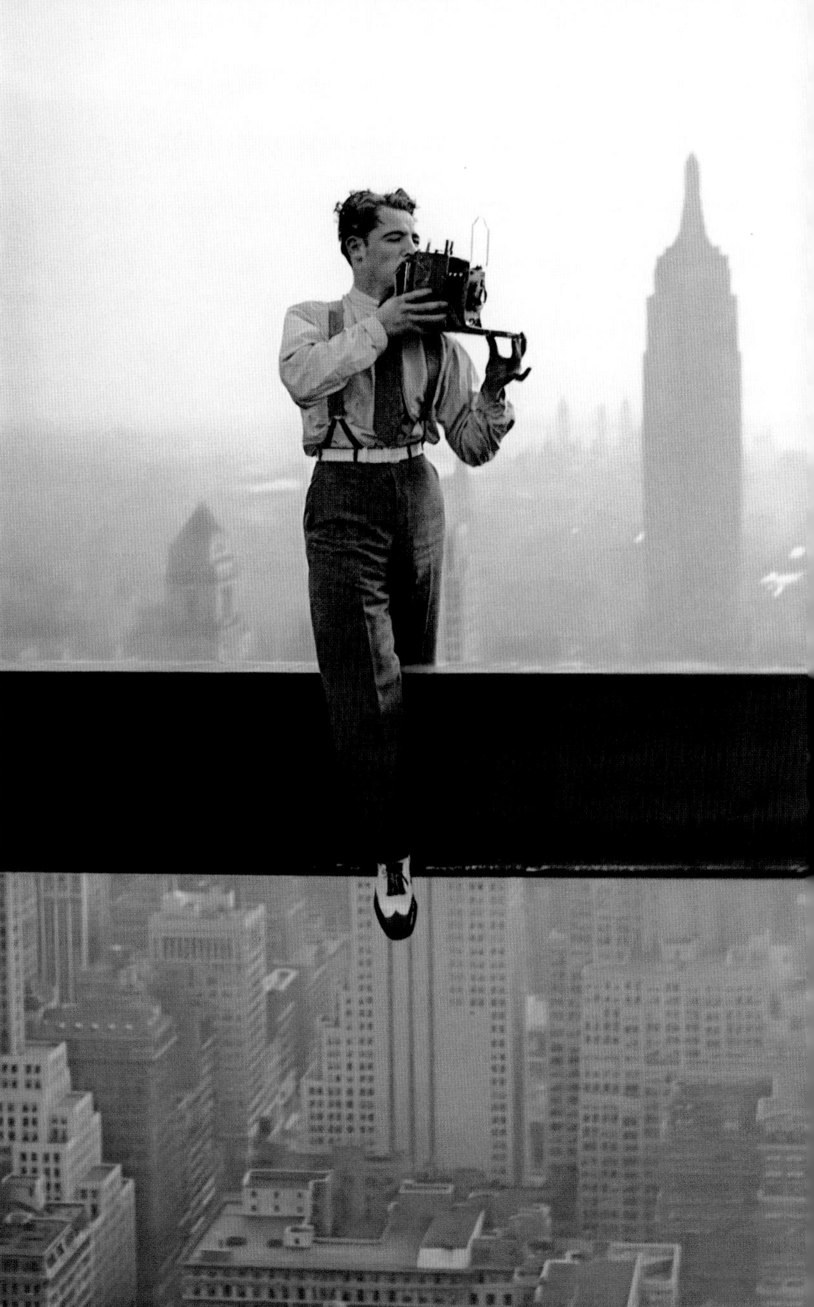

3.8 Thomas Kelley. (Rockefeller Group photo 140A)

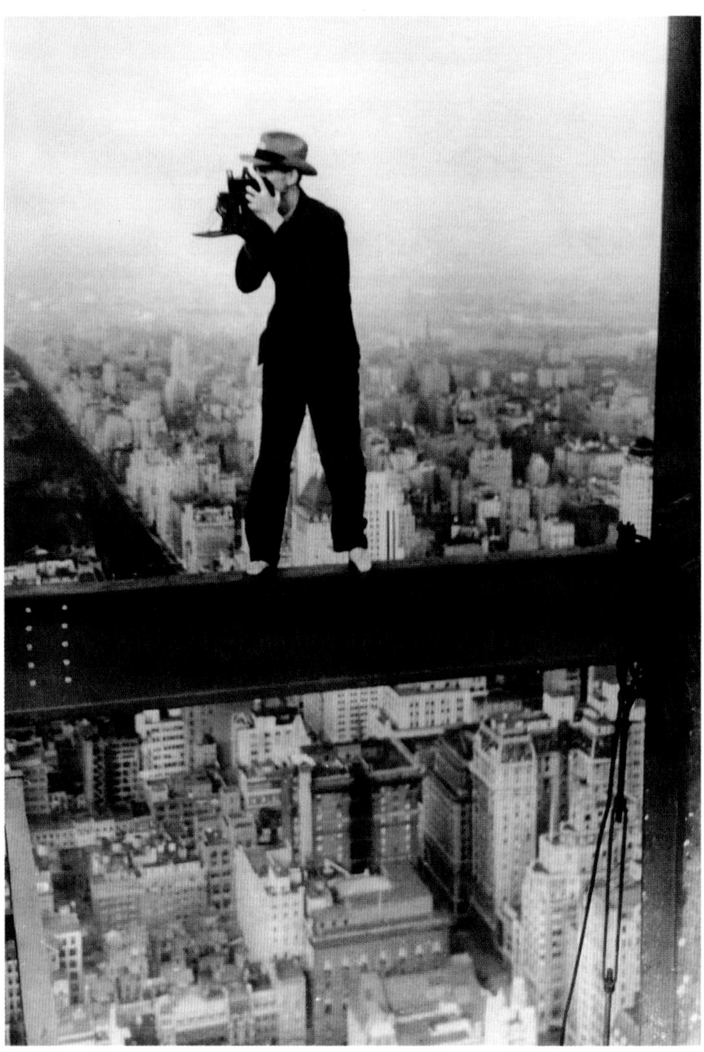

William "Lefty" Leftwich was a debonair and gutsy paparazzo. In his breathtaking portrait, he stands nonchalantly atop a six-inch-wide I-beam over (it seems) the 840-foot abyss. He wears a dark suit, a fedora (note the press card in the hat band), and two-tone wingtips while precariously balancing and focusing his camera.

The tops of buildings on the Upper East Side of Manhattan stretch out directly below him, forming a rough cityscape filled with chasms. The view is to the northeast as a southeast section of Central Park and buildings along Lower Fifth Avenue are visible in the left middle of the frame. It is a visceral photo that speaks volumes about this man.

"He had no fear of heights," his son, Bill Leftwich Jr., told me. "And he was a bon vivant, a man about town, frequently accompanied by Rockettes."[32] Leftwich was also enterprising and opened his own photo agency to sell his photos directly to publications without paying agency commissions. He incorporated the business as Newspictures, Inc.[33]

My research found that over the years, Leftwich operated from varying New York City addresses, including, significantly, 48 West Forty-Eighth Street, which still stands across from Rockefeller Center. That easy availability helps account for the number of pictures attributed to him in the archives. He was the quintessential freelancer, photographing everybody and every event. He took pictures of politicians like FDR and sports figures like Lou Gehrig while developing corporate clients, including Trans World Airlines and Studebaker. Rockefeller Center relied on Lefty for many years.

Some vintage photos that remain with his son document the Center, including Rockettes prancing and a dramatic view of a beam of light soaring into the night sky from the top of the R.C.A. Building. Many of his images form part of the Rockefeller Center Archives.

Leftwich was on the steel structure September 20, 1932, the day "Lunch on a Beam" was taken, and his personal agency, Newspictures, is credited with other photos taken that day—including one strikingly similar to "Lunch on a Beam."

These photos established the presence of three fearless photojournalists atop the R.C.A. Building's steel structure on September 20, 1932. Two, Ebbets and Leftwich, have strong claims to authorship of "Lunch on a Beam." My research did not rule out either one.

The camaraderie between ironworkers and photographers appears to have been genuine, as seen in this photo of a nervy stringer straddling a split-channel beam while taking a shot of an ironworker standing on tiptoes atop an I-beam. A leather box hangs on the photographer's back.

It would have contained 4 by 5-inch celluloid film or glass plates. His face is obscured, but his outfit differs from Kelley's or Leftwich's. It is similar to Charlie Ebbets's, as seen in his self-portrait. We are left to speculate. The workman is also unidentified.

During the photo shoot, different views of the city in the background indicate the photographers were moving around the steel structure, trying various locations, compositions, ironworkers, and activities.

The photographers doggedly grappled with one idea: ironworkers casually eating lunch on a beam. Image #119 shows nine men. They appear to be listening to a radio—maybe a late-season game for the Yankees, who had already clinched the American League pennant.[34] Seven are seated on a beam connected to the steel structure. One is standing. The setting is similar to "Lunch on a Beam," as several men hold the ubiquitous white lunchboxes, and three seem to be eating lunch from other containers. five wear flat caps, two are bareheaded, and one wears a fedora. Crowell's caption read: "While New York's thousands rush to crowded restaurants and congested lunch counters for their noonday lunch, these steelworkers atop the seventy-story R.C.A. Building in Rockefeller Center get all the air and freedom they want by lunching on a steel beam with a sheer drop of over eight hundred feet to the

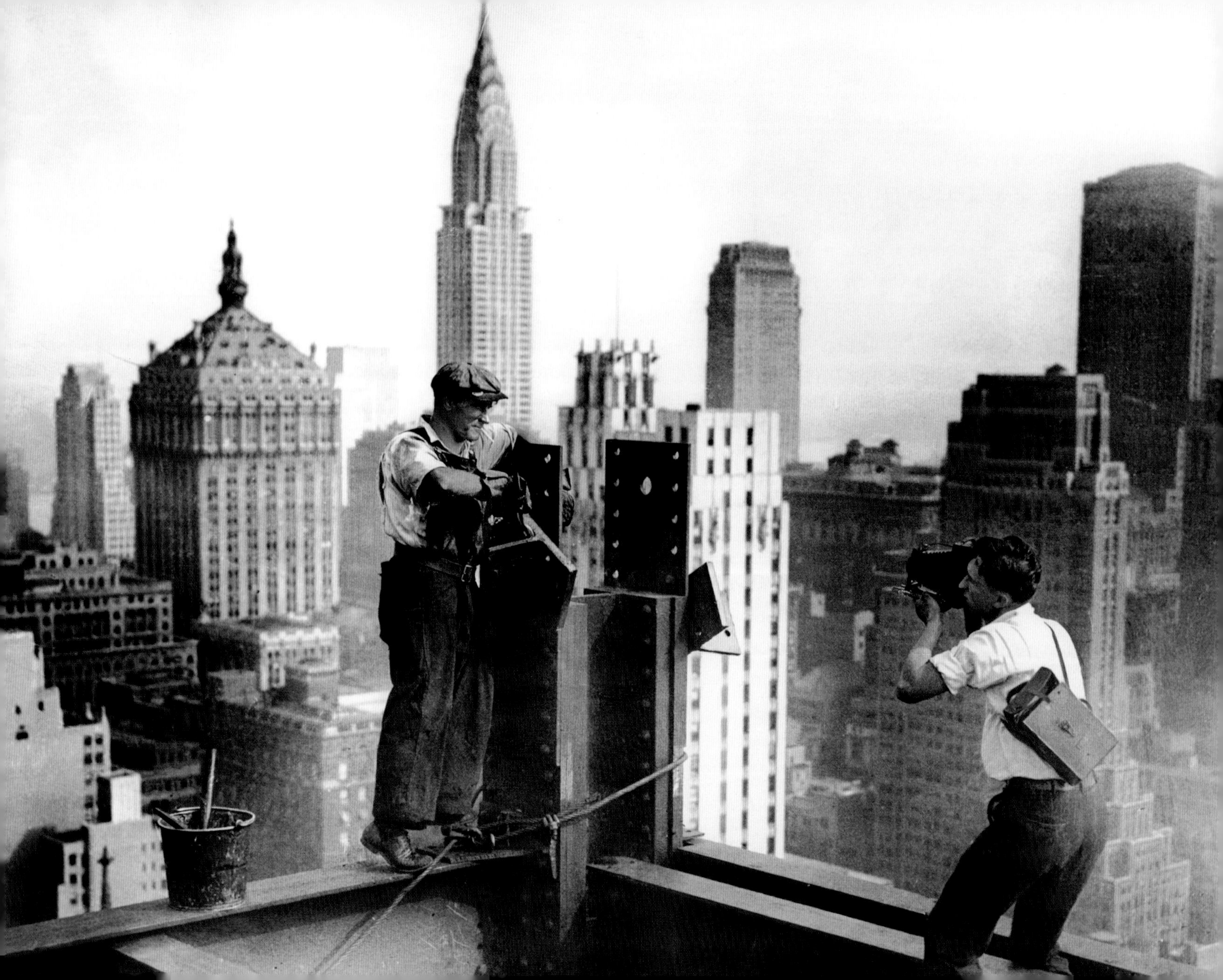

street level. The R.C.A. Building is the largest office building in the point of office space in the world."

The awesome aspect of a loose beam hovering high above the city is missing. It conveys, however, the idea that ironworkers might sit down and eat lunch on a secured beam. Comparison with other photos suggests the standing man is George Urbanneck, the man in the tee-shirt is Joe Curtis, and the fourth man from the left is Joe Jocks. All three are also in the iconic photo "Lunch on a Beam."

The view toward the south shows the Empire State Building and the Hudson River in the misty background. In many of these photographs, the Empire State Building appears as a diminished and shadowy presence, not a magnificent skyscraper towering over the city. Little would suggest that it was the tallest building in the world.

As the day went on, the photographers continued to place different workmen in various configurations while they relaxed, chatted, ate, and mugged for the cameras. Image #118 shows two workers sitting on a split-channel beam eating sandwiches. No white lunchbox in sight. The man on the right holds a liquor bottle like the eleventh man in "Lunch on a Beam." He is also similarly dressed: a flat cap and dark overalls over a light-colored shirt. This photo could be a precursor to multiple men eating lunch on a beam. This photo was taken on the structure's north

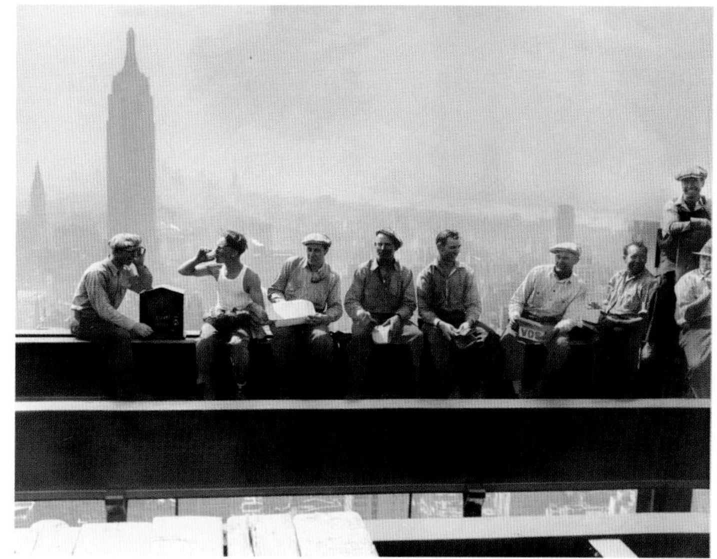

3.11 One of several lunch photos taken Sept. 20, 1932. (Rockefeller Group photo 119)

side, with Central Park in the upper left and the Plaza Hotel in the background.

Eight men stand atop a split-channel beam, silhouetted against a rugged cityscape in Image #112. Buildings stretch out far below them. It is a dramatic, high-contrast image that is more art than publicity. The photographer and the men are unknown.

It was a sanctioned, carefree moment for the ironworkers when they could strut their stuff, show off, and

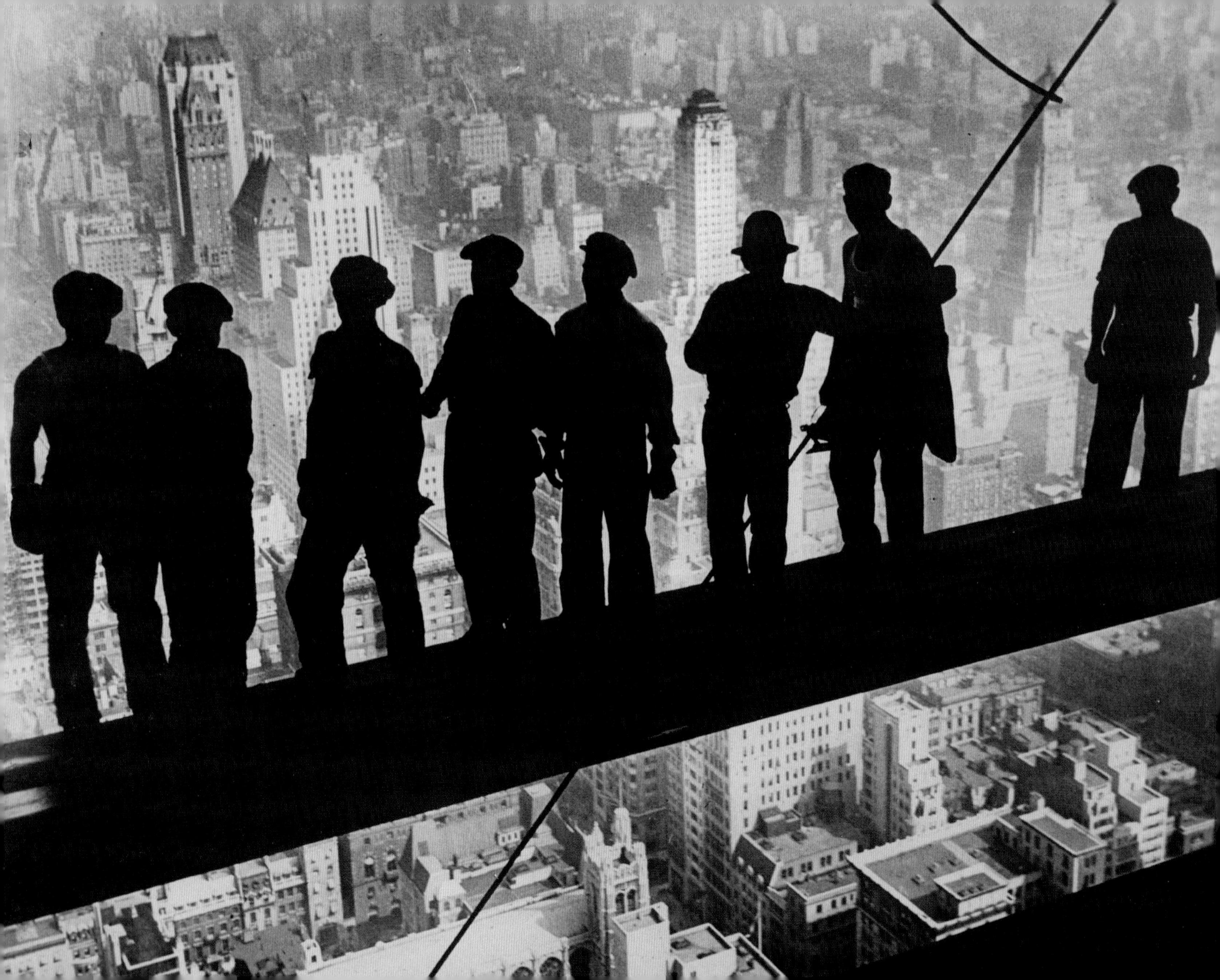

get paid. It was an unusual opportunity for the photographers to shoot choreographed scenes of ironworkers. The combination proved spectacular. The photos grabbed front pages from Buffalo to Berlin. The headlines varied, but most ran Crowell's copy ("While New York's thousands rush to crowded restaurants . . .") verbatim.

When the photographers packed their gear and left the steel structure, the ironworkers resumed the backbreaking job of constructing Rockefeller Center. It was nonstop work, evidenced by the speed with which the buildings were rising.

Considering that the nation was struggling through the worst months of the Great Depression, the pictures may seem frivolous. The number of images taken and the varying locations suggest that a substantial amount of time and freedom had been given to the photographers and ironworkers for this publicity shoot. They served a tangible cause: to attract attention and rent space in the R.C.A. Building. And a less tangible one: the photos not only publicized a building but promoted a vision of the future of New York, America, and even the world: confident, prosperous, hard-working, and fearless.

Don't look down, they said. Don't look down.

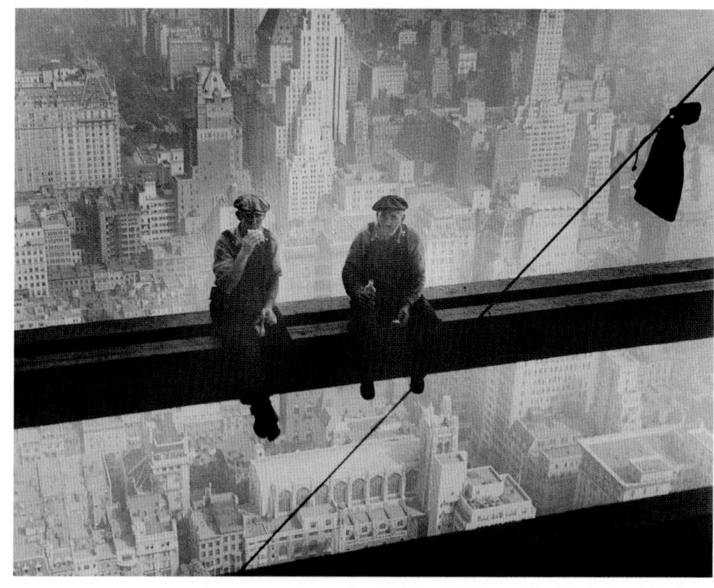

3.13 Two unidentified workers sit on a split-channel beam eating sandwiches. (Rockefeller Group photo 118)

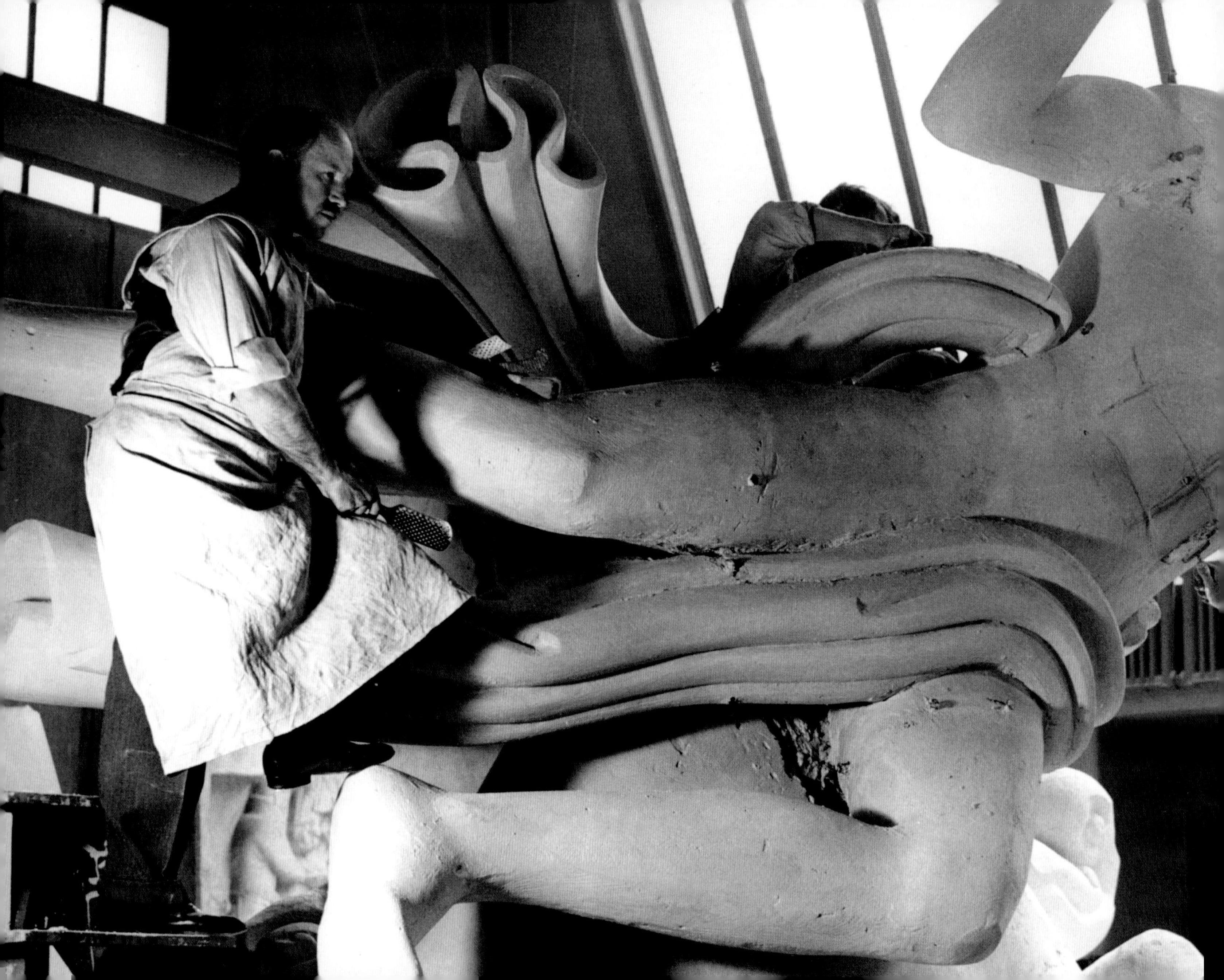

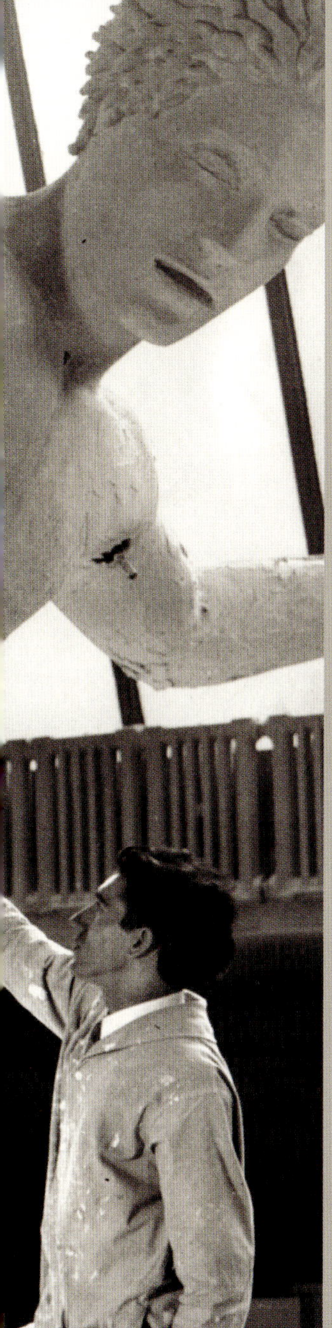

4

MEN AT THE
CROSSROADS

4.1 Paul Manship (left) and his assistant sculpt the plaster model of *Prometheus*. (Rockefeller Group photo 395C)

N 1941, JUNIOR WOULD PUBLISH a personal creed that came to be known as "I Believe." Twenty years later, these words would be engraved on a block of polished black stone in the Channel Gardens and on the Rockefeller Library at Brown, his alma mater:

I believe in the supreme worth of the individual and in his right to life, liberty, and the pursuit of happiness.

I believe that every right implies a responsibility; every opportunity, an obligation; every possession, a duty.

I believe that the law was made for man and not man for the law; that government is the servant of the people and not their master.

I believe in the dignity of labor, whether with head or hand; that the world owes no man a living but that it owes every man an opportunity to make a living.

I believe that thrift is essential to well ordered living and that economy is a prime requisite of a sound financial structure, whether in government, business or personal affairs.

I believe that truth and justice are fundamental to an enduring social order.

I believe in the sacredness of a promise, that a man's word should be as good as his bond; that character—not wealth or power or position—is of supreme worth.

I believe that the rendering of useful service is the common duty of mankind and that only in the purifying fire of sacrifice is the dross of selfishness consumed and the greatness of the human soul set free.

I believe in an all-wise and all-loving God, named by whatever name, and that the individual's highest fulfillment, greatest happiness, and widest usefulness are to be found in living in harmony with His will.

I believe that love is the greatest thing in the world; that it alone can overcome hate; that right can and will triumph over might.[1]

In some ways, the creed reflected Junior's priorities in 1941: contrasting American, social, political, and economic values—"truth," "justice," "God," and "love"—with rising Soviet and Nazi power, along with a rear-guard action—"thrift" and "opportunity"—against what he considered overreach by progressive reformers, labor activists, and Roosevelt's New Deal.

Although these ten principles were literally set in stone, they were not Junior's first stab at a credo. At a ceremony marking the completion of Rockefeller Center in 1939, he described "the fundamental principles and beliefs upon which Rockefeller Center has been built and for which it stands." Although the outlines of his final credo are clear, the focus is tighter on the relationship between labor and capital.

We believe that the ultimate object of all activities in a republic should be the development of its citizens; that such manhood can be developed to the fullest degree only under conditions of freedom for the individual, and that industrial enterprises can and should be conducted in accordance with these principles.

We believe that a prime consideration in the carrying on of industry should be the well-being of the men and women engaged in it, and that the soundest industrial policy is that which has constantly in mind the welfare of the employes [*sic*] as well as the making of profits.

A business, to be successful, must not only provide to labor remunerative employment under proper working conditions but it must also render useful service to the community and earn a fair return on the money invested. The adoption of any labor policy, however favorable to the workers it may seem, which results in the bankruptcy of the corporation and the discontinuance of its work, is as injurious to labor which is thrown out of work as it is to the public which loses the services of the enterprise and to the stockholders whose capital is impaired.

We believe it to be the duty of every citizen to do all within his power to improve the conditions under which men work and live. We believe that man renders the greatest social service who so cooperates in the organization of industry as to afford to the largest number of men the greatest opportunity for self-development, and the enjoyment by every man of those benefits which his own work adds to the wealth of civilization.

But these aims and ideals can be fully achieved only in a world that is at peace. The business men of this country want peace, peace among themselves, peace with government, peace with labor. They are tired, and the public is tired, of strife and discord, doubt and uncertainty, at home and abroad. They yearn for peace. War is often laid at the door of business. On its very face such an imputation is as absurd as it is false. Any intelligent business man knows that, while war may temporarily stimulate certain kinds of business, in the long run it is far more destructive of property and other values and leads to a far greater upheaval in the general business structure than any such stimulation can begin to offset.

I say with confidence that the earnest desire of the great majority of business men throughout the length and breadth of the land is that this country shall keep out of war.

We should, as a people, free ourselves forthwith from any legislative enactments that may prevent our freedom of action in connection with whatever international situations may arise. Having done that, and with the power to act from time to time as the conscience and will of this great nation may determine, we should devote ourselves tirelessly and persistently to the maintaining of peace and the preservation of our priceless heritage—the freedom of the individual, which millions of men and women throughout the world who have already lost it are realizing is worth more than life itself. To that great task, with faith in God and belief in the inherent worth of men, let us as a nation rededicate ourselves.[2]

Through both creeds run the values that Junior professed all his life, as had his father: individualistic, Christian, capitalist, industrious, dutiful, paternal. Those dutiful, paternal instincts had also led Junior to invest a fortune in public education—not only to build the workers and citizens of a great enterprise and nation, but to ensure the public avoided dangerous mistakes (in his view) like radicalism. Or trustbusting. The Rockefellers and their charities were the country's largest private funder of public education. Through the General Education Board, the family gave more than a hundred million dollars to support public schools for Black students in the segregated South. They created the University of Chicago and Rockefeller University, fueled the growth of Spelman College for Black women, and funded institutes across the Ivy League, several themselves devoted to education. Beyond those landmark gifts, the Rockefeller Foundation funded an array of research and educational programs.

Junior's museum philanthropy can be understood as an extension of his program of public education. The restoration of Colonial Williamsburg created a living museum to teach the public about the world that shaped America's founders and their values—which by no coincidence reflected Junior's. To be clear, Junior believed in education for its own sake. But, like his father, Junior believed that with enough education, the American public would come around to his way of thinking.[3]

So, too, would Rockefeller Center steer the public toward Rockefeller's vision. And art would be another tool to educate. In 1931, Hood, the chief architect, approached Junior and sold him on the idea of a coordinated plan for the art and decoration of Rockefeller Center. Junior saw to it that the vision would reflect his own social and spiritual values.

In the spring of 1931, on the recommendation of Raymond Hood, the team commissioned a public philosopher, Dr. Hartley Burr Alexander, to develop philosophic "themes and addendum which outlines the subject of decoration."[4] Alexander, a professor of philosophy at Scripps College at the University of Southern California in Claremont, returned a thirty-two-page manifesto, outlining his vision for "Homo Faber—Man the Builder."

Civilization is . . . what Man adds to Nature . . . men, dissatisfied with the physical environment into which they are born, by their handiwork and arts reshape it, "moulding the World nearer to the heart's desire." The secret of human idealism lies just here: we perceive improvements in the circumstances of our lives as possible, and forthwith we undertake to bring them about, and by the success of such efforts we measure our progress. . . .

Rockefeller City is surely being planned in some such measure. As a monument of human skill and taste and imagination it will be famous throughout the world of men; none will view it with indifference. On American life and society, and on the future development of New York and of the country at large it is inevitable that it will have a profound influence. It will be influential first as a building enterprise . . . for both the nature of its architecture and the character of the venture as a business enterprise are bound to be watched with a keen eye to the following or rejection of its leads. It will be influential secondly in its effect upon American taste, for the conscious effort to create beauty in the Center will compel the development of forms of expression which are novel, and which if successful will open new avenues to American art. finally, it will be influential socially, for it has at least the chance of becoming the first clear expression in our economic life of a new social ideal, that is of human welfare and happiness as centering in the work that we do, and not in some accidental wage; if a whole population, such as Rockefeller City will possess, can be lifted into a finer life in their working hours, then the economic democracy of America will have begun its answer to the Bolshevist challenge. In all of these phases, then Rockefeller is a builder's enterprise, and it is appropriate to announce its theme as "Homo Faber, Man the Builder."[5]

Communication was central to Alexander's vision, which he called "Frontiers of Time." And he went further, describing not only themes, but the appearance and placement of each work of art. Historians have noted that "the proposal was received without enthusiasm."[6] Alexander told Hood that John Todd almost threw him out of his office. And Okrent's *Great Fortune* called Alexander "the worst hiring decision in Rockefeller Center history."[7]

The Art Advisory Committee was formed in March 1932 in response to the furor over Alexander's theme for the Center. Junior found experts from Dartmouth, Columbia, and the Rockefeller Foundation for a second attempt at a vision for the art of Rockefeller Center. The Art Advisory Committee comprised Edward Waldo Forbes, director of Harvard's Fogg Art Museum; Fiske Kimball, director of the Philadelphia Museum of Art; Everett V. Meeks, dean of Yale's School of Fine Arts; Paul J. Sachs, trustee of Boston's

Museum of Fine Arts; and Herbert E. Winlock, director of the Metropolitan Museum of Art.[8]

With his management team at a loss, Junior requested additional guidance from two academics he admired: George Vincent,[9] the president of the Rockefeller Institute, and M. I. Pupin, a Columbia professor and electronics inventor. In March 1932, Vincent submitted "A Decorative Scheme for Rockefeller Center," which reiterated a number of Alexander's ideas, grouped, like Alexander, under an overarching theme: "America in the Pageant of Civilization." Junior was particularly taken by Vincent's subtheme of "The Contemporary World," noting that "it deals with the whole world and not just America."[10]

Pupin's report aligned with Alexander and Vincent. He recommended that the decorative panels for the R.C.A. Building "illustrate the creative power of our civilization on the side of transportation and communication." Some panels would illustrate how "the moving power of electricity" was applied to communications, through images of "telegraphy, telephony, radio transmission, and television."[11]

It fell to Merle Crowell, the Rockefeller Center publicist, to stitch all of these suggestions into a grand theme for the art: "New Frontiers and The March of Civilization."[12] This he divided into four subthemes: "Man's Progress toward Civilization of Today," "Man's Development in Mind and Spirit," "Man's Progress Along Physical and Scientific Lines," and "Man's Progress in Industry and the Character of the Nation."[13]

"This theme," Crowell wrote, "is intended to interpret our American civilization of the moment, its manifestations, its meanings, its promises. We are considering specifically the pictorial representation in Rockefeller City of where we have arrived and what we are going through as a people, physically, mentally, and spiritually . . . as well as what we are about to go through. The past will be brought in naturally and briefly as background, but the points of special interest will be developed from our life today."[14]

These themes hewed closely to Alexander's original vision. "Indeed, the way Crowell discussed the 'New Frontiers' was virtually identical to Alexander's claims about the same subject," wrote William Buxton, a scholar of communication studies. "Since there were no longer new territories to explore and settle, civilization would now develop in an inward and upward manner. This would involve cultivating 'the comparatively unexplored and undeveloped territory within ourselves.' What Crowell had in mind was not only 'the spiritual significance of life,' but also 'a significant adventure in human relations.' Echoing Alexander's allusion to various forms of institutions, Crowell went on to note how 'new frontiers' would be embodied in medical science, in general science, and in education. His plans for the Central (Radio) Building were also quite in line with those of Alexander, namely, the use of the two long available spaces for the representation of 'the pageant of transport' and 'the pageant of civilization.'"[15] These themes—human development redirected upward, the modern workplace an "adventure in human relations"—would resurface months later in a photo shoot, once again managed by Crowell.

For his part, Alexander was unimpressed by any departure from his vision. His contempt dripped into his 1935 essay, "More Than This, What Need Any Art Tell?" Alexander praised a young California artist, Millard Sheets, as a maker of art for art's sake and contrasted him with "picture-writers, who conceive their scribe's office to be that of rebuking our sins, and all of spotty time's, and there are scolds who berate in paint our stupidities, not always concealing their own, and there are pedants of the brush who conscientiously prick out our walls with multigraphs of the masterpieces of yesteryears. Instructions in oil, sermons in paint, monitions in fresco, all meant to remind us that Art is a Mission and that our reform is its affair, all these flourish, and doubtless there is place for their passing cleverness in the daily cartoon, in Rockefeller lobbies, in the gossip files."[16]

Nevertheless, Alexander's influences are visible throughout Rockefeller Center. It was he who named the promenade between the British and French buildings "The Channel."[17] With Todd and Brown's tight timetables for construction, most of the American artists were commissioned before Crowell and company purged Alexander's name from the public story. Over the main entrance to the R.C.A. Building, for example, sculptor Lee Lawrie's three panels, "Wisdom," "Sound," and "Light," hew closely to Alexander's vision for "A Voice from the Clouds." And in Radio City Music Hall, Ezra Winter's "Quest for the Fountain of Eternal Youth" followed Alexander's instructions with a degree of specificity usually reserved for paint-by-number kits. Critics have called it one of the weakest artworks in Rockefeller Center, but Winter's academic, hazily didactic mural delighted Junior.[18]

The most famous sculpture in the Center is the monumental, gilded Art Deco figure *Prometheus* in the flowing fountain of the Lower Plaza by the American artist Paul Manship.

The architects gave him little time to produce a masterwork that would dominate the Lower Plaza: one year from approved sketch to installation. Manship's simplified forms, clean sinuous lines, and sweeping slender curves meld classical and modern. After World War I, he spent

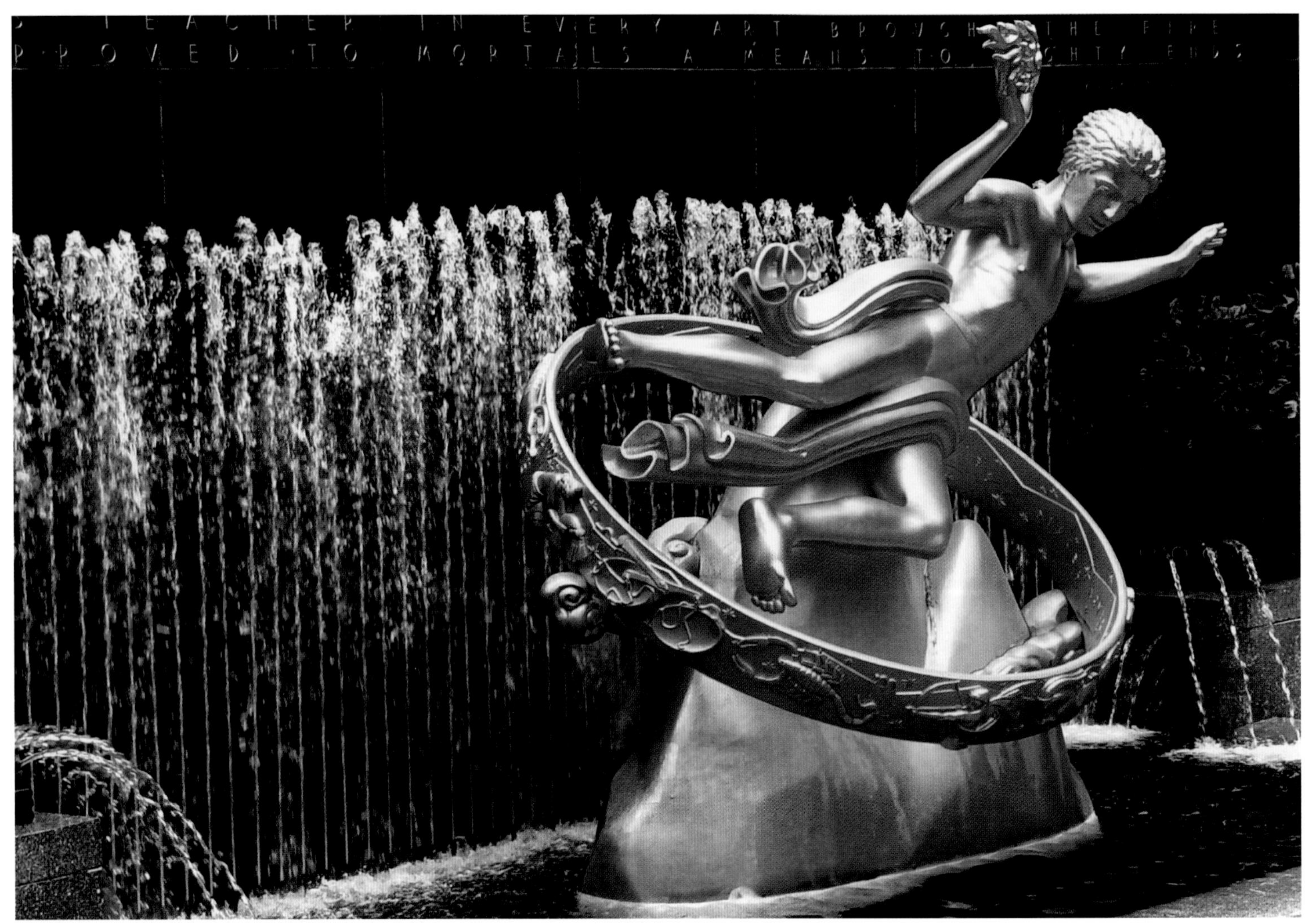

4.2 *Prometheus* by Paul Manship. (CR photo)

five years in Italy, Greece, and the Middle East to study the techniques of classical and Renaissance sculpture, monuments, and iconography. In 1925, he returned to the United States, where his work was immediately successful. *Prometheus* is said to be the most photographed sculpture in New York City.

By 1930, the Art Deco movement had swept urban architecture and design. The movement's sleek and opulent modernism, culture-spanning classical motifs, and monumental scale reflected new building technologies—especially improved steel, and the path it offered into the sky.

For businesses, Art Deco was the perfect visual language to communicate success, power, and prospects.[19] The Cunard building (1921) adorned the sixty-five-foot domed ceiling of its Great Hall with Edward Winter's sweeping frescoes of the history of navigation. The Chrysler Building (1930) incorporated exposed steel into its gleaming Art Deco facade, where eagles perch in the style of the automaker's hood ornaments. Inside the lobby, Edward Trumbull's canvas mural *Transport and Human Endeavor*—then the largest painting in America—depicts Chrysler's assembly line.[20] The Empire State Building (1931) announced its triumph not only with its record height but also with the geometric lines, sunburst motifs, and opulent materials of Art Deco. For the lobby ceiling's gilded celestial mural, the builders turned to a commercial designer, Leif Neandross of the Rambusch Decorating Company.[21]

Manship's *Prometheus* reflects the persistent influence of Hartley Burr Alexander's mythological themes. The story of Prometheus communicates endurance, strength, and sacrifice. The mythological Titan dominates the scene, surrounded by the elements of fire, water, and earth. His gilded, nearly nude figure plummets through the sky while bearing a fiery torch to mankind. The mountain-like pedestal at the base of the statue symbolizes the earth, the basin, the seas, and the ring with the signs of the zodiac, the heavens.

In Greek mythology, Prometheus stole fire from the Olympian gods and gave it to humanity huddled in darkness. Mankind took the fire and advanced civilization toward immortality—a quality reserved to the gods. The offended Olympians captured Prometheus and punished him for his crime. Zeus chained him to a rock, where a vulture would peck out his liver every night, only for it to regrow and the torment to repeat the next day.

Manship's sculpture celebrates the duty of the strongest to help the weakest, and symbolizes the burden of privilege. Manship suggested the inscription, a quote from

Aeschylus, carved into the red granite wall behind the figure: "Prometheus, teacher in every art, brought the fire that hath proved to mortals a means to mighty ends."

In the architects' vision for the open spaces of Rockefeller Center, only one site was as important as Prometheus's perch in the Lower Plaza: the narrow forecourt of the International Building on Fifth Avenue, across from Saint Patrick's Cathedral. "Any work placed here had to be a forceful expression of authority and strength, dominating the site without compromising the architecture."[22]

In other words, a Titan.

In 1934, the architects approached Lee Lawrie, their go-to sculptor and the Center's most prolific artist. Lawrie was an architectural sculptor—a sculptor whose work is integral to the building's design. Over his long career of more than three hundred commissions, Lawrie's style evolved with the architects who employed him, from Beaux-Arts to Art Deco. His productive partnership with the architect Bertram Goodhue included the Nebraska State Capitol Building, where he first worked with Hartley Burr Alexander.

Lawrie created the mighty cast-bronze Art Deco Titan *Atlas*. One of twelve works Lawrie created with Rene Chambellan, *Atlas* is a companion piece to Manship's *Prometheus*; their Art Deco style and myths are interwoven.[23]

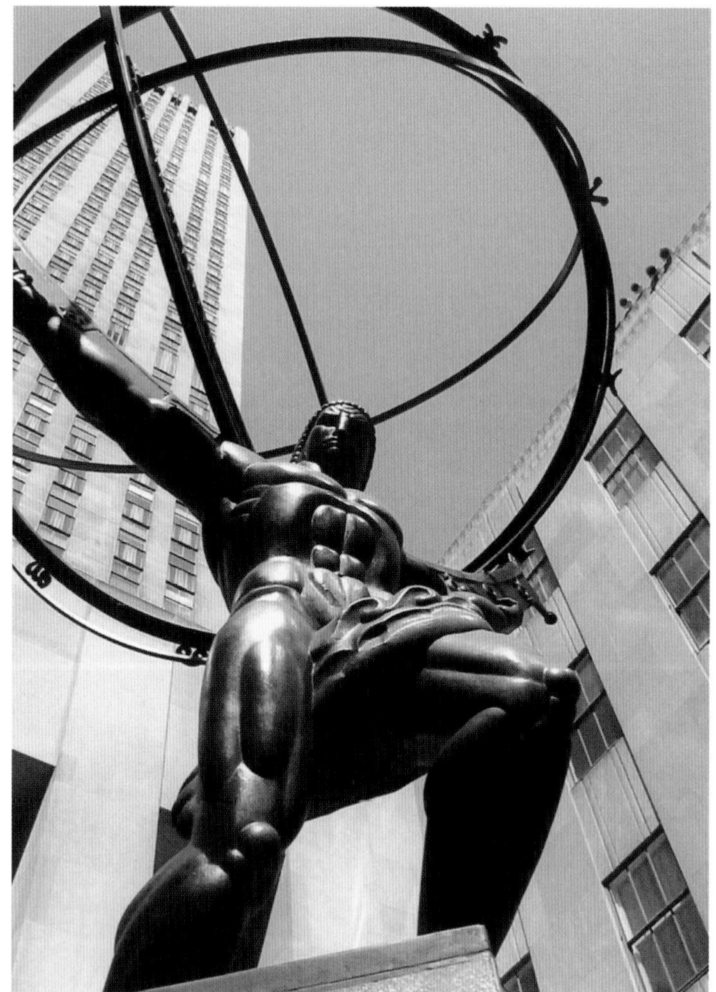

4.3 *Atlas* by Lee Lawrie and Rene Chamberlain. (CR photo)

As a brother Titan, Atlas joined the ten-year war against the Olympians to determine which gods would control the universe. And like his brother, Atlas paid for his defeat. Atlas was made to carry the Earth and heavens on his back for eternity. The statue depicts that never-ending duty. *Atlas* stands on a high pedestal in the narrow courtyard of the International Building. He bears on his shoulders an armillary sphere, the celestial vault. The sphere's north-south axis points toward the North Star.

Both *Atlas* and *Prometheus* are huge, powerful, and sumptuous. They are literal titans, one persecuted for the gifts he gave mankind, the other shouldering the weight of the world. It is hard to imagine more obvious symbolism for Rockefeller's namesake.

If *Atlas* symbolizes Rockefeller's vision at the front of the International Building, the bas-reliefs of Gaston Lachaise complement it at the rear. In 1935, Gaston Lachaise had a successful retrospective exhibit at the Museum of Modern Art but, amid the Depression, was struggling for work. Like his mother, Abby, Nelson Rockefeller admired and collected Lachaise's risqué artwork, and he arranged a contract for Lachaise. Lachaise chose a theme that paid tribute to the workers who built the Center: *To Commemorate the Workers of the Center*, a duo of limestone bas-reliefs set into the rear facade of the International Building. His muscular, nearly naked ironworkers wear kilts in the fashion of Egypt's pyramid builders. They defy gravity as they float on an I-beam—a sculptor's reflection of "Lunch on a Beam."

A titan at the fore, his noble workers at the back.

Lachaise was one of a dozen international artists enlisted to promote the global reach of Rockefeller Center. Rockefeller was positioning his development as a World Trade Center, a generation before his sons would bestow that name on their own project. In 1932, an act of Congress made Rockefeller Center a free port, allowing businesses to import goods duty-free and store them on the premises—a commercial *coup de maître*. To the English and French Buildings, the developers discussed adding buildings for Germany and Italy. (Lee, worried about Germany's instability and rising fascism, advised Junior to quietly pursue the idea but avoid any public announcements until the situation was better understood.) The German building was dropped when Hitler's Nazi party seized power in 1933. The Palazzo Italiano was subsumed into a catch-all International Building. The ingenious decision to rent the second floor to the US Passport Service for one dollar per year attracted paying tenants to the International Building: steamship companies, airlines, trade offices, luggage stores, and travel agencies.

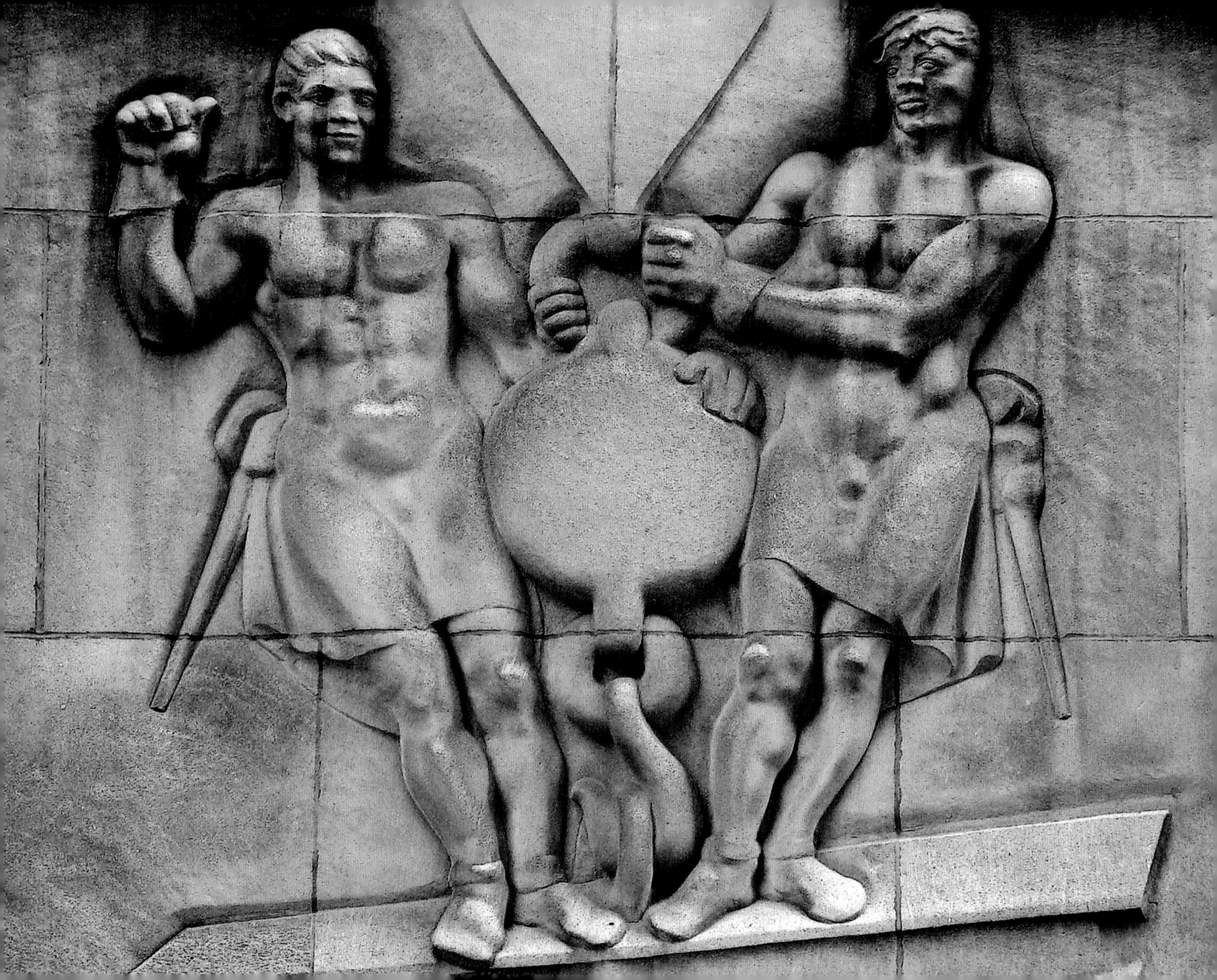

By the fall of 1932, no international artists had yet been commissioned—a lacuna in Rockefeller Center's international image. On September 2, 1932, Todd and Hood set out on a voyage that Crowell announced with typical bombast: "John R. Todd, head of the builders and managers of Rockefeller Center, and Raymond Hood, one of the architects prominently identified with the big mid-city building project, will sail on the French liner *Paris* . . . to contact a notable group of English, Italian, French and Spanish artists relative to their execution of murals in the Great Hall of the seventy-story R.C.A. Building."[24]

Crowell's announcement was light on artistic detail, but laden, as usual, with big numbers: Ten panels, each "at least seventeen by twenty feet" were planned for "the spacious main lobby, or Great Hall, of the world's largest office building."

Crowell dangled the promise of further news. "The names of the European artists to be considered were not announced," he wrote. In fact, Hood and Todd were aiming high. They reached out to Henri Matisse and Pablo Picasso. Matisse refused. As Hood told Junior: "We explained our scheme of decoration of the great hall to him but without going any further or even coming to the point of discussing what we had to spend, Matisse very amiably but firmly told us that he did not feel that his work would be shown to good advantage in such a setting, and that he would not be honest in accepting a commission to do the work."[25] Picasso did not respond at all.

Down the list, Hood and Todd had more luck: José María Sert and Frank Brangwyn, leading muralists from Spain and England, were both enthusiastic and agreeable to the terms—financial, logistical, and artistic. And at the same time, Hood and Todd were negotiating by cable with one more international artist, the foremost muralist of his time: Diego Rivera.[26] The plan taking shape: Rivera would paint the central mural in the lobby of the R.C.A. Building, flanked by murals by Sert and Brangwyn.

Junior had insisted he must personally approve sketches before any contracts were given. But, on one occasion, Junior deferred to his wife Abigail and their son Nelson. The Rockefellers already knew Rivera. With two friends in 1930, Abby Rockefeller had founded the Museum of Modern Art to champion contemporary artists. Nelson, who shared his mother's taste, joined the museum's board and helped raise money. Through that association, Abigail became friendly with Diego Rivera and his wife, the painter Frida Kahlo, and over the course of a few years became quite close and entertained them when they were in New York. Abigail collected their art for her personal collection and, in 1931, helped sponsor a retrospective of

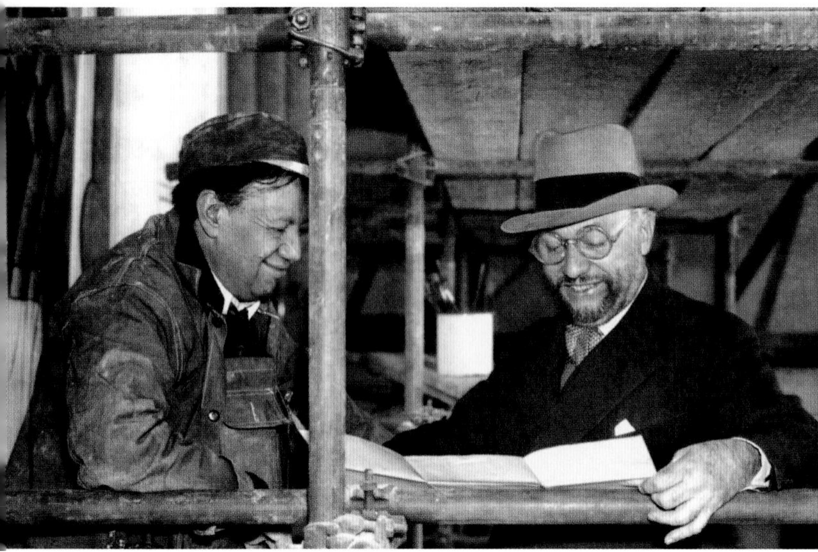

4.5 Diego Rivera and Jose Maria Sert at work in Rockefeller Center, 1933. (Rockefeller Group photo)

Diego's work at MoMA. It was a record-breaking one-man show for which Rivera painted eight mobile mural panels, all before he was awarded the fresco commission at the Center. Abigail's taste in "modern art" was completely foreign to her husband, who collected Chinese porcelains and established the Met Cloisters, a branch of the Metropolitan Museum of Art, to showcase medieval art.

"I can't tell you how pleased we all are that Rivera is going to do the art panel for the entrance of the #1 building at Rockefeller Center," Nelson wrote to Clifford Wright, an English sculptor and Rivera protégé. "I feel this is perhaps the most important piece in the development and that he is, without question, the man to do it."[27]

The Rockefellers knew perfectly well that Rivera was a Communist, a fact he proclaimed at every opportunity. But he seemed a Communist they could work with. He had been kicked out of Mexico's Communist Party, and by fall 1932 had accepted a major commission at the Detroit Institute of Art, funded by the family of Henry Ford. The choice was seen as controversial but daring and bracingly modern, for both the artist and the Fords, and soon, for the Rockefellers. "As for Rivera," Junior wrote to his architects, "although I do not personally care for much of his work, he seems to have become very popular just now and will probably be a good drawing card."[28]

John Todd presented Rivera with a four-page contract, which said nothing about the subject of the mural but gave Rivera thirty days to submit a preliminary sketch. Once approved by the architects, the sketch was to be "faithfully and closely followed." Rivera had until April 1, 1933, four months from the sketch to completed mural, which the contract assumed would be on canvas. He would be paid $21,500 in installments.

Rivera insisted on changes. His mural would be in color—not the gray palette that Sert and Brangwyn had agreed to, and it would be a fresco, not a painting on canvas. In fresco painting, the artist rapidly applies watercolor to wet lime plaster on a wall or ceiling, so that the colors penetrate deeply and chemically fix as the plaster dries. The ceiling of the Sistine Chapel is a fresco. So is *The Last Supper*. A fresco is as permanent as the building, or at least the wall, it adorns. Did Rivera anticipate the furor to come?

Diego Rivera, John Todd, and Joseph O. Robertson (or their secretaries) signed the contract. It was dated November 2, 1932.

Rivera submitted a series of drawings for approval, with the theme "Man at the Crossroads, Looking with Hope and High Vision to the Choosing of a Course Leading to a New and Better Future." Todd and Nelson asked for a less crowded sketch, and Rivera obliged. The final pencil sketch filled 71¼ by 31 inches of paper. Only so many details of the 63 by 17-foot fresco could be clearly depicted, but the theme seemed still to align with Junior's credo and Dr. Alexander's thesis, "New Frontiers and The March of Civilization."

At the center, three men representing different aspects of life hold hands: a worker, a farmer, and a soldier. Behind them appears to be a movie screen. Rivera described his vision as a "more complete balance between . . . technical and ethical development."[29]

Rivera showed Abby and Nelson the sketch in November 1932. Hood and Junior also saw it. The Rockefellers were comfortable with Rivera and thought that he would interpret "Man at the Crossroads Looking with Uncertainty but with Hope and High Vision to the Choosing of a Course Leading to a New and Better Future" in a manner that would enhance the Center, or at least its publicity. Even if the artist's Communist sympathies leaked into the plaster, that would only demonstrate the sophistication of Rockefeller Center: international hub, cosmopolitan, a city within a city. As benignly risqué as the Rockettes' kick line, which debuted the following month.

But this time, the Rockefellers had chosen a partner who danced to his own tune.

The central figure was now a single worker, at the controls of a vast machine. Long ellipses of light radiated out, filled with microbes and planets—lenses on the micro- and macrocosm. To the left, Rivera painted warplanes, gas-masked troops, and society ladies smoking, swilling cocktails, and playing cards while mounted police beat protesters. To the right, juxtaposed against the violence and debauchery of capitalism, Rivera painted a parade of workers, red-babushka'd women and soldiers, marching together under red banners; young athletes; and a diverse,

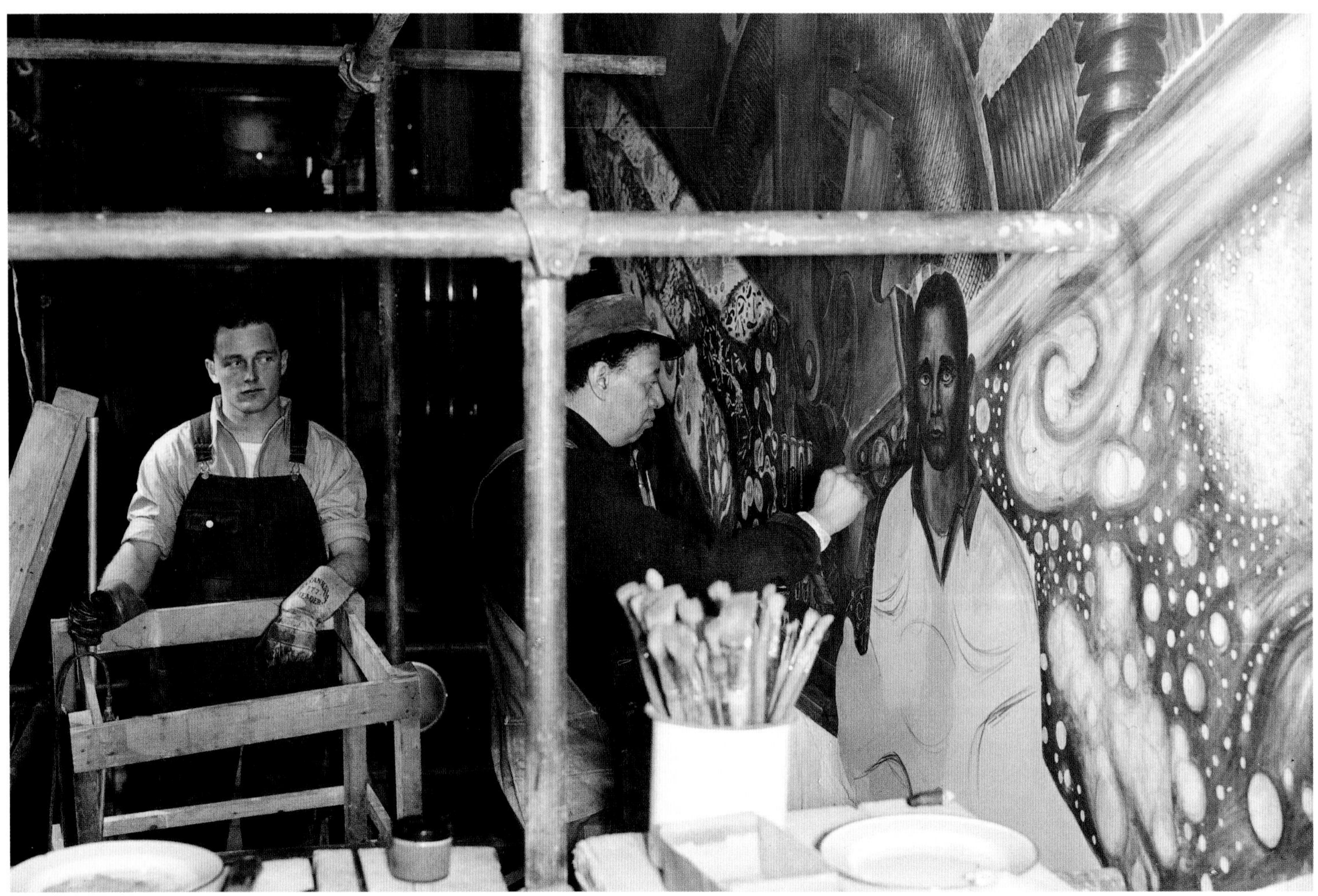

4.6 Rivera paints a worker. He would discover that his model was Hugh Curry Jr., the grandnephew of a Tammany Hall boss. (Rockefeller Group photo)

harmonious crowd. The trio—worker, farmer, soldier—had moved to the right of center, and now one of them was Black.

Rivera needed controversy—it could ignite his energy and his painting. The divided reaction to the Detroit murals had only increased his fame. He hoped his next mural would provoke the Communist Party, which had expelled him for backing Trotsky over Stalin and now ridiculed him for selling out to capitalists. As he painted, he expected a commotion—an outcry from the left and right, but there were no protests. He invited Joseph Lilly of the *New York World-Telegram* to a preview showing. The April 23, 1932, headline read: "Rivera Perpetuates Scenes of Communist Activity for R.C.A. Walls and Rockefeller Jr. Foots the Bill."

Still, there was no uproar. Rivera doubled down. "If you want communism," he said, "I will paint communism." To the trio of men holding hands, he added one more: the iconic, bearded bald head of Vladimir Lenin.[30]

A few days later, ceiling painters dripped white paint on the mural. Hood, the architect, was called down to examine the damage and repairs. As he scrutinized the fresco, he caught sight of the new face. "Who's that?" he asked. "Trotsky?"

At last, Rivera got the reaction he wanted. To say a furor exploded among all classes of people is to understate

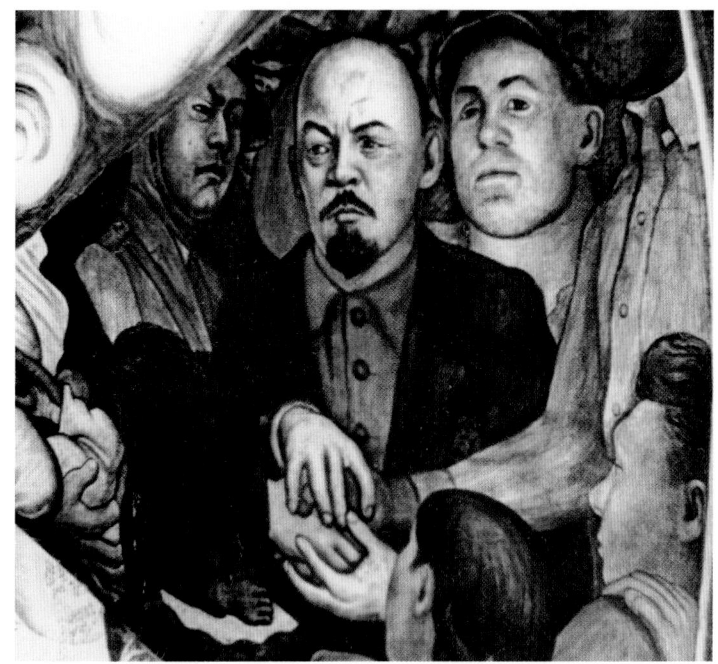

4.7 Detail of Rivera's fresco showing Lenin. (Rockefeller Group photo)

the public's reaction and Junior's displeasure.[31] Headlines called for the mural's destruction. Protesters gathered to demand it stay.

It fell to Nelson, as Rivera's champion in the family, to get Lenin out of the picture. After all, Rivera had accommodated changes to his sketch. Nelson began the negotiation with a tactful note to Rivera: "While I was in the No.

1 building yesterday viewing the progress of your thrilling mural, I noticed in the most recent portion of the painting you had included a portrait of Lenin." After a bit of hemming and hawing, Nelson cut to the chase: "As much as I dislike to do so, I am afraid we must ask you to substitute the face of some unknown man where Lenin's face now appears."[32]

Rivera replied, somewhat disingenuously, that Lenin's head was included in the original sketch, if only as "a general and abstract representation of the concept of a leader, an indispensable human figure." He offered to balance Lenin with such American heroes as Abraham Lincoln, John Brown, or Nat Turner in place of the louche socialites. But he drew a line in the sand: "Rather than mutilate the conception I should prefer the physical destruction of the concept in its entirety but preserving at least its integrity."[33]

That was the end of Nelson's involvement. After his kid gloves came Hugh Robertson's iron fist. On May 9, Robertson dispatched a phalanx of security guards through the protest and into the R.C.A. lobby. He ordered Rivera down from the scaffolding, handed the artist a check for the last fourteen thousand dollars of his twenty-one-thousand-dollar contract, and escorted Rivera and his team out of the building.[34] Rockefeller Center workers taped brown paper over the mural.

And there it sat for the next nine months, as architects agonized over "the Wailing Wall," as they called it among themselves. Hood reached out again to Picasso, who this time responded with a list of demands designed to be refused.[35] The fresco's plaster proved impossible to separate intact; Rivera's fresco could only be removed by destroying it.[36] And so it was.

Saturday, February 9, 1934, dawned as the coldest day in New York history: thirteen degrees below zero. Extra guards patrolled Sing Sing prison, where ice floes on the Hudson River presented a tempting means of escape. Strong gusts blew through the new canyons of midtown Manhattan. Rockefeller Center's fountains were in no danger of freezing; they had not yet been turned on. That night, workers entered the lobby with hammers and wheelbarrows. They smashed the fresco off the wall. Plaster chunks, paint still visible, were carted out in wheelbarrows.

Years later, I asked Nelson, who had championed the artist, why he didn't at least have the head of Lenin chopped out of the wall and delivered to his office. "On a silver platter?" asked the vice president, his face like an anxious little boy. "You don't know the trouble I was in with Father."

I have always suspected that Nelson took the fall for his mother, to whom he was devoted and, in this situation, protective. He paid a heavy emotional price with his stern father, who preferred his values like his R.C.A. murals: black and white.

4.8 Rivera's mural was covered with brown paper. (Rockefeller Group photo)

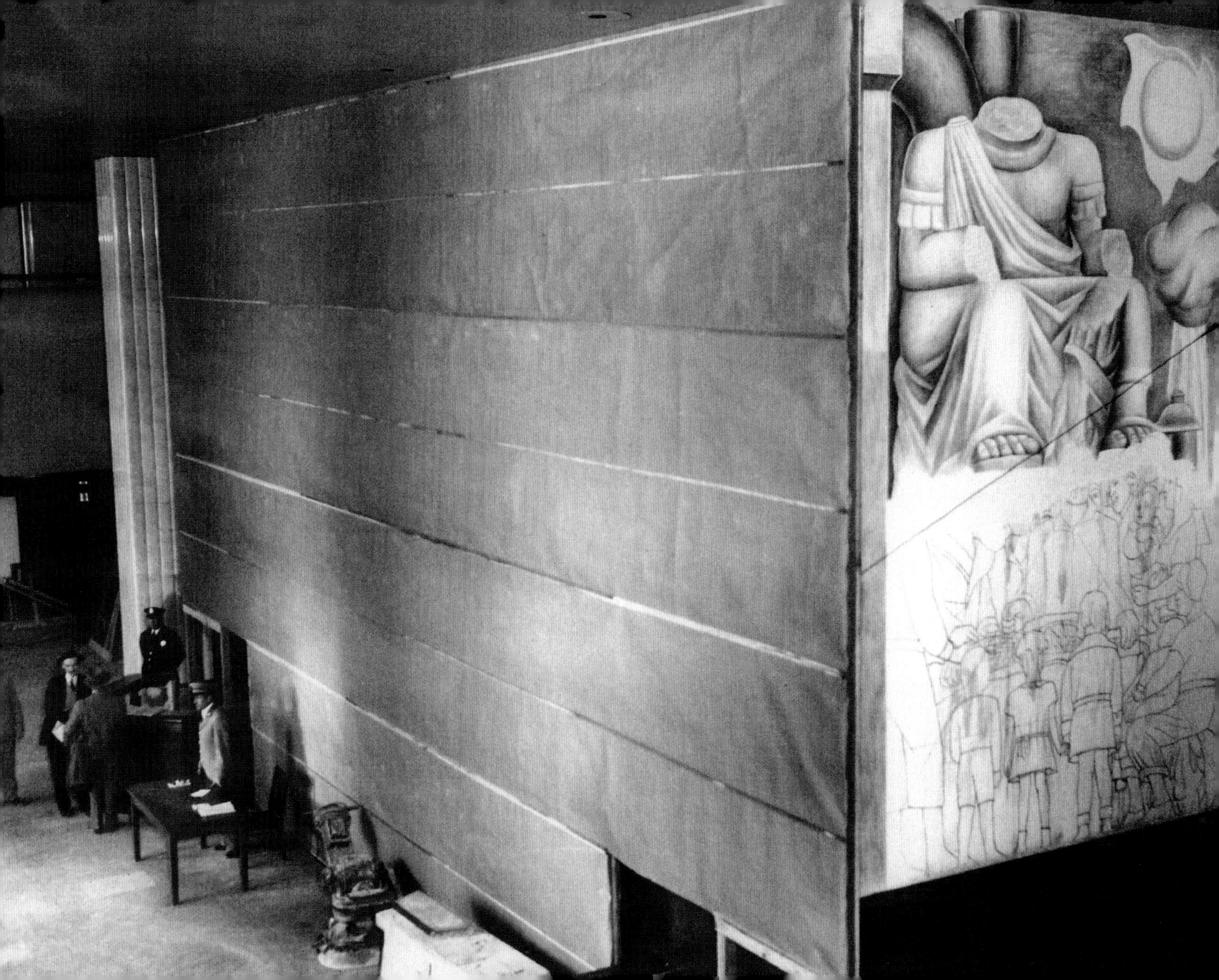

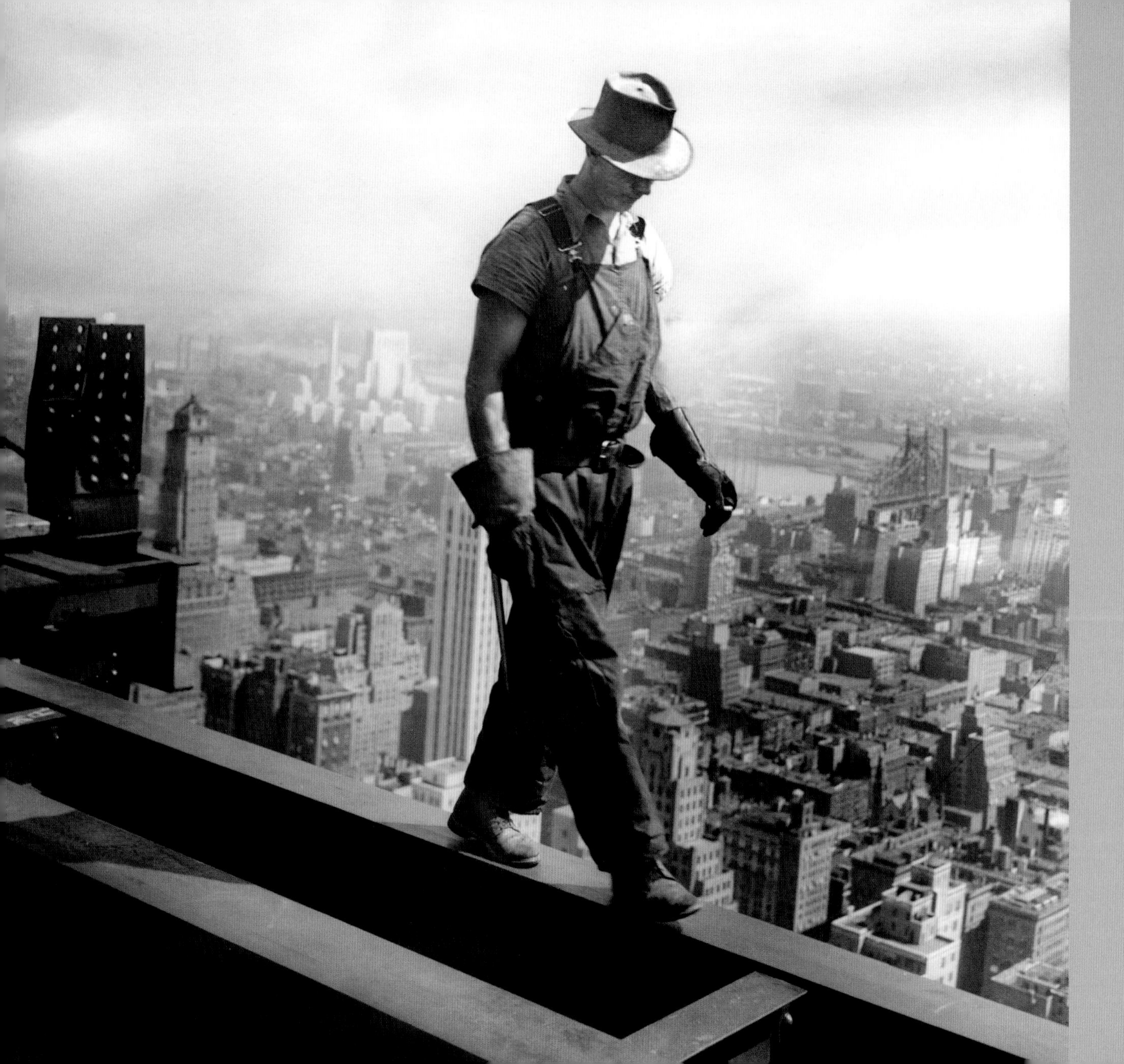

5

"ALL WE GOT IS HARD LUCK"

5.1 "Lone man walks on a Beam." (Rockefeller Group photo 252)

C HRIS THORSTEN WAS BORN AROUND 1889, aboard a fishing boat moored to a dock in New Orleans. Like his father and brother, he worked on herring boats, but unlike them he didn't die at sea. In 1907, he left the water for ironwork and New York City—a common path in the early twentieth century. In 1939, he granted a remarkable interview to a writer, Arnold Manoff, who was profiling laborers for the Works Progress Administration. Manoff marveled at Thorsten's physique—"200 pounds, 6 foot 2 flat, hard muscle. Back is bent in a long curve, no hips, long thin legs, hands are twice the size of ordinary man's hand, fingers abnormally thick and straight. A huge head sitting squarely on a lean young neck. Face set like iron but immensely warm. Clean gray eyes, fine well-proportioned features solid and sharp. Reddish tan complexion, deep set eyes, graying blond hair."

Here is Thorsten's story, as told to Manoff:

I remember one job. It was the Parcel Post Building 43rd and Lexington Avenue, you know the one. I worked straight through five days and four nights. We made money in those days. I was with the hoisting gang. The only time we got off was two hours for breakfast 1 hour for lunch, one hour for supper and one hour at night. Then I went into the saloon and I went to sleep. They couldn't wake me with a sledge hammer. I felt kinda ashamed of myself that I couldn't take it. Fallin asleep and all that. We wuz loadin 32-ton girders on that job. My friend Charlie Walker wuz workin with me. He wuz hookin on in the raising gang. That wuz a good job, we made money on that job. I been in this racket 32 years. You wouldn't believe I wuz 51 years old. Take a good look. You wouldn't believe it would you? It's a hell of a racket.

Now take that Sixth Ave. El job. They're rushin that job.

Plenty of men get killed there. The first man gets killed standin on the railroad tracks. Friday another man gets killed. The burners don't wanna go down. Dawn by Canal Street the first man was killed. They dropped a whole load of steel. I was on a job once and my friend George Morgan got killed.

We're just sittin there jokin you see. He was tyin on a safety railin on the scaffold and a beam rolled. The next mornin we had to go over and work where he fell down. I had him in mind and I got stuck between a beam and I landed in the Good Samaritan Hospital. Three vertebrae broken and the collar bone. Here you can feel the bump where the back was broke. Go on feel it. You ain't an Iron worker unless you get killed. He Sam I'll knock wood, I was never on a job where we lost a derrick. Yeh I know plenty of booms fold up. Everybody knows Lehman is behind this Sixth Ave. El job. They can't get men from the Union to go down there. Well they're rushin it. A man don't have time to watch out for himself.

There'll be plenty of men killed before this job is over. If I had the money I'd put it in steel. They figure these things. Take a building like the Chrysler Building. Who gave the estimate on that? Take the Empire State Building. Who's gonna give the estimate on that? Take the designer. He's gotta know. What I mean is this. When they get up to the 86th floor. There's some tonnage in that building and somebody gotta know where to put it. There was one or two of our men killed on that job. Men hurt on all jobs. Take the Washington Bridge, the Triboro Bridge, plenty of men hurt on those jobs. Two men killed on the Hotel New Yorker. I drove rivets all the way on that job. When I got hurt, I was squeezed between a crane and a collar bone broke and all the ribs in my body and three vertebrae. I was laid up for four years. I'll tell how I got hurted. There wuz an airplane factory cross the way from where I was working.

The motors were runnin and you couldn't hear a thing. I had a sign up there and I was leanin over the rail and squish I got caught between the beam and the rail.

Once dawn in Maiden Lane we wuz workin and we wuz singin dirty songs. You know "It ain't gonna rain no more no more." You know, I can't tell ya. Ya know, "Mary went to the grocer to buy herself a duck," that kind of stuff and they had to send the cops up to stop us from singing because they could hear us. That place is like a canyon.

Once dawn in Georgia two colored ladies wuz walkin along the street. They see some of the boys comin out of the saloon. You know. Foolin around. One colored lady says to the one. Ya see dam guys. On Friday they walk a narrow little plank away up in the air and on Saturday, the sidewalk ain't wide enough for them.

They drink like hell. There wuz Three Star Hennessy. He threw his card away and went snakin. Another place I worked there wuz two genuine snakes.

We ain't got any stories around here. All we got is hard luck. If they'd give the damn work back to the contractors, we'd all be workin. I don't get this WPA set-up at all. You take Sam here. They fired him on the WPA for drinkin once or twice. That ain't no way for them to act.

I ran away from New Orleans when I wuz a kid. Yeh I'm an old herring catcher. What can a man do if his whole family is herring catchers?[1]

Time after time, as I interviewed ironworkers' families, I was told the Great Depression hit the construction trades hard and ironworkers harder than most. The families were proud of how they survived and thrived.

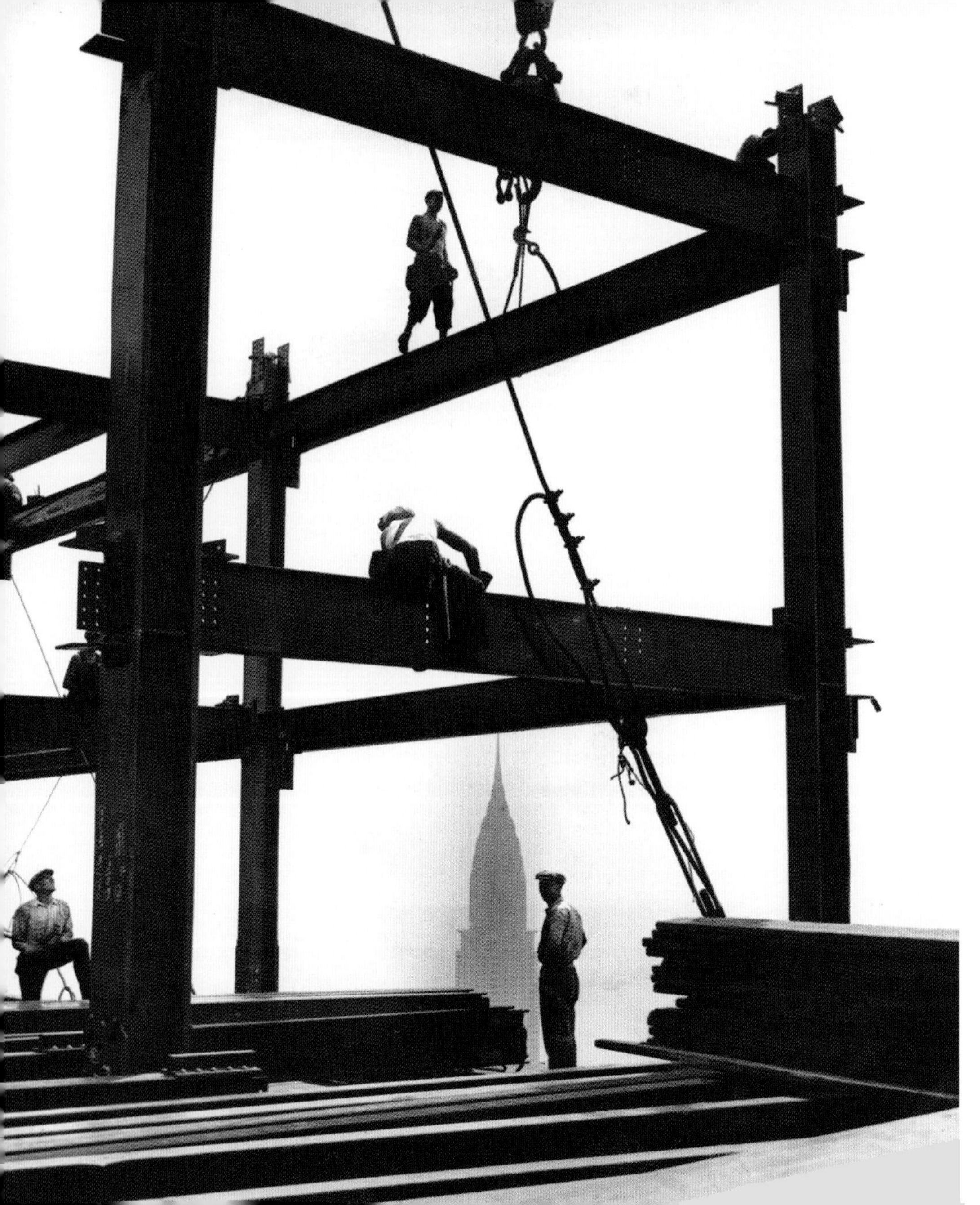

5.2 "As the world's largest building greets a rival. In the background is the Chrysler Building." (Rockefeller Group photo 10)

A few men found work in high-rise construction at Rockefeller Center, almost the only game in town. "There was a lot of talk about Radio City and the Triborough Bridge, good jobs to come, but the Triborough remained in the talking stage for years," recalled McClain, an ironworker, in his memoir. "There was a lot of courage behind Radio City, behind the steel and brick, the human skill and energy assembled to create one of the great monuments of our country."[2]

For New York's immigrants, this dangerous work became a vehicle for assimilation into American culture, because ironwork is teamwork as each man coordinates with and is dependent on others no matter where they came from. Recalling the thick accent of one superintendent—"a cigar-chewing Swede of the old school," McClain described communication on the site as "strictly a mind-reading proposition."[3]

One misstep could be deadly. Among the perils: The job went on no matter the weather. In New York, steel beams become icy cold and slippery in winter and sizzling hot in summer. The higher the structure, the stronger the wind, buffeting incoming beams and scattering sparks from the riveters' forges, always burning on the highest levels.

The year before, one such spark had ignited the upper floors of the rising Starrett-Lehigh Building on West Twenty-Sixth Street. "While the flames were at their height to the accompaniment of a crackling like that of a multitude of firecrackers, a gasoline drum went hurtling into the air and then bounced down through the building," the *New York Times* reported. "At times, heavy ten-foot planks would break loose and go sailing to the street, but from such a height that firemen had ample time to gauge them and get out of the way." The flames burned too high for water to reach, even as the maximum pressure "burst one line of hose after another."[4]

To reduce that risk at the R.C.A. Building, fireproofing crews followed the riveters up the rising towers, sealing the floors below from the fire threat above. But that work posed its own dangers. On August 22, 1932, carpenter Antonio Graziano, forty-seven, was working with a crew from the Knickerbocker fireproofing Company on the thirty-seventh floor of the R.C.A. Building. As he stood on a sawhorse, balanced on two planks over an open shaft, an ironworker shouted from five floors above: "Look out below!" A bull pin—an iron bolt weighing about six pounds—had slipped free, and as it tumbled down the open shaft, it struck Graziano in the head, breaking his neck and sending him sprawling to the floor below. Although he survived without paralysis, his serious injuries ended his career.[5]

Injuries were so common that ironworkers considered them part of the job.

"You ain't an iron worker if you ain't had bones broken, fingers chopped off," another New York ironworker told Manoff, the WPA interviewer, in 1939.[6]

For his part, McClain nearly lost his left arm building the Bronx County Courthouse in the early 1930s, when a crane mishap sent beams collapsing around him. "The first aid doctor gave me the customary jolt of good whiskey and poured whole bottles of mercurochrome into the crushed flesh," McClain said. "He kept me talking while he put on a tourniquet and the ambulance pulled up."[7]

McClain was lucky to fall where he did, when he did. New York had some of the nation's strongest worker protections, which its governor, Franklin Roosevelt, would later as president introduce to the nation with the New Deal. "New York compensation was the best in the country at that time, and it was a great comfort to know that my family would be taken care of," McClain wrote.[8] But in the 1930s, in the midst of the Great Depression, federal safety laws and the Occupational Safety and Health Administration had not been established, and the work went on six days a week no matter the reasons or the seasons.

Families told me there was no job security or paid time off, and little insurance. If an ironworker wanted to be paid, he showed up, "in defiance of gravity and common sense."[9] Rockefeller Center was, for the time, uniquely steady employment. It was a coveted high-risk job with hard-earned pay, as many steel jobs were performed on narrow beams on the edge of an ever-deepening abyss.

Bill Sears, a Mohawk ironworker born in 1949, told me he had witnessed eight or nine men suffer serious injuries and saw three others take what he called "the final plunge," two in New York and one in Hamilton, Ontario. "When it happens, you get the hat out and pass it around for the widow or the family," he said. "Everyone goes to the wake and the funeral and there's a lot of reminiscing about the jobs you worked on together."[10]

Even today, as hazardous as steel construction is, ironworkers say it is enormously satisfying. "Not many men would do this" is both a boast and a lament. Few men can point to a skyscraper and say, "I built that." Pride, gratification, and good benefits have helped ironwork evolve into a respected blue-collar job often handed down generations from fathers to sons and recently to daughters.

Throughout researching this book, ironworkers taught me some (sanitized) lingo—improvised shorthand for a tool or situation that has become a universal vocabulary used on construction sites everywhere. It is often amusing and sometimes obscene, like Thorsten's lewd songs that drew the police.[11]

The ironworkers' job is to raise and assemble the structural steel columns and beams that form a skyscraper's grillage, or steel skeleton. In 1932, high-altitude ironwork, without hard hats, work boots, safety harnesses, or nets, came with a high possibility of injury or death. With that distressing prospect in mind, men risked their lives to go to work. Ironworkers have a saying: "We do not die. We are killed."

It was hard-earned money in 1932. It is hard-earned money today.

The structure of a steel building comprises two elements. Columns are the vertical posts that bear the building's weight and convey it to the bedrock. Beams are the horizontal supports that connect the columns and create the floors of the building. These structural steel I-beams vary in length, width, height, and weight.

The grillage is not stationary or rigid; it flexes and sways in the wind. This ability to sway slightly, called deflection, helps protect the building from the forces of air pressure. The higher you go, the stronger the wind; the higher the building, the greater the deflection. The oscillation would unnerve most people. At the top of the R.C.A. Building, 840 feet up, deflection would have averaged over a foot on a normal day. Constructing the grillage and walking iron in the constantly changing environment takes guts and a dancer's agility.

Three large albums in the Rockefeller Center Archive overflow with positive news clips heralding the progress of Radio City's exciting new construction. Tucked away in one of them, I found two small but significant news clippings from the *New York Herald Tribune*. The first is dated January 28, 1932. "Girder hits two in Radio City," was the headline. "Two ironworkers employed in the construction of Radio City were injured yesterday when a beam they were unloading slipped and struck them. They were Salvatore de Pasquale, of 514 East 113th Street, who suffered a possible fracture of the right leg, and Andrio Deilnorno, of 424 East Eleventh Street, who suffered a possible fracture of the right shoulder and concussion of the brain. They were taken to Reconstruction Hospital." Was Deilnorno permanently disabled? Out of work for a substantial time? Was the family hungry? I found no record of his fate.

The second is dated August 24, 1932. John Fitzpatrick, a stoneworker, "lost his footing" and fell fifteen stories to his death. Both articles underscore how one slip could spell disaster.

In 1935, three years after these events, Merle Crowell claimed that "Seventy-five thousand tons of structural steel were erected with the occurrence of only eighty-three accidents causing lost time, out of a total of more than five hundred thousand man-hours of work."[12] Who was hurt,

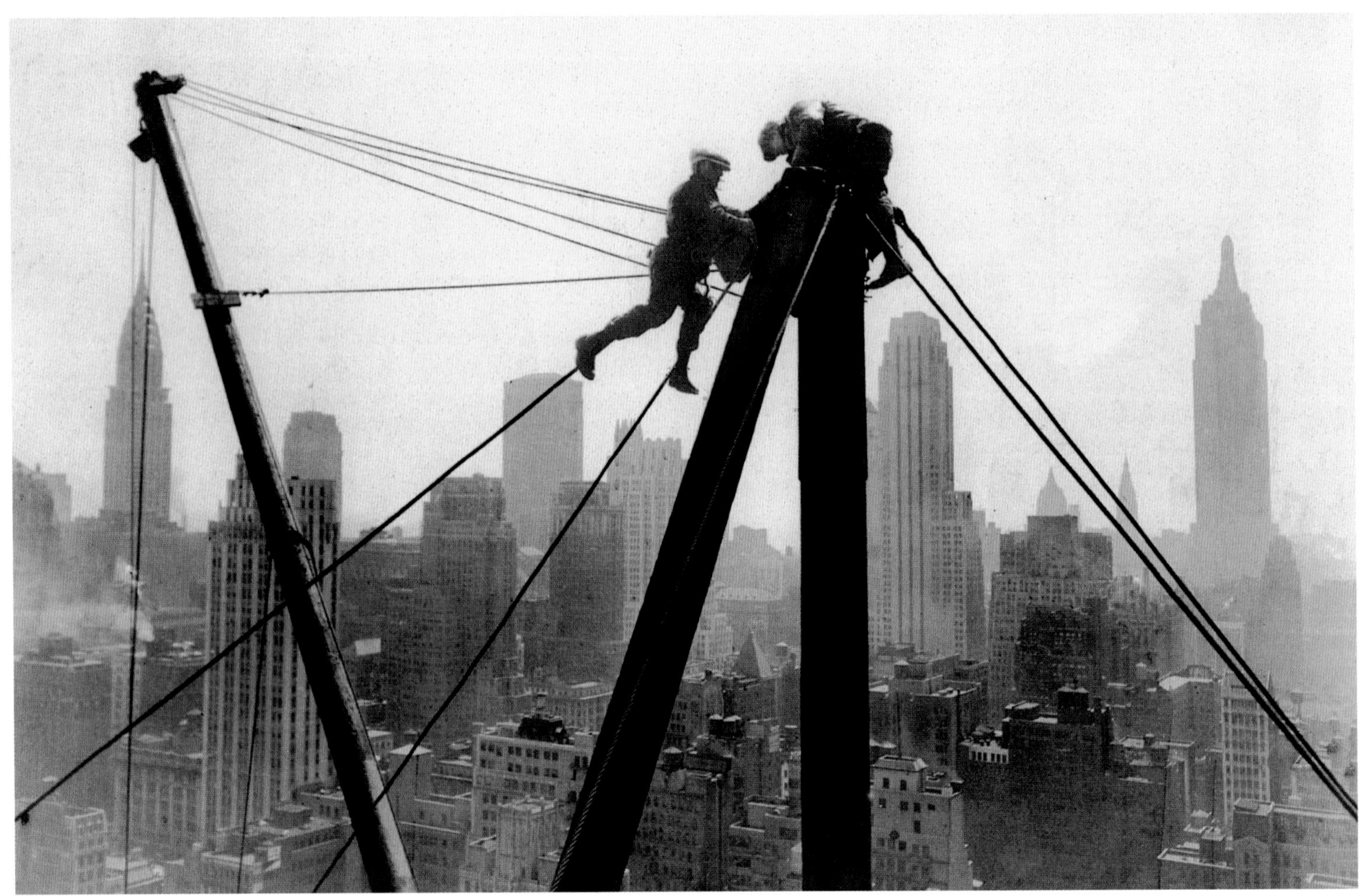

5.3 "Guiding Radio City into the Skyline. Two steel workers atop girders helping to raise the buildings of Rockefeller Center into rivalry with the other skyscrapers of midtown Manhattan." (Rockefeller Group photo 2 by Charles F. Doherty)

when, or how? That was nothing he wanted to crow about.

Exactly how many workers were injured or died building Rockefeller Center is unknown, but there is no doubt some did. Even today, after nearly a century of safety improvements, ironworkers remain among the most frequently injured or killed workers in construction.[13]

Bob Walsh joined the Ironworkers union in 1963 and now serves as an executive of Ironworkers Local 40 in New York City. He is a third-generation ironworker whose grandfather emigrated from County Cork, Ireland. His father was killed by a collapsing crane when Walsh was eleven. He is proud of his family's tradition as ironworkers; his sons are ironworkers, as is one grandson—totaling four generations of Walshes walking iron.

In the 1960s, Walsh was a young ironworker; his first job was on the Verrazzano-Narrows Bridge. It would be the longest suspension bridge in the world, with a center span of 4,260 feet and two suspension towers topping 693 feet. It crosses the Narrows, a tidal strait and shipping route separating the New York boroughs of Staten Island and Brooklyn. The bridge is high above the water.[14] The site is windy, and the tidal current can be deadly. The ironworkers feared for their safety, with good reason. Three men died falling off the construction. After the third death, the workers asked for safety nets. They were refused and called a strike. five days later, the temporary safety nets went up. They saved many lives, Bob told me—including his own.

"I was young and rushing to get everything done," Walsh said. In his haste and inexperience, he fell from the bridge. The net broke his ribs but saved his life.

It wasn't his only fall. Later, he fell onto the top of the inspector's shed and then a catwalk. How did it happen? I asked. "The same reason: young and eager." We talked about those incidents, sixty years ago. "Things have changed," he said. "Things have improved."[15]

Although ironworking remains dangerous, the net that saved Walsh's life was one example of improving safety through the twentieth century. Another, Walsh said, was training. "In the 1930s, there were no apprentice training schools," Walsh told me. "Workers were learning on the job. That was downright dangerous."[16]

Many great photos were taken by photographers who are still unrecognized. Some images are so distinctive that just a glance tells who shot the photo. The dramatic photo "Guiding Radio City into the Skyline" is one of them. Charles F. Doherty's image beautifully chronicles the spine-chilling scene. It was published in the *Herald Tribune* about six months before "Lunch on a Beam." In it, two unnamed ironworkers work without safety lines or

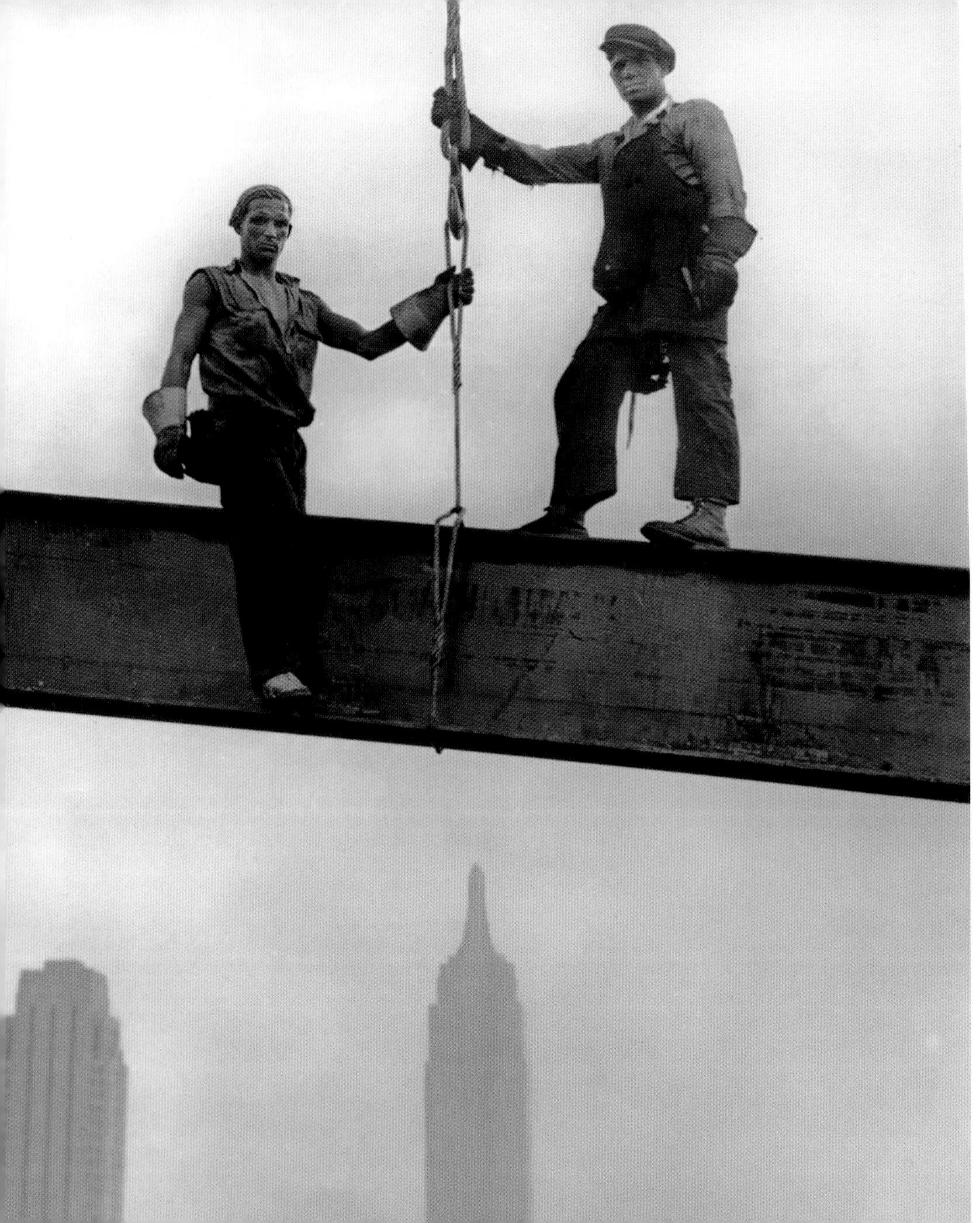

5.4 A raising gang lifts the beam into place. (Rockefeller Group photo 40)

nets. Somehow, they have reached the apex of two long, wooden stiff-leg girders. The Empire State Building and the Chrysler Building loom in the distance. The scene is harrowing, as the men hang like spiders, with eight guy cables spreading from the top of the girders like the beginnings of a web. The men are part of a raising gang.

Walsh explained that traditionally, ironworkers are organized into *gangs*—not of hoodlums, but of specialties. Even today, the ironworkers work in gangs. There are about six different gangs, and each performs a specific job. A journeyman ironworker prides himself on his ability to work with any gang. The raising gang gets the job going by moving the steel into place. The raising team is highly coordinated and focused from the moment the beam is hooked up, leaves the ground, is manually grabbed, and is temporarily bolted into the steel skeleton. Ironworker Bill Sears told me, "You must work fast. Grab the beam. Drop the tagline and bully the temporary bolts in as the next piece is coming up."[17]

Raising is the most daring and fastest-moving job within the gangs. Usually, the most agile and youngest of the workers do it. They consider themselves the audacious alpha dogs of high steel. That job puts them constantly in danger atop the grillage. They often work with a steady partner, sometimes for years; they say they can anticipate each other's moves without words. Sears said communal familiarity is paramount within the raising gang. Many say working with cousins, brothers, fathers, and sons, or in the same community, as with the Mohawks (see chapter 8), makes the men feel more secure.

Ironworkers depend on their brute strength and ability to persevere in hazardous situations, whether hanging on a stiff-leg derrick or scaling steel columns to grab the next beam and set it into place. There were no walkie-talkies, safety nets, harnesses, or even hard hats in 1932, just the ever-present danger of "going into the hole." McClain explained: "In the ironworkers' parlance, all things below him are in the hole."[18]

Within the raising gang are the connectors, who temporarily attach the beams with provisional bolts to the existing structure, incrementally forming the iron structure. The team must be strong, agile, and alert, as any misstep or swinging I-beam can result in a fall.

The ironworkers' leatherwork belts may hold fifty pounds of tools and bolts. A single bolt could weigh as much as eight pounds.[19] Spud wrenches have different-sized spanners to tighten or loosen bolts on one end, and tapered spikes on the other. The spikes help align bolt holes to make the initial connection. Large iron bars also help align the holes or pry steel beams. A heavy hammer nicknamed a "beater" does just that.

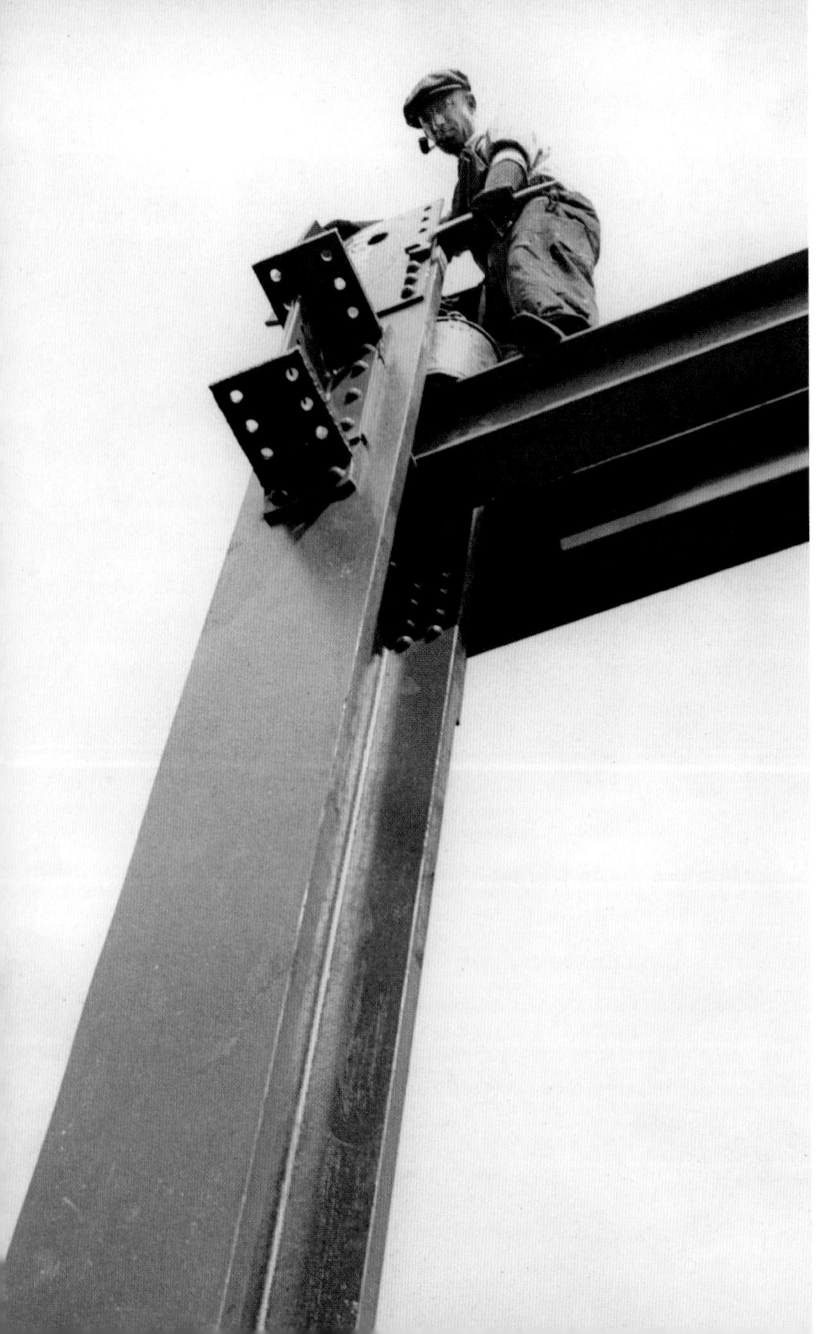

Next, the bolter-ups follow the raising gang and secure the newly placed beams with additional bolts. These men heft a pail or leather bag full of iron bolts from area to area. They are followed by the plumber-uppers, who level the beams, ensuring horizontal and vertical alignments. Older ironworkers usually perform this work as it is considered safer, less arduous, more judicious, and perhaps wiser. Once they are done, the riveters arrive.

In the 1930s, a four-man team of riveters permanently secured the joints by hammering in hot rivets. The team was paid by the number of rivets set each day. The team included a worker dubbed a "heater," whose small, three-legged forge heated four or five rivets at a time over a bed of coals. It took a rivet about three minutes to become red-hot and malleable.[20]

With protective gloves and eighteen-inch tongs, the heater pulled a ready rivet from the forge and tossed the glowing meteor to his comrades,[21] stationed anywhere from a few to as far as fifty feet away, and two or three stories above or below. When a reporter asked a heater on a Rockefeller Center rivet gang what the trick was, the answer was nonchalant. You have to get the "feel" for it, the heater, Arthur Bianchi, said. Proficiency took four to six years. Perfection took anywhere from ten to fifteen, and a lot of misses along the way.

5.5 A bolter-up secures the beam. (Rockefeller Group photo 125)

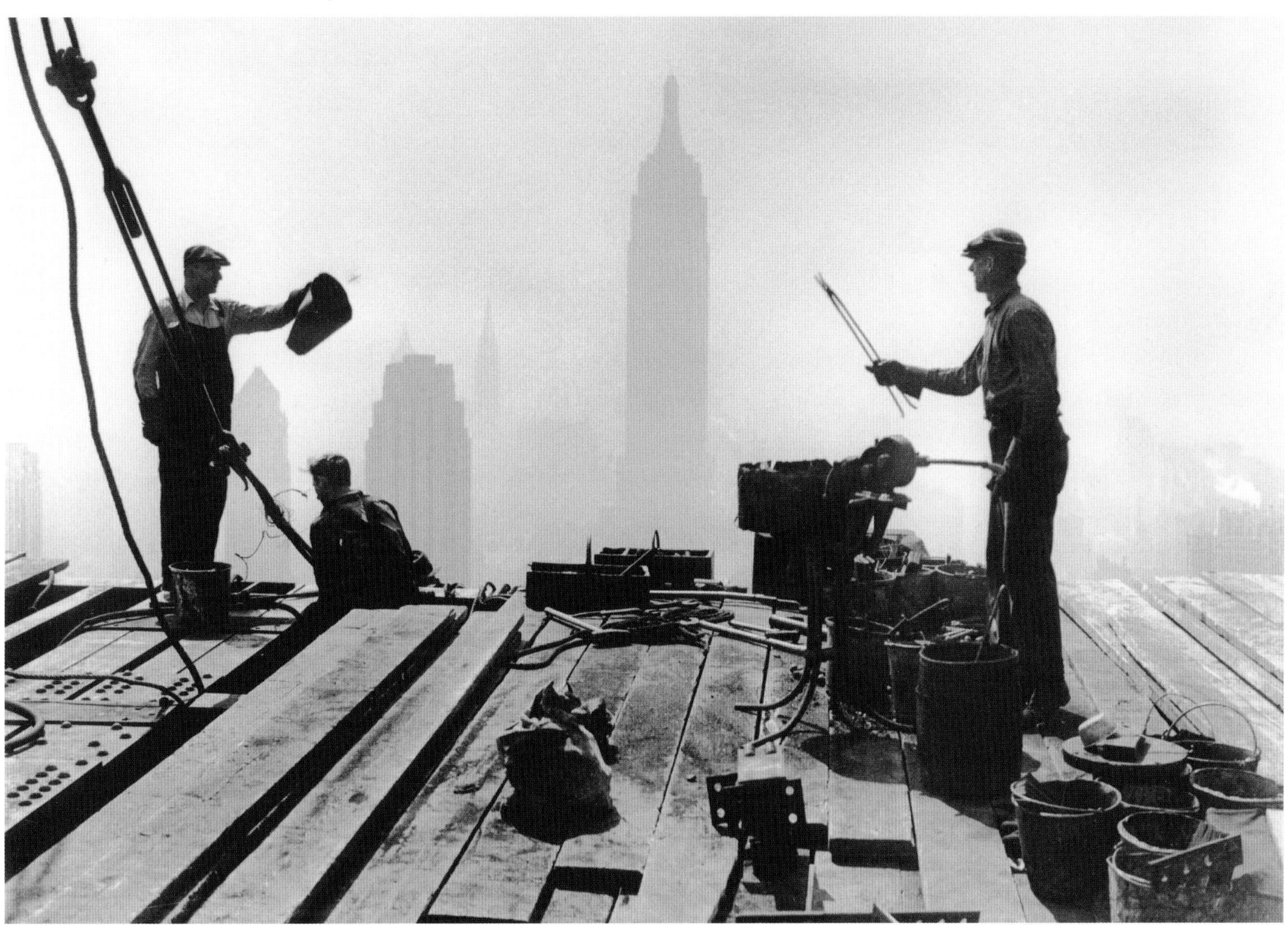

5.6 A rivet gang's heater throws a rivet to the catcher. (Rockefeller Group photo 132)

At the other end of that long, fiery throw was the second man in the rivet gang: the catcher, who caught rivets with a funnel-shaped iron bucket called variously the "catching can" or the "cannonball catcher." Keeping the rivet from ricocheting out of the bucket was its own art, performed with a quick twist at the moment of impact.

With work gloves and tongs of his own, the catcher inserted the glowing rivets into the beams through holes prepared by the final two men: the driver and the bucker-up. The bucker-up braced the mushroom-shaped head of the glowing rivet with his goose-neck dolly, a twenty-five-pound iron tool. On the other side of the connection, the driver placed his pneumatic rivet gun—also twenty-five pounds, plus 125 pounds of air pressure—over the stem. The gun pounded for forty seconds, flattening the rivet's stem against the steel beam. The men had sixty seconds from the moment the heater pulled a rivet from the coals to the last ring of the rivet gun before the rivet cooled, contracting to tighten the join.

It was hard work and loud. It wasn't uncommon for riveters to go deaf. The worker had to lean into the pounding machine to set a rivet. The team (apart from the heater) rotated the work to give the driver a break. An inspector followed the riveters, tapping each rivet with a hammer. Good joins rang like a bell. Bad ones clunked, riveters said, "like a bad quarter." An even heavier rivet gun, the hell-dog, was used to extract bad rivets.[22]

On most days, at least four gangs of riveters worked. On some days, there could have been many more; Crowell indicated that four hundred ironworkers were present on the R.C.A. Building in August 1932. Perhaps a mild exaggeration: Testimony from a workplace injury suit put the exact number at 363 ironworkers, including twenty-one riveting gangs.[23]

Crowell boasted that "The 60,000-ton structural steel framework was erected by Post & McCord in one hundred and two working days, between March 7th and September 26th."[24] When I asked Bob Walsh, the union executive and an ironworker, if that was possible, he said: "At that time, there had to be many gangs working at the same time to raise that much steel and then rivet it in six weeks."[25]

By the end of World War II, high-strength bolting and welding replaced rivets for most steel-frame constructions. Welding required fewer (if any) holes and lighter or no connection plates compared to the pre-war process of riveting.

The gangs repeated these operations until September 26, 1932, when they "topped out" the steel frame of the R.C.A. Building with the final beam. Ironworkers gathered at the top of the steel skeleton to celebrate a job completed. A lone ironworker rode the last I-beam, with American flags attached, to the summit amid the cheers of the

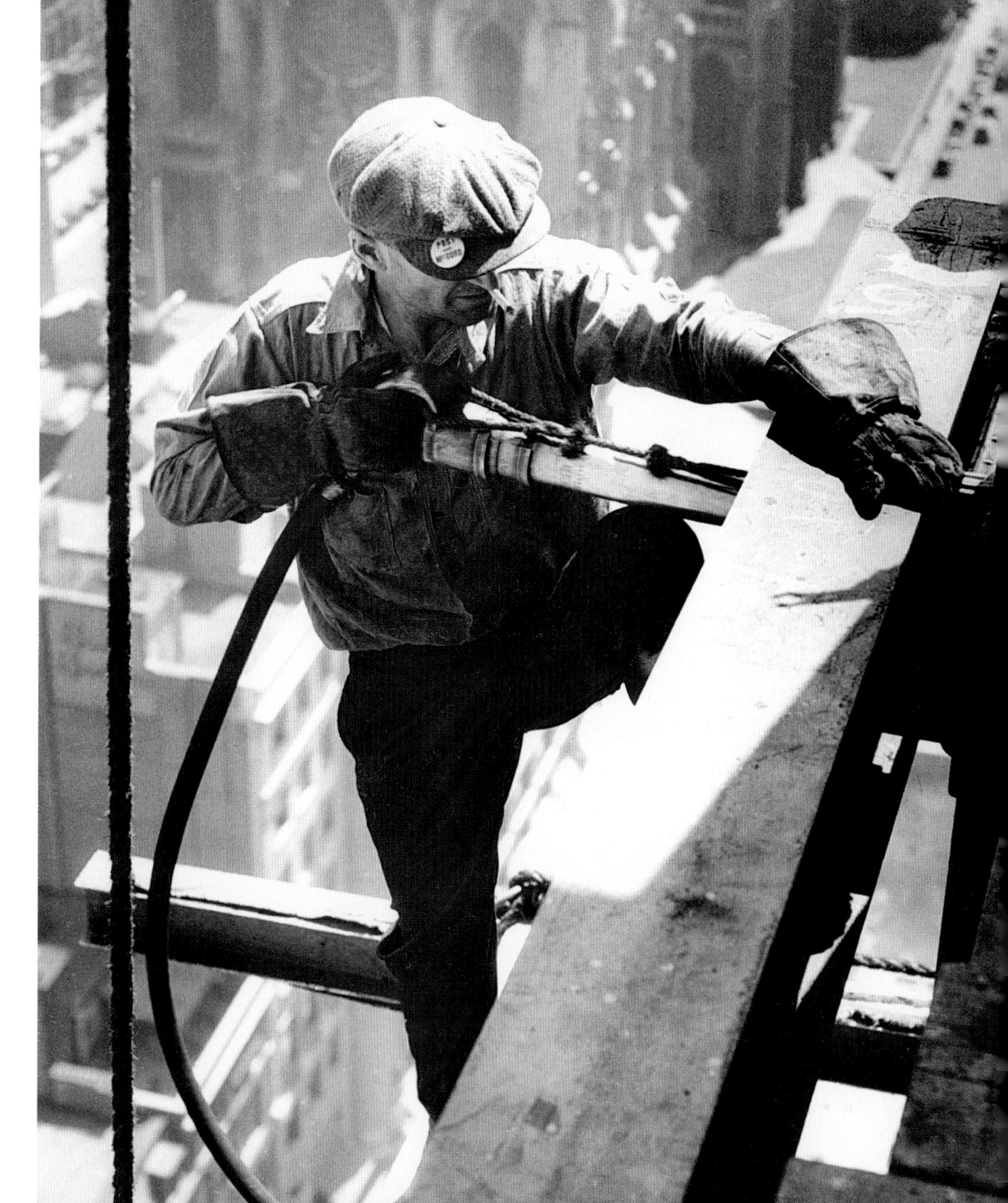

5.7 A riveter fastens a girder on July 27, 1932.
(Rockefeller Group photo by Charles Doherty)

ironworkers and George Atwell, their pipe-smoking boss.

It was a milestone in the construction of Rockefeller Center. The final stone would be set eight months later, in May 1933. By then, the Depression had hollowed out the nation's economy and morale. Almost half of all construction jobs had disappeared.[26] The one bright spot was bridges: The George Washington Bridge had just opened, and work on the Golden Gate Bridge was just beginning.[27] But other construction projects were scarce. The $1.05 per hour an ironworker could earn at Rockefeller Center went a long way in the Depression, even if it represented a 15 percent pay cut from the boom times, and even if an ironworker had to alternate his work days with another man. Nor was completion of the R.C.A. Building the end of work in Rockefeller Center, where construction would continue until 1939.

For a New Yorker in the fall of 1932, not all news was doom and gloom. The state's popular governor, Franklin D. Roosevelt, won the White House in November 1932. It's likely that Junior, a Hoover man, would have agreed with at least one bit of FDR's inaugural address on March 4, 1933: "Our greatest primary task is to put people to work." But the president's most famous quote could have come from the mouth of an ironworker: "The only thing we have to fear is fear itself."

There were other bright spots. The Yankees swept the 1932 World Series, with Babe Ruth anchoring the famed Murderers' Row. He made baseball history on October 1, 1932, in the fifth inning of Game 3 against the Chicago Cubs in Wrigley Field. The Babe gestured toward the stands and then walloped the ball out of the park. The legend of his called shot was born. It was the tenth and final World Series for the greatest hitter who ever played. But he wasn't the ironworkers' favorite. That honor went to his teammate, Lou Gehrig, whose father was a metalworker.

The fourth and final game was played the next day in Yankee Stadium. It was a sweep for the Yankees. That day, Sunday, October 2, also marked the first time that a newspaper published "Lunch on a Beam," though the caption that ran below it in the *New York Herald Tribune* was "Builders of the City Enjoy Luncheon."

The photograph was more than a lark. It captured the mood of its time, and the mood of its place—peril tempered with optimism; men meeting hardship with fortitude, even joy. The photographers had delivered Merle Crowell's vision of the perfect photograph: a group portrait of the nation, where every American could find himself in the picture.

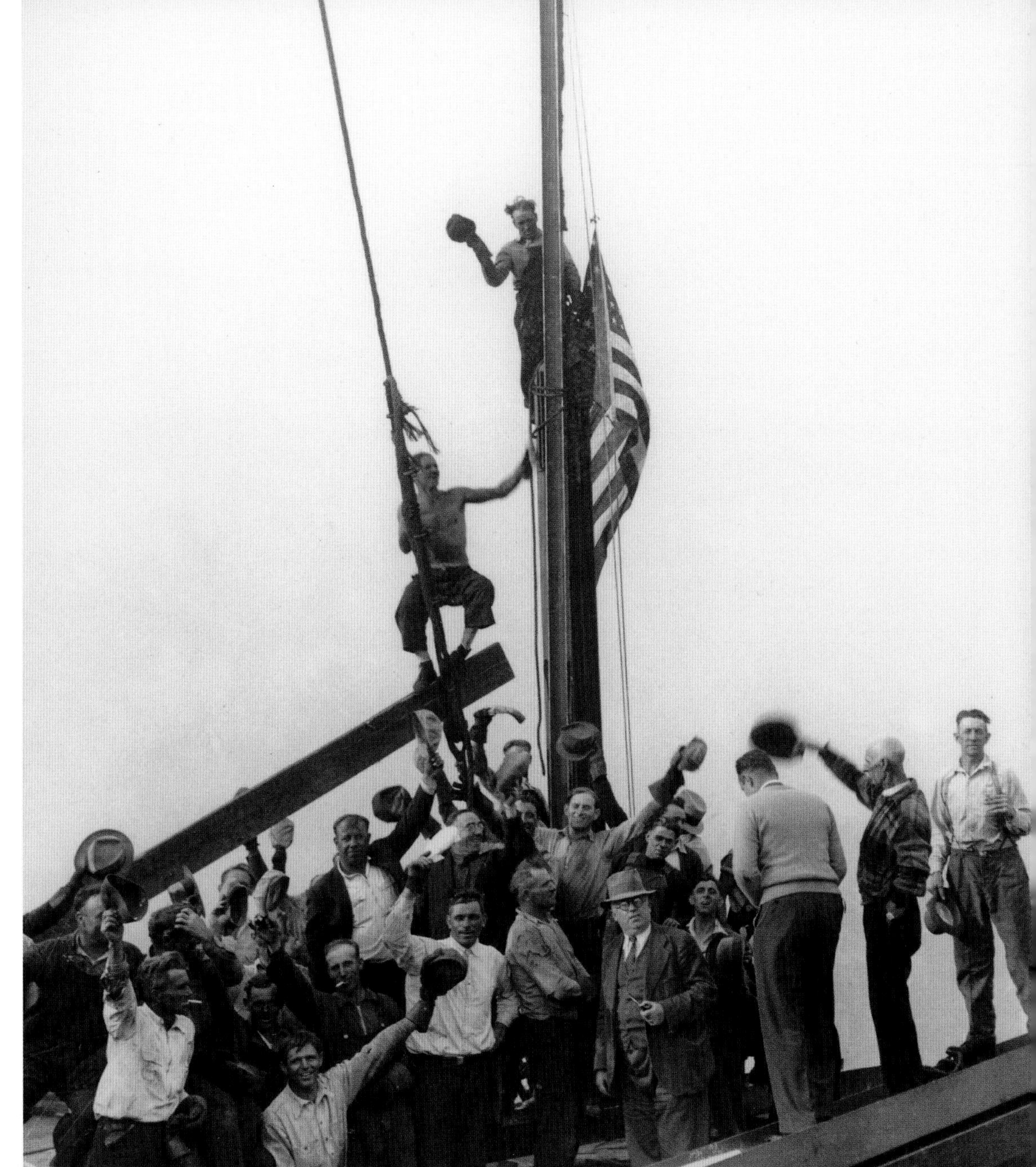

5.8 A "topping-out" ceremony celebrated the completion of the R.C.A. building's steel frame on Sept. 26, 1932. Other photos of the ceremony, taken from different perspectives, raise the tantalizing possibility that multiple photographers shot other scenes arranged that day, including "Lunch on a Beam." (Rockefeller Group photo 137)

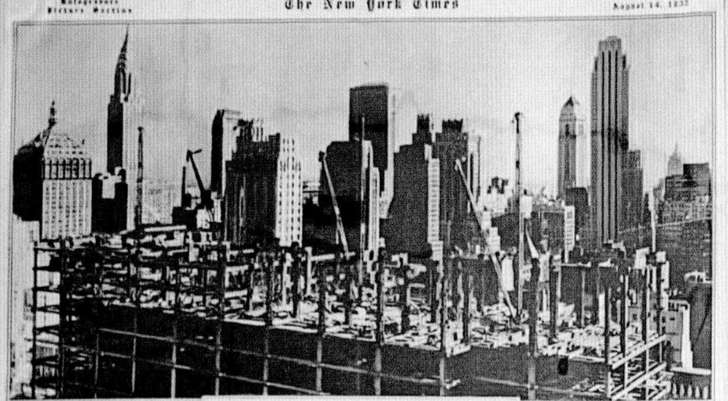

A RECENT STAGE OF SKYSCRAPER WORK IN THE MIDST OF ROCKEFELLER CENTER, THE R. C. A. BUILDING, Which Will Contain More Office Space Than Any Other Building in the World, as It Now Appears Against the Background of the Midtown Skyscrapers.

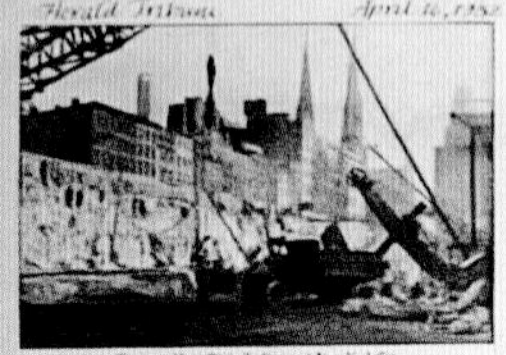

Herald Tribune — April 16, 1932

Clearing a Huge Pit in the Center of New York City.

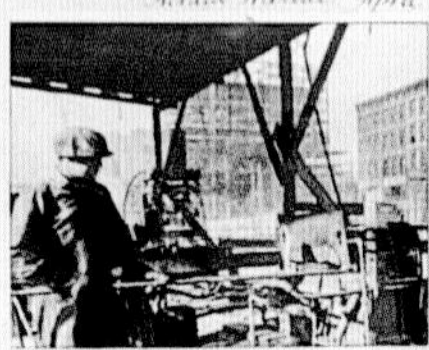

Herald Tribune — April 16, 1932

Forging Drills.

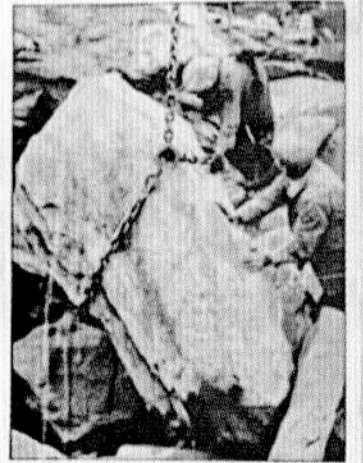

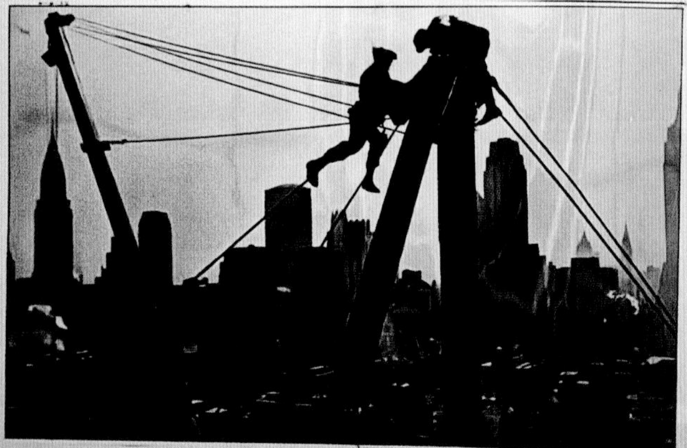

Herald Tribune — April 24, 1932

Girding Radio City Into the Sky.

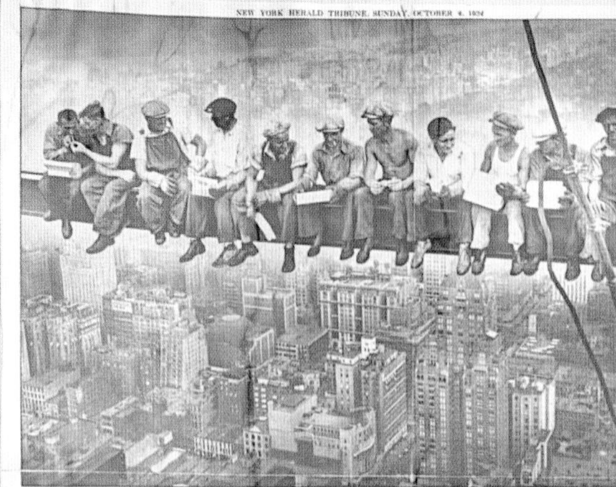

Builders of the City Enjoy Luncheon
Steel workers during the noon hour on a girder of the RCA building 800 feet above Rockefeller Center. The last steel for the structure has been raised.

City's Foundation
The bedrock that supports Manhattan as it appears in the excavation for Radio City. The spire of St. Patrick's Cathedral can be seen in the background.

Herald Tribune — April 16, 1932

Boring in a Cliff
Right — Workmen drilling into the rock between the area bounded by Fifth and Sixth Avenues and Forty-ninth and Fifty-first Streets where Radio City will rise.

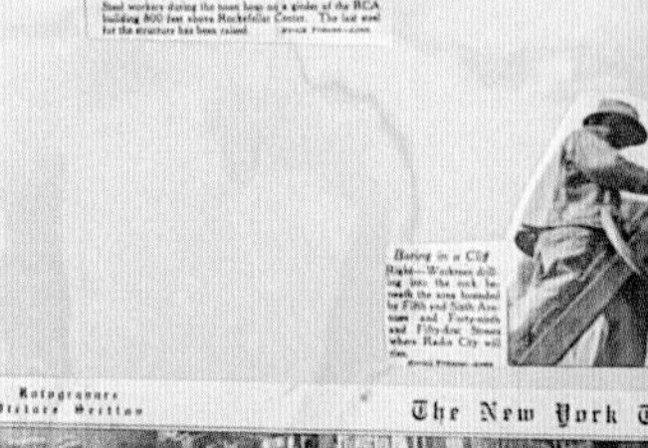

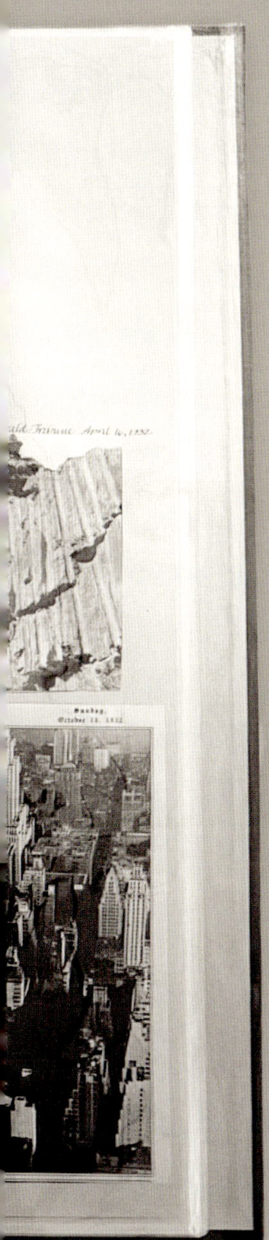

6

"LUNCH ON A BEAM" AND VARIATIONS

6.1 A bound volume of news clips at the Rockefeller Center Archive. (CR photo)

Picture Merle Crowell (or likely an assistant) hunched each morning over a stack of newspapers and magazines, scissors in hand, painstakingly harvesting the fruits of his labor. Today, the Rockefeller Center Archive preserves those news clippings in an oversized cloth-bound album. Open it, and the pages sprawl across ten square feet of conference table. Inside, you will discover "Builders of the City Enjoy Luncheon." The first time I did so, I was amazed by its impact. The newsprint is surprisingly well preserved, barely yellowed since the day the Yankees won the World Series.[1] It shares a page with other articles about the Center's construction, showing excavators at work and autogyros—the first helicopters—buzzing past the near-complete R.C.A. tower.

There is no answer recorded for why the photo taken September 20, 1932, was not published until October 2, twelve days later. Perhaps it was promised as an exclusive to the *New York Herald Tribune*. The paper's Sunday photo supplement—where the photo ran—would have been printed several days in advance, which may have kept the photo from running on Sunday, September 25. But this is speculation, complicated by the fact that rotogravure (picture) sections usually appeared twice a week. These sections documented high society, classic art, parades, politicians, and goings-on about town. The text was limited; brief captions accompanied the pictures. At fifteen inches wide by ten-and-a-half inches high, "Builders of the City Enjoy Luncheon" dominated page four of the supplement.

The scene is stunning. Eleven ironworkers perch precariously hip-to-hip on an I-beam suspended 840 feet above the ground. The beam appears detached, hovering above the city, while the men casually chat and smoke, inured to any danger. It can cause vertigo to the viewer. The caption informs the reader that these men are taking a lunch break, albeit in defiance of death. To illustrate that absurdity, six of them hold white cardboard lunchboxes.

Rooftops, Central Park, the Upper West Side, and the Hudson River are visible below and in the misty background. In the bottom left foreground, the end of a beam protrudes. It is barely discernible as it is a similar color and shape to the rooftops. In the right foreground, a twisted steel guy-wire bisects the image and continues out of the top of the frame. Neither connects to the beam supporting the men.

That's what I saw. But I wondered what "Lunch on a Beam" looked like through an ironworker's eyes. So, I asked Bill Sears.

William Sears,[2] a Mohawk ironworker and son of a formidable ironworker nicknamed "Big John Sears," stood six-foot-five and weighed 360 pounds. His great-great-grandfather was the first ironworker in the family, starting about 1898. Bill said, "It's a way of life."[3]

Bill always wanted to be an ironworker. In 1964, the sixteen-year-old quit school, enlisted in the Army, and was sent to Vietnam. After returning home, he joined an ironworkers' apprenticeship program and Local 440. five years later, he was hired to help build the Twin Towers of the World Trade Center. In 1978, he helped install the towers' antennae at 1,728 feet—the highest any ironworker had ventured above the ground. At a Christmas party celebrating the completion of the second tower, Nelson Rockefeller (then governor, and still feting construction workers) presented Bill and his fellow ironworkers with platinum keychains and pens.

Forty-one years later, on September 11, Bill was in Manhattan and saw news footage of the second airplane hitting the towers. "Holy s—t," he said. "That's my building."[4] He was one of the many ironworkers who helped clear the site. Bill maintained his roots in the Kahnawake Mohawk Reserve and invested in Native businesses. He was also a force in the Mohawk Warrior Society and participated in the Oka Crisis in the 1990s. This involved seventy-seven violent days, many injuries, and two deaths over land disputes with the Canadian government. Along the way, he earned his nickname: "Wild Bill Sears."

Bill became the historian of New York's Ironworkers Local Union 440 and to me, a friend and important source of facts and awesome tales. I asked Bill what he sees when he looks at "Lunch on a Beam." Although he knew it well, he scrutinized it. "The men are sitting on two I-beams parallel to each other, which forms a configuration termed 'split-channel beam construction,'" he said. "Each beam appears to be sixteen inches high and eight inches wide, with a four-inch channel or opening between them. These parallel beams provided a twenty-inch platform for the men to sit on. The guy-wire—the steel cable—hanging on the right side of the picture would have been connected to the derrick. They are quite safe."[5] Despite his reassurance, it still didn't look to me like a tempting lunch spot, but Sears's perspective differed from most.

"Lunch on a Beam" (see frontispiece) stands among the most famous photographs ever made. The men are unknown, the photographer uncertain, but the gravity-defying picture lives on. *Time*'s 2015 publication, *100 Photographs: The Most Influential Images of All Time*, notes that the image captured "a turning point in our human experience." The fearlessness of the eleven men symbolized hope at a difficult period in America's history. It has become a celebrated image known worldwide and reprinted countless times.

The photo was taken on September 20, 1932, and, since that time, has been preserved in Rockefeller Center Archives as "Lunch on a Beam Photo #110." The subjects' stories, or even their names, were not. For nearly a hundred years, the eleven men have been world-famous and anonymous.

In the archive's oldest print, the bright yellow paper of a press release is glued to the verso. It reads: "Lunchtime 800 Feet Up at Rockefeller Center. New York: A remarkable photo of steel workers nonchalantly eating lunch on a steel girder 800 feet above the street level during the construction of the R.C.A. Building—70-story structure in Rockefeller Center, New York City."

Also typed on the back are the words: "#110 Copy Negative—Newspictures: (No. 344) Exclusive Herald-Tribune roto Oct 2, 1932." Written in pencil is: "Taken Sept 20 1932." Written in ink: "Don't give out!" Although the photo is today one of the most reproduced in the world, that stricture supports the idea that it was promised as an exclusive, at least for a time.

The *Herald Tribune* captioned the photo: "Builders of the City Enjoy Luncheon." It was taken on a warm autumn day. The ground temperature was in the low eighties. The men wear light clothing or overalls: one is shirtless, one is in an undershirt, five wear heavy work gloves, and nine are in the ubiquitous worker's flat cap. Feet in various shoes dangle loosely below or rest on the narrow flange of the I-beam.

In the foreground, a forbidding chasm amplifies the gaping space beneath the beam. The acute downward view of the dark foreground sucks the viewer in. The vast background fades into the distance. The men appear at ease and acclimatized to the height, and most seem indifferent to the photographer.

It's the viewer who gets dizzy.

There are four distinct groups of men in the lineup. From the left, the first two men are busy lighting a cigarette. The following two men are chatting. The next three men share something that excludes the others. The next three hold their own conversation. The eleventh man, holding what appears to be a liquor bottle, is isolated and the only man confronting the camera.

Look closer, and we find the two men at the left end are absorbed in sharing a light. Their gaze focuses on the burning ends of their joined cigarettes.

The first man's bare head, dark-haired, tilts forward as he hunches over the open white lunchbox that rests on his knees, steadying it with his left hand. One foot rests on the flange; the other is hooked on its edge. His right hand holds a cigarette to his mouth as his body shields it while his neighbor attempts a light. He wears a dark, long-sleeved shirt and dark trousers.

The second man wears bib overalls and a dark, short-sleeved shirt. He is bare-headed, and his hair appears lighter. His left arm reaches across his body, flexing a powerful bicep, as he lights the first man's cigarette. His right elbow rests casually on his thigh. His ankles are crossed, and his left foot hangs down. He appears unmindful of the exceptional setting and is preoccupied with lighting his neighbor's cigarette.

The third man wears a cap, bib overalls, a white short-sleeved shirt, and leather work gloves. His face is lined, and he appears heavier and older than his companions. His gloved left hand lies casually on his hip, and his right forearm on his thigh. The heels of his shoes rest on the flange of the I-beam. He has turned slightly toward the fourth man and seems engrossed in conversation.

The fourth man wears a white short-sleeved shirt, dark trousers, ironworker's gloves with large cuffs, and a dark cap. He sits erect, his face in profile. His long legs hang past the beam, exposing his white socks. He holds a white lunchbox with the letters "VO" or "VOS" on the side. He appears to be conversing with the third man.

The fifth man wears a white shirt with rolled sleeves, bib overalls, and work gloves. His light cap is turned backward. A white lunchbox hangs at an angle from his right hand between his knees. He slouches forward and rests his elbows on his thighs while his feet dangle above the abyss. The bottom of his pant leg is ripped. He gazes at the lunchbox of the sixth man.

The sixth man also looks into his lunchbox, which he holds in his lap with gloved hands. A cigarette hangs from the corner of his mouth. He wears a light-colored cap, a dirty, long-sleeved shirt, dark trousers, and work gloves. His shoes are hooked on the I-beam flange. He appears shorter and radiates machismo.

The seventh man is lean, leathery, and bare-chested. He wears a light cap and dark pants. He holds a sandwich with both hands while turning his head to talk to the sixth man. His feet are hooked on the flange of the I-beam. He seems comfortable and confident taking an 840-foot-high break from hanging iron.

The eighth man appears to be the youngest man on the beam. He wears a dark cap, a long-sleeved white shirt, dark trousers, and work gloves. He leans forward, resting his elbows on his thighs while holding a cup with both hands. His focus is on the lunchbox held by the ninth man. His heels are hooked on the flange.

The ninth man holds an open lunchbox and wears a light-colored cap, a loose white tank-top undershirt, and the only light-colored trousers on the beam. This indicates that he might also work as a mason—or, as Bob Walsh said, "just wore white trousers that morning." His white socks are visible above his shoes, hooked on the flange.

The tenth man's face is in profile and partially obscured by his cap and the guy-wire. He wears work gloves, a cap, bib overalls, and a shirt with rolled sleeves. He holds a lunchbox with both his hands and has turned his head. He appears to be listening to the conversation between the eighth and ninth men.

Only the eleventh man on the far right looks directly at the camera. He is wearing a cap, a long-sleeved, open-collar shirt, and bib overalls, and has rested the heels of his shoes on the flange. Squinting, he appears intent and, despite Prohibition, holds a liquor flask on his left knee.

Looking at these eleven confident men, one gets a sense that having lunch on a beam is routine. The ironworkers' casualness conveys the moxie it takes to construct a building, especially a skyscraper. It all seems so natural—relaxing and chatting on an I-beam high above the city, but these are hardly ordinary men in ordinary jobs. They are the ironworkers who built Rockefeller Center girder by girder and beam by beam and risked their lives slamming iron to do it.

In 1932, when they came to work and climbed the web of steel, they faced a two-fold danger—they could risk falling off the high steel or go hungry; the Great Depression presented this unprecedented confluence. "The pay was good; you had to be willing to die."[6]

The Bettmann Archive holds the oldest—and possibly original—glass negative of "Lunch on a Beam" at the Iron Mountain National Underground Storage Facility in Boyers, Pennsylvania. I called Ken Johnson, an art historian and former director of historical photography at Corbis, which owned the Bettmann Archive until 2016.

Johnson and I had crossed paths a decade earlier, helping a team of Irish filmmakers make a documentary about "Lunch on a Beam." He is one of the few living people to have handled the glass negative (or its pieces—at some point, it was broken into shards). When Corbis acquired the Bettmann Archive in 1995, Johnson said that the glass negative was stored in a manila envelope. "It had a missing corner," he said, "and was broken into five pieces."[7]

I wanted to pick Ken's brain. What he told me sent me in a surprising new direction.

While at the Bettmann Archive, he had seen an image "on a weird photography site" almost identical to "Lunch on a Beam."

"Oh," I asked, "'Hats Off'?" That second photo of the men on the beam, waving their caps as they grin at the camera, was well known, if not as famous as "Lunch on a Beam."

But Johnson said no—a third photo. Johnson recalled the subjects' slight movements—a lowered cigarette, a shifted glance—and suggested the third photo was taken a few seconds before or after (he suspects after) its famous doppelganger. To his eye, the timing raised tantalizing evidence of a second photographer: The cameras used that day—Graflex Speed Graphics—took some time to change glass negatives or film between shots. If one photographer couldn't change film that fast, perhaps two (at least two) photographers stood side by side recording the scene, as they had the topping-out ceremony.

I recalled that conversation when I came across a news clip one ironworker's family had preserved, from the October 5 edition of the *New York Evening Journal*.[8] Under the headline, "A 'Heavenly' Lunch in Rockefeller Center's Skyline," the caption struck familiar Crowellian notes: "Lunch hour crowds hold no terror for the workmen on the new 70-story R.C.A. Building in Rockefeller Center. Seated on a steel beam (It's 800 feet to the street below), they enjoy their noonday repast far from the madding throngs. The R.C.A. Building is the world's largest in point of floor space."

At first glance, the photo appeared to be "Lunch on a Beam," but a closer look revealed something else.

It shows the same men. The same beam. The same background. Even the same six lunchboxes. But slight changes in the men's poses—nothing as dramatic as "Hats Off"—confirmed the existence of a third version of "Lunch on a Beam." The rumor was true.

I couldn't believe my eyes.

But where did it come from, and why had it disappeared? A search led me to Ullstein-Bild, Germany's oldest photo agency, which held a print distributed by the Associated Press on September 30, 1932. The photo was published in the *Berliner Illustrirte Zeitung* (Berlin Illustrated Magazine) on October 28, 1932, with the following caption, translated here from German:

BREAKFAST BREAK

When you walk the streets of NYC, you will notice dozens of empty floors in skyscrapers and new massive buildings going up in important areas of the city, which will house thousands and thousands of offices. Even the smartest New Yorkers don't know how and if this contradiction between relentless optimism to construct and the ongoing depression can be resolved. The skyscrapers are their pride and, at the same time the economic indicator, which is calling for stormy weather.[9]

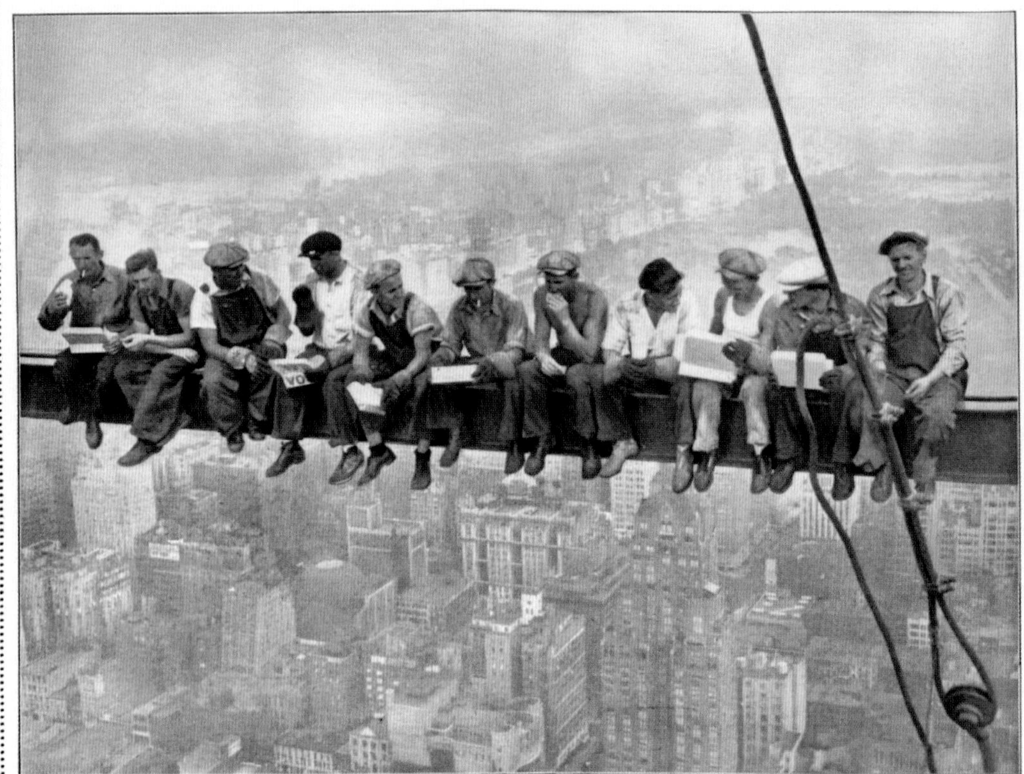

Frühstückspause.   Fot. A. P.

Wenn man durch die Straßen New Yorks geht, fällt einem zweierlei auf: In allen Wolkenkratzern stehen Dutzende von Stockwerken leer, an sehr wichtigen Punkten der Stadt werden neue Häusergebirge errichtet, die Platz für Tausende und Tausende von Büros bieten werden. Wie und ob dieser Gegensatz zwischen einem unerschöpflichen Bau-Optimismus und der noch nicht weichenden Depression zum Ausgleich kommen wird, wissen auch die klügsten New-Yorker nicht. Die Wolkenkratzer sind ihr Stolz und zugleich ein Wirtschaftsbarometer, das auf schlecht Wetter zeigt.

6.2 "Breakfast Break" in *Berliner Zeitung*, Oct. 23, 1932. (City Library of Berlin)

The tone is strikingly gloomier than the American press. The ostensible subject, the eleven ironworkers, is not even mentioned. The Great Depression had hit Germany harder than any other industrialized country. After World War I, the Weimar Republic had relied on loans from US banks to finance Germany's massive debts. When the crash of 1929 led US banks to recall foreign loans, Germany reeled. By the end of 1932, the German economy was running at half its capacity, and one in three Germans was unemployed. Nazi propaganda fanned resentment against foreign banks and "the smartest New Yorkers" who ran them. Three months after *Berlin Illustrated* predicted stormy weather, the dire conditions helped pave the way for Adolf Hitler's rise to power.[10]

A close comparison of "Breakfast Break" and "Lunch on a Beam" suggests more than a few seconds may have passed between the taking of the two photos. Crucially, where no food is visible in "Lunch on a Beam," three men are now actually eating in "Breakfast Break." The man on the far left has lit his cigarette, is now smoking, and is about to take a bite of his sandwich. The fourth man is also about to bite into his sandwich; the seventh man has most of his sandwich in his mouth. And the flask has moved from the eleventh man's left hand to his right. A smile has replaced his stern expression in "Lunch on a Beam."

Time enough for one man to eat a sandwich is time enough for another to switch glass plates in his camera. Perhaps we are back to one photographer after all. What else do these two nearly identical images tell us? For one thing, the differences help explain how "Lunch on a Beam" embedded itself in the public imagination. When the photo captivates the viewer—as it surely does—the capture begins with two men on the left, bent toward each other, sharing a light. Their simple interaction sets the tone for the photograph, which becomes a harmonious organization of a group of groups—a classical composition.

Consider another composition of men gathered for a meal, arranged in a line but interacting in groups: Leonardo's *The Last Supper*. Both works invite the viewer to "read" from left to right, and each begins its story with a group at the left. In *The Last Supper*, the three men on the left look questioningly toward Christ, directing the viewer's gaze toward the focal point of the painting. In "Lunch on a Beam," the two men on the left lean in to light a cigarette, and the middle man draws the viewer's attention as he looks away, ignoring everyone. In both images, the leftmost group begins the story.

Without the two men leaning in to light a cigarette, the composition of "Breakfast Break" remains static. The viewer may regard each man individually or the group as a whole, but without those interactions, there is no animating force, so "Breakfast Break" appears more contrived. Is it a dud? No, but it lacks a story. It is an adequate publicity shot. I began to understand why one picture became an icon and the other languished in an *Aktenschrank*.

And the difference is simply two men sharing a light.

After "Breakfast Break" was taken,[11] a critical request was made: The men were asked to raise their hats and look at the camera. The result was a third photograph, known today as "Hats Off."[12] It captured most faces' frontal views. Otherwise, little was altered. No man had moved from his spot. Even their feet remained in place. Two of the men who had held lunchboxes in "Lunch on a Beam" disposed of them in "Hats Off." Six boxes were now four. The eleventh man raises his flask—now in his right hand, as in "Breakfast Break." Ever detached, the sixth man looks away with his hat still on.

"Hats Off" is framed slightly closer and higher than "Lunch on a Beam," with less space below the men, who recede from right to left. The cityscape below them is smaller and brighter, and the background fades away. Our attention is drawn to the men's smiling faces. They are having fun and celebrating the completion of the R.C.A Building's frame. The viewer's fear for the men in "Lunch on a Beam" has been replaced with joy.

Other aspects of the picture are significant; the small end of an I-beam jutting into the lower left foreground of "Lunch on a Beam" is gone, and only the tip of the pulley appears in the lower right corner. The raised right arm of the first man on the left is cut off above his elbow. The photographer might have moved. But when I asked Clint Saunders, a professor of photography, he suggested another explanation: "Maybe two photographers stood side by side."[13]

Which brings us back to the possibility that more than one photographer was making versions of "Lunch on a Beam." Thomas Kelley Jr. told me it was not unusual, in his father's experience, for multiple photographers to work the same set-up shot in a photo shoot. Differences in composition and character suggest this may have been the case that day.

"Hats Off" provides an opportunity to see the faces of nine of the men in full. The sixth man looks away. The tenth man's cap and the cable mostly obscure his face, although in "Hats Off," he has turned his covered head toward the camera and raised his gloved hand.

The three photos help us understand how one photo rose above them all. "Hats Off" is a great image but does not chill the spine like "Lunch on a Beam." "Breakfast Break" shares the arresting perspective of "Lunch on a Beam," but its composition tells no story. Only "Lunch on a

6.3 "Hats Off" provides a third view of the ironworkers. (Rockefeller Group photo 111)

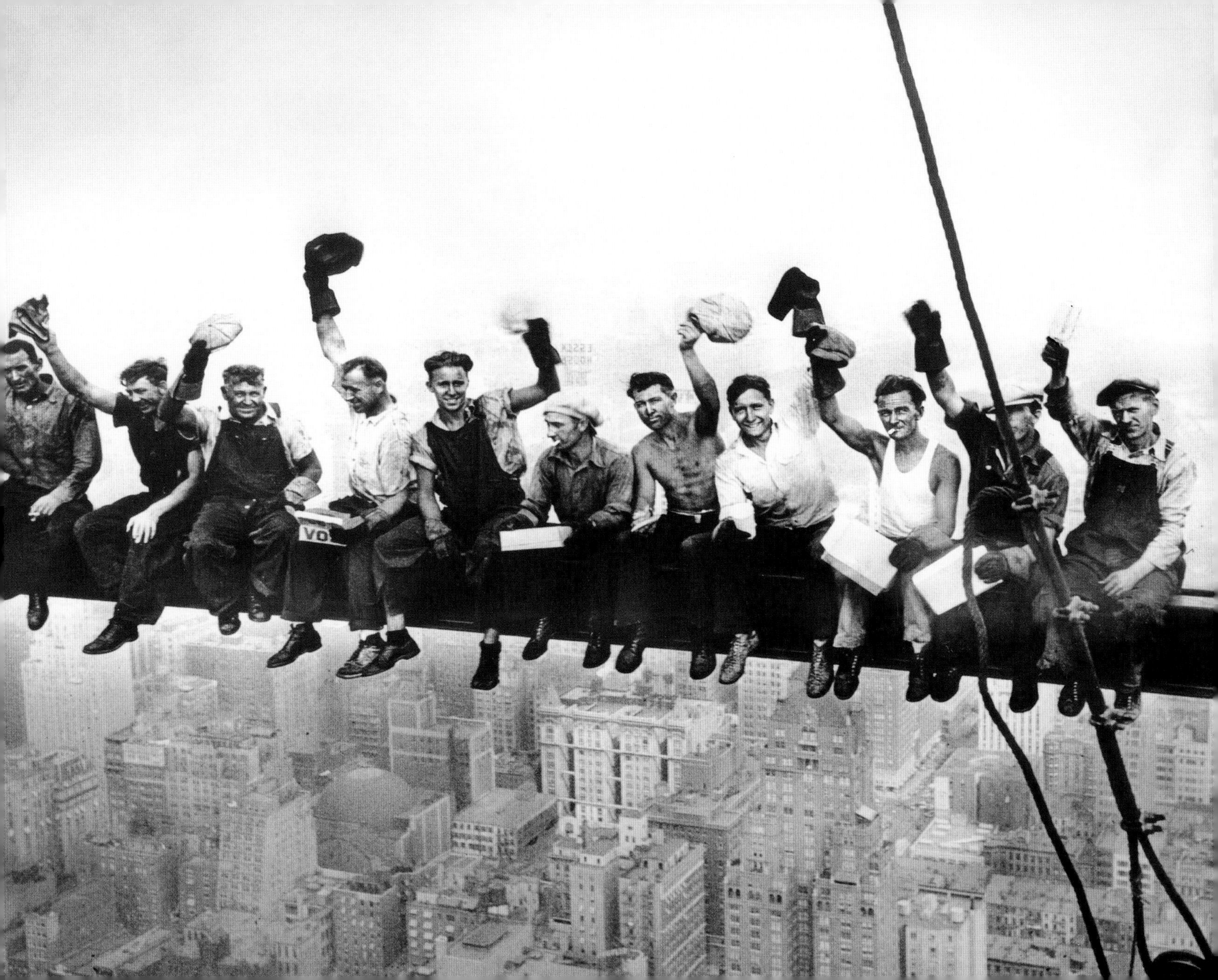

Beam" combined the artistry, danger, and human connection to become an icon.

But the questions remained: Who was behind the camera, or cameras? And who were the men on the beam?

· · ·

Evidence suggests that the photos were taken in this sequence: "Lunch on a Beam," then "Breakfast Break," and then "Hats Off." We can reason that the men sat down, then lit up, and then smoked and ate. After the first photo, the eleventh man switches his bottle from his left hand to his right, where it remains for "Hats Off." After the second photo, two men dropped their empty sandwich boxes—not eight hundred feet to the street, but perhaps a dozen feet to the unseen planks below.

Most people assume that the same photographer took both "Lunch on a Beam" and "Hats Off" (and "Breakfast Break," to the extent anyone considered it at all). But we know several photographers were there that day. And evidence, both stylistic and tangible, points to at least two different photographers. Some of that evidence is recorded on the backs of the three photographs.

The Archive's captions for "Hats Off" and "Lunch on a Beam" are identical: "Lunchtime 800 Feet Up at Rockefeller Center, New York." But other details recorded on the archive's oldest prints are different.

On the back of "Lunch on a Beam," Rockefeller Center's publicity department noted the following:

Acme holds the negative

Copy Negative—Newspictures (344)

Exclusive Herald-Tribune roto October 2, 1932

[Noted in pencil] Taken Sept 20 1932

[Noted in pen] Don't give out.

The note "Acme holds the negative" seems to rule out one possible photographer: Leftwich was self-employed and did business under his own agency, Newspictures. But the very next line complicates the story: "Copy Negative—Newspictures (344)." These markings suggest that Rockefeller Center's PR Department had initially ordered prints through Acme but later had a copy negative made by Leftwich, whose studio across the street made him a convenient and dependable source.

The Acme attribution for "Lunch on a Beam" left the photographer up for grabs. It could be any stringer they had paid. But Charlie Ebbets's family has offered a strong case that he shot "Lunch on a Beam."

Rockefeller Center Publicity Department stamp marks are on the back of "Hats Off":

Rockefeller Center 30 Rockefeller Plaza New York

This Picture Is for Your Unconditional Release

 Circle 6-3440 Photographic Department

Credit Photography by Newspictures, Inc

48 West 48th Street New York City

Medallion 3-3737

The second stamp attributes the photograph to Newspictures, Inc., William Leftwich's corporation. This provides specific, tangible evidence that Leftwich made "Hats Off."

The numerous stamps, notations, and measurements on the back of the Ullstein-Bild photograph reflect the history of a print that was distributed internationally, published, and later archived.

It bears more than a dozen stamps, labels, and handwritten notes. Stamped in black ink at the center is:

Note to editors: Sept. 30, 1932

Under each reproduction of this photo must be carried the following credit:

"ASSOCIATED PRESS PHOTO"

Title picture may not be syndicated, rented or

loaned, nor used for advertising purposes.

The Associated Press

Beside the stamp is a green label, partially obscured by tape. It reads:

Veröffentlichung darf nur erfo—

mit Genehmigung und unter Nennun—

The Associated Press, Be—

A. P. Photos

Bilderdienst der Associated Press of Ar—

Nachf. von Pacific & Atlantic Photos U. m—

Berlin SW 68 Markgrafenstr

Fernspr. A7 Dönhoff 125

Below that, a white label reads:

Verlag Ullstein. No. 6084z

The white label partially obscures a red stamp:

zu benchigar Verw—

Above that stamp, in red pencil:

EDV 133057

The space around the labels is filled with the following notations, handwritten in black pencil:

Foto: Lewis W. Hine

55.5 [along diagonal line]

11.5 in [along horizontal line]

Frühstuckspause

It is stamped "230??" A white label reads:

Verlag Ullstein. No. 6084z

A green label reads:

The Associated Press Berlin A.P. Photos [and an address
in Berlin]

The distribution of this copy of "Breakfast Break" through the Associated Press complicates the search for its origin. But one glaring error on this archive photo raises an interesting story, one that keeps percolating up no matter how often photography historians attempt to correct it: the (certainly mistaken) handwritten credit to photographer Lewis W. Hine.

Hine was an important photographer of the early twentieth century. He was known for his photographs of industrial and construction workers, especially on the Empire State Building, but he did not photograph Rockefeller Center. The mistake is a common one, and Hine has been miscredited with "Lunch on a Beam" by many, including the Smithsonian Institution.[14]

Lewis Hine was a pioneer in many fields. He was a sociologist and educator concerned with exposing the appalling conditions of immigrants and factory workers as America progressed into the machine age. He exposed the abuses of child labor and the unsafe conditions men and especially women faced as heavy industry grew. He did this with a relatively new tool—the inexpensive and portable camera.[15] Hine realized the power that photography could have as a truth-teller and record keeper. "Photography," he said, "can light up darkness and expose ignorance."[16]

In 1905, Hine photographed people passing through Ellis Island. He wanted to show immigrants as complex individuals, working hard to provide a better life for their families. Inspired by his mentor, the social reformer Frank Manny, Hine sought to instill in the public "the same regard for contemporary immigrants as they have for Pilgrims who landed at Plymouth Rock."[17]

In 1930, he was hired as a commercial photographer to document the yearlong building of the Empire State Building. He chose to focus on the workers. Working alongside the ironworkers, he devised new and risky methods like a crane-lifted basket he sat in as he shot his pictures a thousand feet above Fifth Avenue.

In 1932, Hine published *Men at Work,* a book of industrial photography that included several of his Empire State Building photographs. Hine's work likely influenced all construction photographers working at the time, especially in New York. But that influence was his only connection to "Lunch on a Beam."

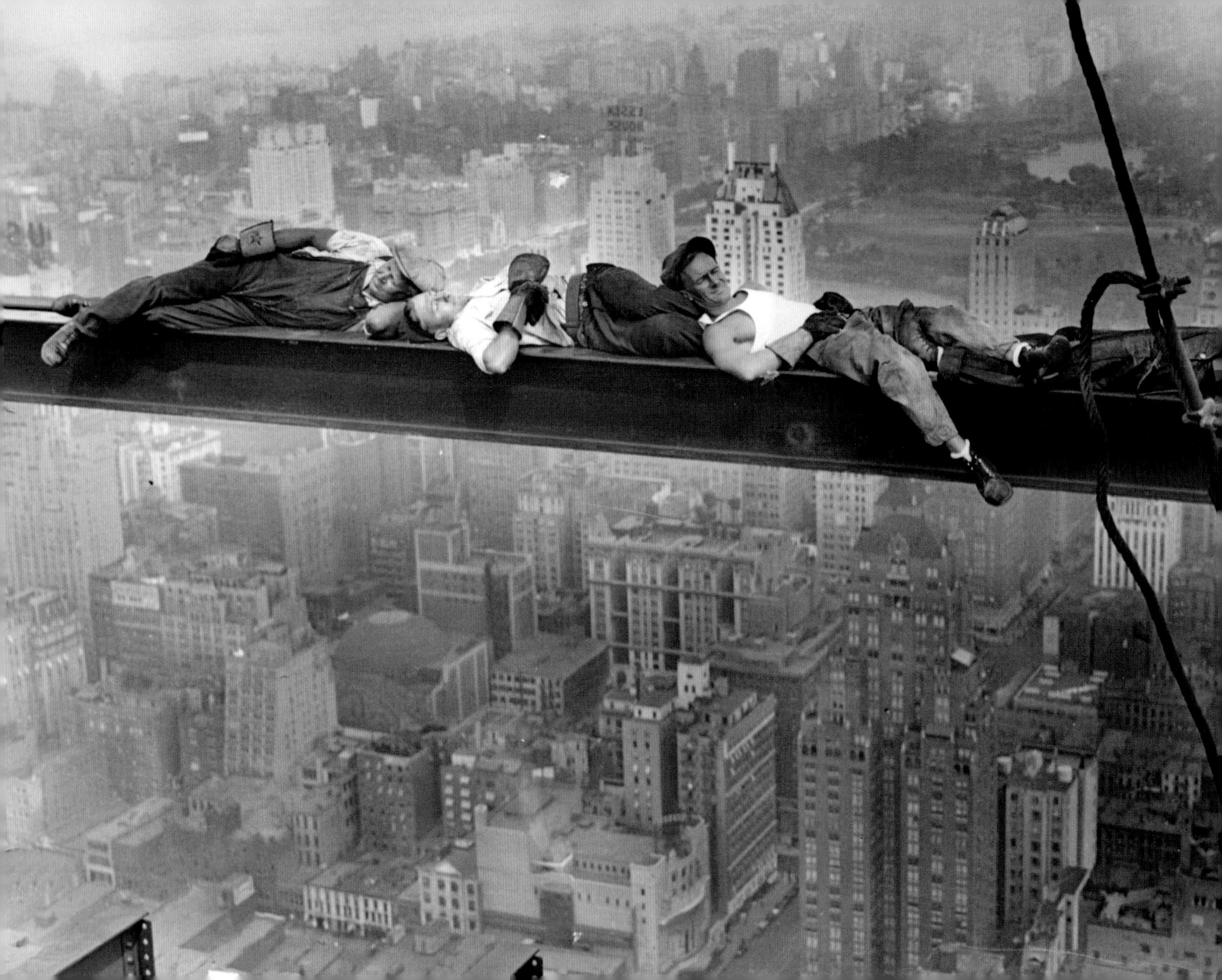

ESSEX
HOUSE

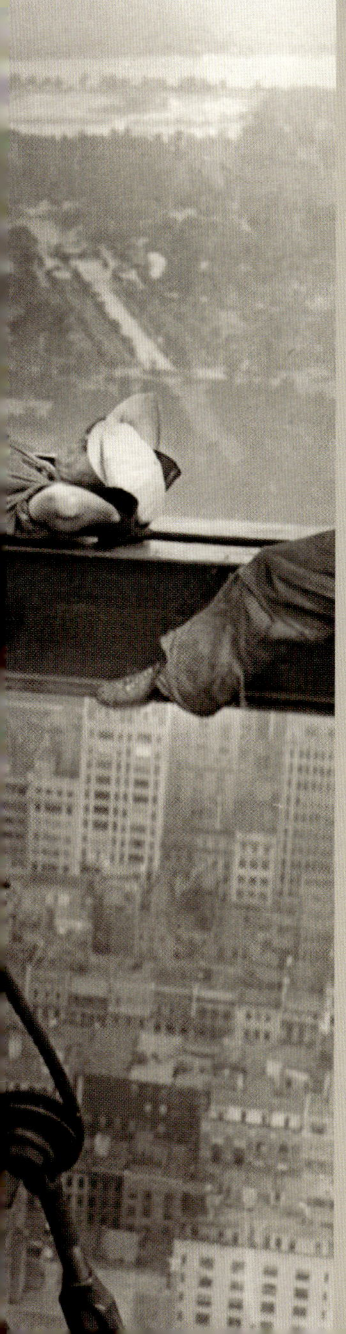

7

INTO THE ARCHIVE

7.1 Appearing to nap on a girder, from left: Joseph Eckner, William Birgir, Joe Curtis, and John Portla. (Rockefeller Group photo 120)

WAS FORTUNATE to follow in the footsteps of researchers who previously sought to identify the eleven men on the beam. And I was fortunate to do so with unprecedented access to original records in the Rockefeller Center Archive.

The archive is both a joy and a frustration. For more than sixty years, it did not exist—at least not as a research archive. When the Rockefeller Group sold Rockefeller Center in 1996, employees of the Public Relations Department scrambled to preserve its history. Books, photographs, and files—some older than Rockefeller Center itself—were pulled out of dumpsters, thrown into unlabeled boxes, or stacked at random onto old shelves in a newly designated "Rockefeller Center Archive Center."[1] In the thirty years since then, the archive has moved at least four times. The most recent move, in 2022, was the first to an archive space worthy of the name, with room to organize and access the trove within.

As I researched this book, I cross-referenced photos of ironworkers at the Rockefeller Center Archive and compared each man in "Lunch on a Beam" with his photo in "Hats Off" and eventually "Breakfast Break." The next step was to compare those faces with other photos in the archive, a precious few of which identified the subjects in their captions.

As the Rockefeller Center Archive was not digitized, I searched by hand for photos that identified ironworkers by name. Of the tens of thousands of images at the archive, I found ten. And even those were suspect. Did the photographers take notes as they scrambled over the steel structure and shot pictures? Did they identify subjects later, squinting at negatives? Did Merle Crowell, or an assistant, fill in names after the fact? Would the publicity maestro let any doubt stand in the way of a good story? The thing that seemed to matter was the scene itself, and rarely the individuals in it—unless that individual's name was Rockefeller.

Against those doubts, the fact that most photos of the ironworkers bore no name gave me hope: If Crowell's team was going to make it up, why hold back?

At the same time, I examined images sent to the archive by the families of ironworkers and sought out evidence in contemporary publications.

For help wading through the confusion and possibilities, I talked to Clint Saunders, an associate professor of photography at Dakota College in Bottineau, North Dakota. He had shown an interest in who the photographers were at the time Rockefeller Center was built and, like me, he was curious about the names of the eleven men on the beam. We compared notes and began to scrutinize archival photos. We continued this exchange of ideas for nearly two years.

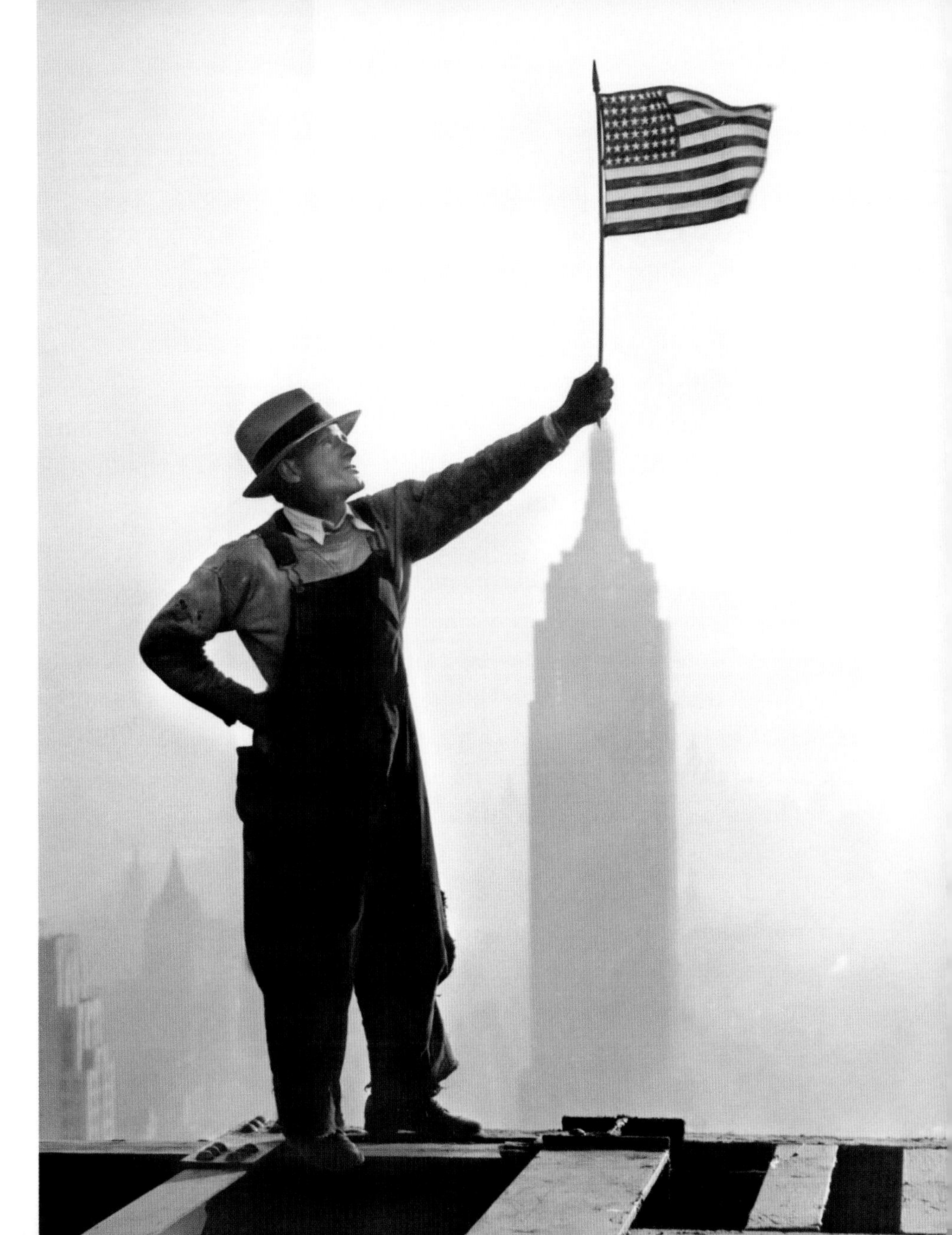

7.2 Joseph McCloskey holds a flag "above" the Empire State Building. (Rockefeller Group photo 297)

Planting a flag atop the Empire State Building is another example of the playful shots taken that day in 1932.[2] Joseph McClosky doesn't seem concerned by brazenly standing on the edge of a narrow beam, holding a small American flag flapping in the breeze. The caption reads: "NEW YORK: Puzzle—How can you hold a flag over the Empire State Building and still be nearly a mile away? Here's the answer—just get on top of the R.C.A. Building in Rockefeller Center, the world's largest office building, and do it. And if you still don't believe it can be done, here's Joseph McClosky showing you how."

McClosky's confidence is apparent: his cocksure posture, hand on hip, head thrown back, hat on. There is even a not-too-subliminal message: McClosky dwarfs the Empire State Building, which he tops with his flag like a toy. McClosky is easily recognizable but, unfortunately, is not one of the men in "Lunch on a Beam."

These antics reflect a frantic publicity effort. Simultaneously, six Rockefeller buildings were underway, and with them was a significant campaign to sell all that upcoming space. The ultimate hype man, Crowell presented the rise of Rockefeller Center as a wondrous event. He pitched flashy and bold ideas. He sought magic moments. What he couldn't find, he invented.

"Steelworkers Resting on a Beam," taken September 20, 1932, shows a preposterous arrangement of four men napping on an I-beam high above the city. The men lie on the same girder as "Lunch on a Beam," "Breakfast Break," and "Hats Off." The view looks to the same northwest direction at a slightly different angle. The ends of beams jut out in the lower left foreground, and part of a vertical I-beam intrudes on the right side of the photo. This section of the I-beam stabilizes the scene, removing the impression of a floating beam. The same twisted steel cable bisects the right half of the image.

The caption reads: "A noon-day siesta on a narrow steel beam 800 feet above the street level is nothing in the lives of these steelworkers at Rockefeller Center. Photo shows, *left* to *right*: Joseph Eckner, William Birgir, Joe Curtis, and John Portla, resting after their morning's labors."

Of all the photos taken that day, this one makes me most anxious.

Two of the men's legs dangle disconcertingly off the beam. Like "Lunch on a Beam," the sprawling cityscape below heightens the sense of risk and underscores the alarming distance to the ground. Their very casualness makes me fearful for the men. I get queasy thinking how they got out there and then lay down. How will they get up? I foresee catastrophe.

This image also provides a good view of the top of the beam, confirming Sears's observation that it is a split-channel beam, twenty inches across. The caption names the men participating in the stunt, and a comparison with photos "Lunch on a Beam," "Breakfast Break," and "Hats Off" suggests the following identifications, from left to right.

The man identified as Joseph Eckner is the third man on the beam. The similarities in attire are spot-on. He wears dark overalls, a white short-sleeved shirt, and a light-colored cap. Saunders reached the same conclusion.

The man identified as William Birgir is the eighth man on the beam. The hat, white shirt sleeves rolled to the elbow, dark construction gloves, ears, eyes, mouth, and hair are a match. Birgir is also one of the only men also identified in a photo from outside the archive, which we will discuss later.

The man identified as Joe Curtis is the ninth man on the beam. He wears a white tee shirt, a white cap, dirty light-colored trousers, and dark work gloves. In "Hats Off," his white socks show just above his high, dark shoes. We have seen him before, the second of nine men eating lunch safely on the planked floor in figure 3.3. He also strongly resembles the single reclining man in two other archive photos. But here, we encounter a complication: Those captions identify their subjects as "Harry Brender" and "Joe

Holton" (see figures 7.14 and 7.15; we will return to this question below).

The man identified as John Portla is the tenth man on the beam. He wears a clean white cap and dark overalls over a gray shirt. The shirt sleeves roll to his biceps, and his partial profile is a match, though less definitively so. Again, a discussion with Saunders about his clothing, including his white cap and the partial view of his face, convinced us that he is the tenth man on the beam.

We can identify four more ironworkers in another staged scene, "Make Yourself at Home." The archive kept two nearly identical takes (figures 7.8 and 7.9) in which the four men sit close together where two beams meet at a corner. They eat lunch and appear to listen to a radio.

The radio is a prop that appears in at least half a dozen photos taken in different locations around the grillage that day. Perhaps surprisingly for the top of the R.C.A. Building, the brand was not Radio Corporation of America, but instead Jackson Bell, a smaller West Coast radio manufacturer. Bob Donner, who restores vintage radios, told me that collectors today prize Jackson Bell radios for their distinctive front grilles, with designs that aficionados have dubbed "Peter Pan," "Tulip," "Sunrise," "Sunburst," and "Swan." The grille in these photos is a "Sunburst," a perfect fit for the Art Deco aesthetic of Rockefeller Center, which

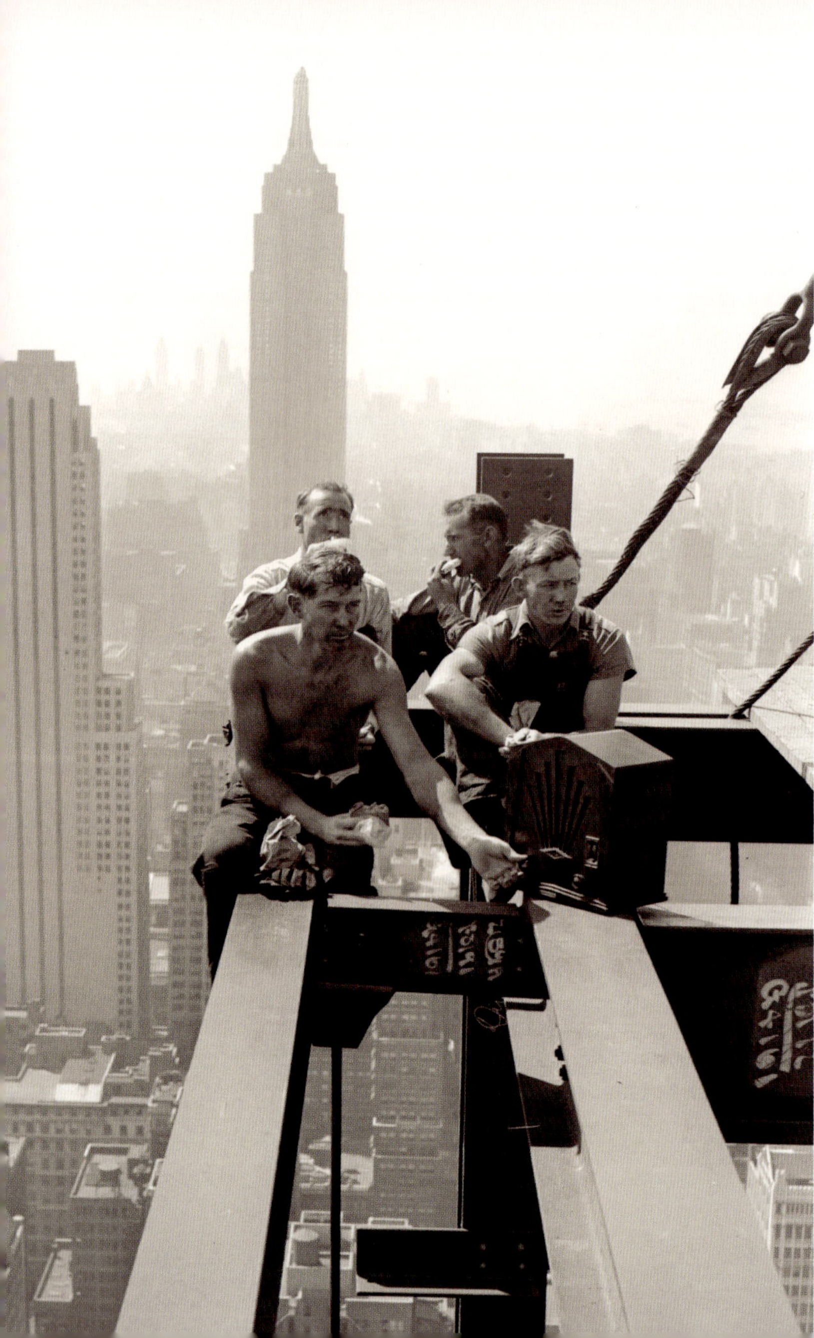

suggests the careful intention behind these photographs.[3]

The Empire State Building behind the four men tells us that they are sitting near the southeast corner of the R.C.A Building, the camera pointed in the opposite direction from "Lunch on a Beam." The photographers were working in all areas of the site, with ironworkers continuing to participate in the photo shoot. The caption reads: "Lunchtime on The World's Largest Building: NEW YORK—"Make yourself at home'—that's the motto of these steelworkers at ROCKEFELLER CENTER as the noon-day whistle blows for lunch, 70 floors above the street level. It's only an 800-foot sheer drop to the street below but they seem more interested in the radio than that fact. Left to right, Howard Kilgore, George Kovan; in the rear, left to right, George Comsky and John O'Rielly."

We can match three of these men—Kilgore, Kovan, and O'Rielly—to "Lunch on a Beam." The man at the back left drinking from a canteen, identified as George Comsky, does not appear to match any of the eleven men in "Lunch on a Beam."

Once again, the identification is complicated by other photos in the archive. Another photo taken at the same

7.3 "Four-man lunch" identifies Howard Kilgore (front left), George Kovan (front right), George Comsky (back left), and John O'Rielly (back right). (Rockefeller Group photo 123A)

corner (figure 7.4) identifies the shirtless man not as Kilgore, but as "James Kovan."[4] (One could suspect that no one was taking careful notes on the sixty-ninth floor that day, and that Merle Crowell's publicity department may have been happy to fill in the blanks.) The caption reads: "James Kovan, crack steel worker at ROCKEFELLER CENTER, New York City, takes a fifteen-minute rest after lunch on a steel beam on the sheer edge of the R.C.A. Building, 69 stories above the street." The man's face is partially obscured by the light cap pulled over his eyes, but he otherwise resembles the shirtless seventh man in "Lunch on a Beam." His right leg casually dangles off one side of the beam. Nearby lie a paper-wrapped sandwich and the familiar radio, which he once again pretends to tune with his left hand. This time, instead of the Empire State Building, the photo is framed to show the pinnacle of the Chrysler Building, the East River, with Brooklyn and Queens in the background.

As with the lunch theme, photographers kept returning to the idea of a nap. While Kovan (or Kilgore) napped on the southern edge of the building, back on the north side another ironworker lay in the same northern area as "Lunch on a Beam" (figure 7.5). The caption reads: "Harry Brender, a crack steel worker at ROCKEFELLER CENTER, New York City, resting after lunch on a steel

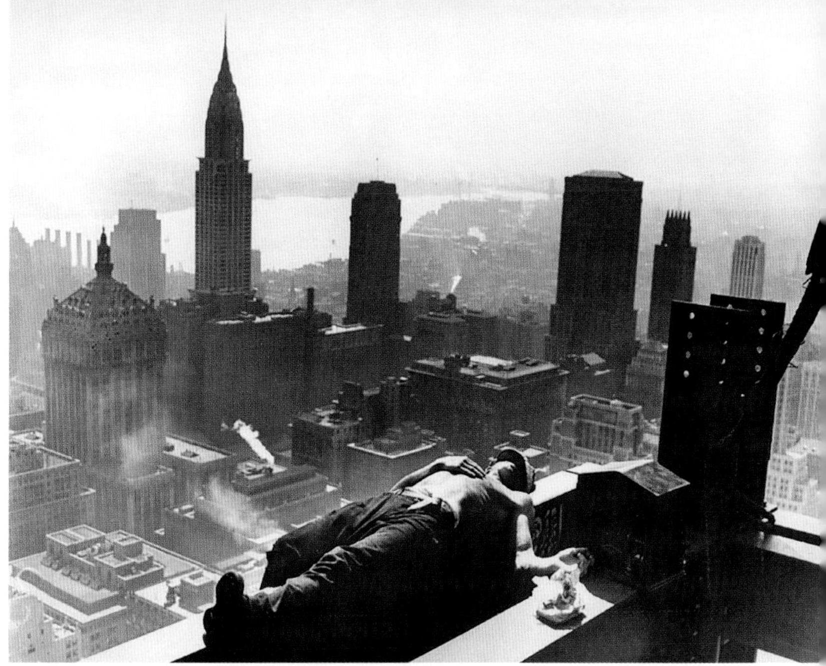

7.4 Another photo at the same corner identifies the shirtless man as "James Kovan, crack steel worker." (Rockefeller Group photo 121)

beam on the sheer edge of the R.C.A. Building, 69 stories above the street." The photo was taken on the north side of the grillage with Central Park and the upper west side of the city on the left of the background.

Cropped tighter on its subject than "Lunch on a Beam," the Brender photograph includes fewer buildings in the background. The Ziegfeld sign appears below the beam in both images. Brender lies on his back, hands crossed behind his head. He wears a white tank top, dark pants,

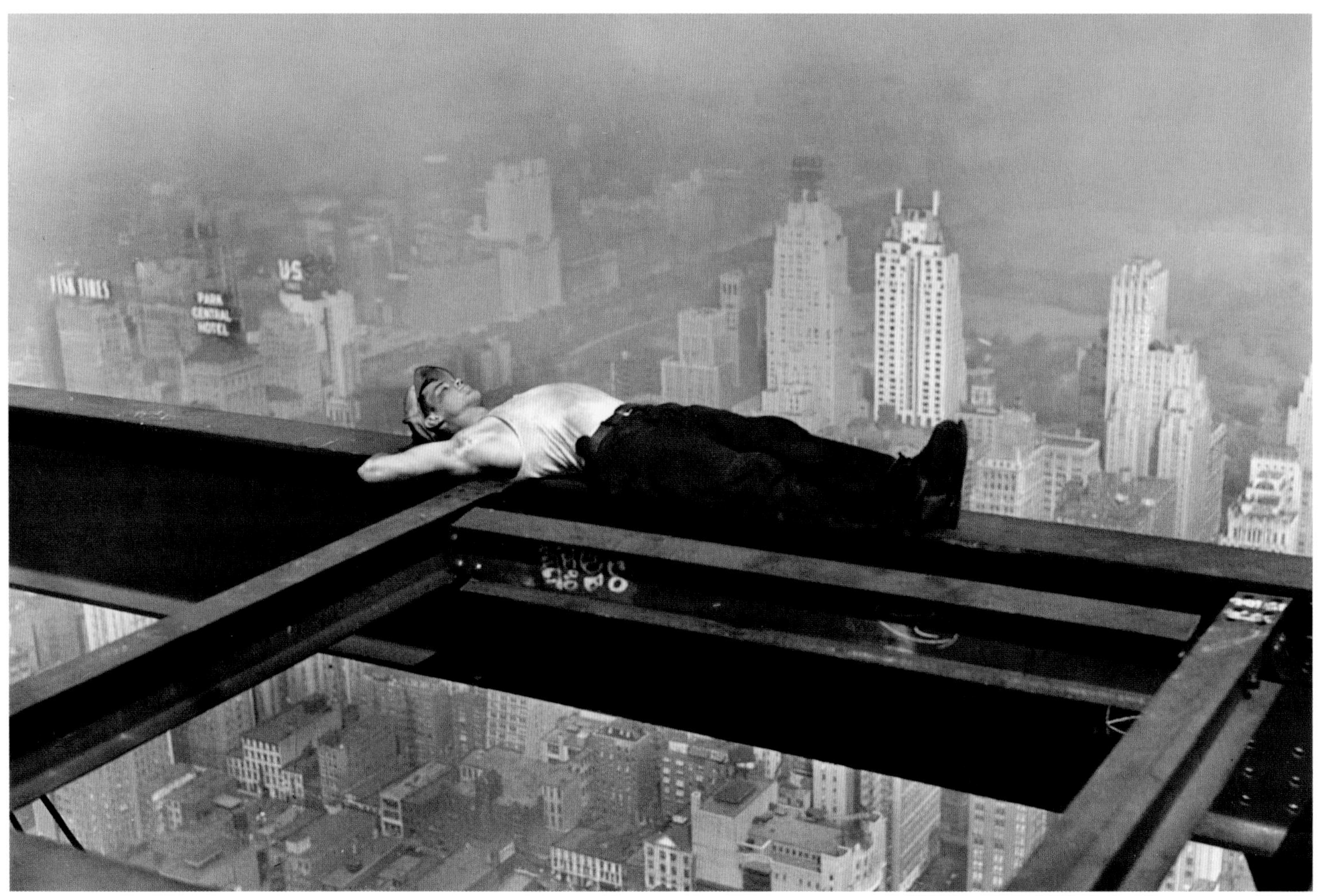

7.5 A man identified as Harry Bender. (Rockefeller Group photo 238A)

7.6 A man identified as J. Holton. (Rockefeller Group photo 238B)

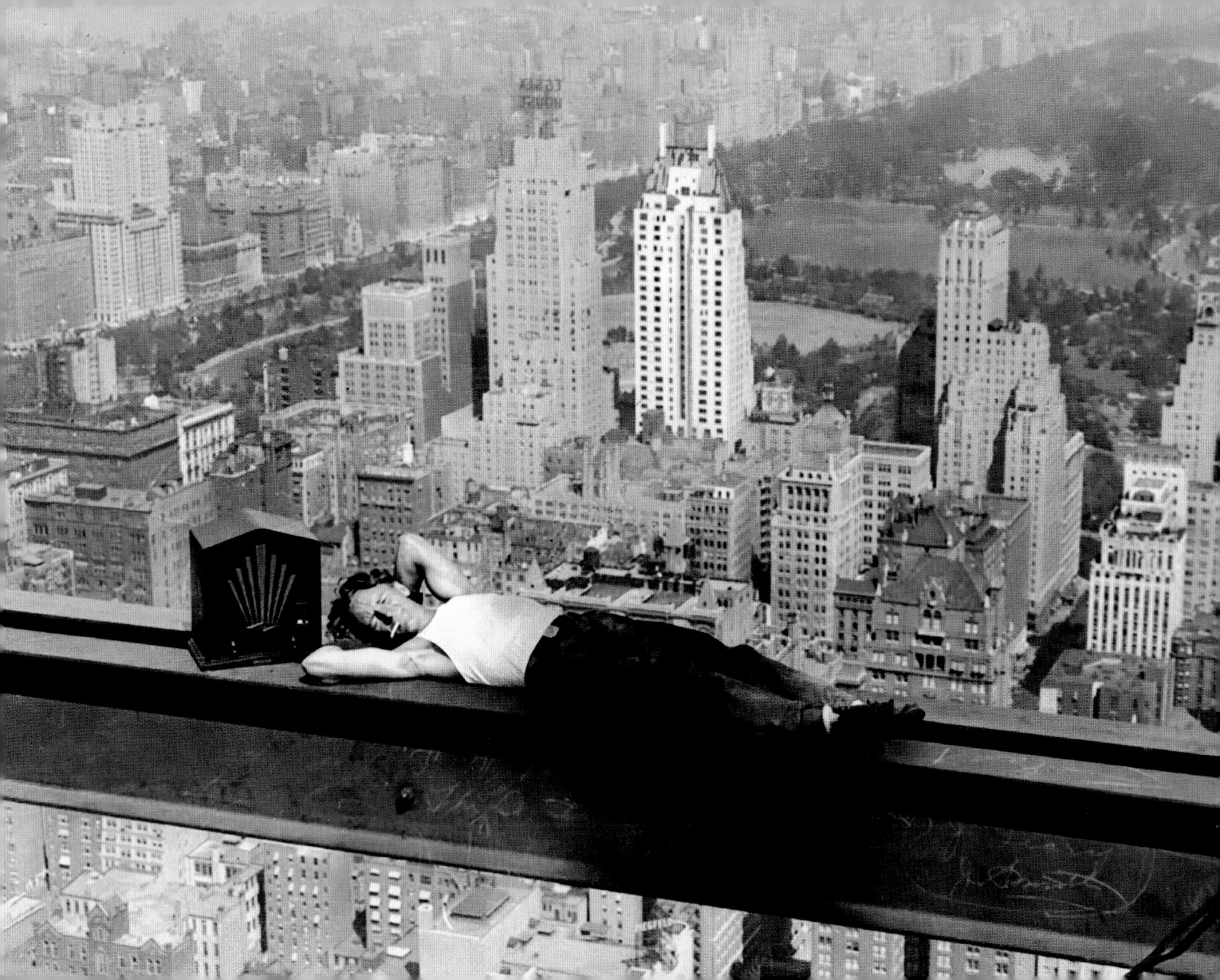

and a light cap pushed back on his head. His eyes are closed, and he faces the sky.

A second photo (figure 7.6) in the same location appears at first glance to be the same reclining man. But the caption identifies this man as "J. Holton, crack steel worker." A sea of buildings stretches below Holton, who lies on a split-channel beam. The caption reads, with poetic flair: "TIS SLEEP THAT KNITS THE RAVELLED SLEEVE OF CARE: New York—J. Holton, this is no place to toss about in your sleep. Here is J. Holton, crack steel worker at Rockefeller Center, John D. Rockefeller's $250,000,000 Radio City development, taking a 15-minute luncheon snooze on a steel beam, 800 feet above the street. And, for nonchalance, he must have his music nearby on edge of the R.C.A. Building—69 stories above the street."

The headline ("Tis sleep . . .") is a quote from *Macbeth*. Shakespeare quotes pepper Crowell's columns in his Rockefeller Center magazine.[5] It makes me wonder: Who was Crowell, or who was he trying to be? Pompous? Playful? A farmer's son and Colby man striving among Rockefeller's Ivy Leaguers? And who was his audience? There, at least, we know: newsmen, his former trade.

Like Brender, J. Holton wears a white tank top and dark trousers, and his head rests on his folded arms. He smokes a cigarette and looks directly at the camera. The chiseled faces of Brender and Holton, though at different angles, share a strong chin, straight nose, and medium eyebrows. The strong resemblance may explain why the Rockefeller Center publicity department catalogued these photos as 238A and 238B, a filing system used for multiple takes of the same photo.

The 1930 US Census does not record a "Harry Brender" in the New York region, but it does record a New York City ironworker by the name of Harry Brenner. I conferred with Saunders, who shared my frustration. "The fact that one of these is named incorrectly suggests that other photos might also be named incorrectly, which adds an entirely new level to the magnitude of this project," Saunders said. "Is he James Holton or Joe Curtis?"[6]

Or neither?

Small differences suggest that the men identified as Holton and Brender are indeed different men. Although both the Holton and Brender photos look northwest, with Central Park in the background, the men lie on different beams, and the camera angle is steeper in Holton's photo. A radio, absent in the Brender photo, appears in Holton's. Holton is bareheaded, although he could have removed his cap between takes. His tank top is stained. His pants are shorter, exposing white socks. Most tellingly, he wears a different belt: Where Brender's buckle appears to be a prong style, Holton's is a flat, military-style plate.

Different belts. Different men. But is either of them Curtis, the man napping with three fellows in the siesta photo (figure 7.2)? Curtis folds his hands on his waist, concealing his belt. No help there. He wears a clean shirt like Brender, white socks like Curtis, and gloves like neither man. Like Brender, he wears a cap, but it is darker.

The sum of these details suggests three different men.

At least two other photos in the Rockefeller Center Archive identify workers on the R.C.A. Building grillage who are not among the eleven in "Lunch on a Beam." In the first, two men stand atop the northwest corner of the R.C.A. Building. Behind them is Central Park and the Upper West Side. The caption reads: "Heart Failure to You—Relaxation to Them: New York. It's an 850-foot drop to the street and there's usually a stiff breeze at this height above New York City. What would mean heart failure to most of us street-bound mortals is just a happy hiatus in the day's job to these two workmen as they light a cigarette on the top of the R.C.A. Building, the world's largest office building in Rockefeller Center. Left to right: Joseph McClosky, Edward Smith, Rockefeller Center workmen."

Notably, the caption describes McClosky and Smith as "workmen," not ironworkers (or "steel workers," terms the press office used interchangeably). They dress differently from men identified as ironworkers in other photos. Smith (right) wears a dark work jacket, wide-legged striped trousers, and a worker's cap. McClosky wears wide-legged dark overalls; a soiled, light-colored, long-sleeved shirt; and a fedora (as he does in figure 7.1, where he holds an American flag at the pinnacle of the Empire State Building). Here, the flag is planted on the beam as McClosky leans over it to light his cigarette off Smith's. The gesture recalls the first man in "Lunch on a Beam," leaning over to light his cigarette off his neighbor's.

The meticulous composition here suggests something similar was going on in "Lunch on a Beam": The arrangement of the eleven men, the groups of groups, was no accident, but instead carefully choreographed by the photographer. Where Merle Crowell quoted Shakespeare, the photographer quoted Leonardo.

In the second photo that named men who weren't on the beam, two workers ride a hoist ball. The caption reads: "Weave Web of Steel: Two of Brooklyn's ace steel workers, Jack Anderson of 476 E. 60th St., and John Poole, of 1563 E. 65th St., are swinging high above terra firma while they do their bit to build the massive R.C.A. Building in the Rockefeller Center (Radio City), Manhattan. The building will tower 70 stories and will contain 26 recording and broadcasting studios and enough equipment to broadcast to every human being on earth."

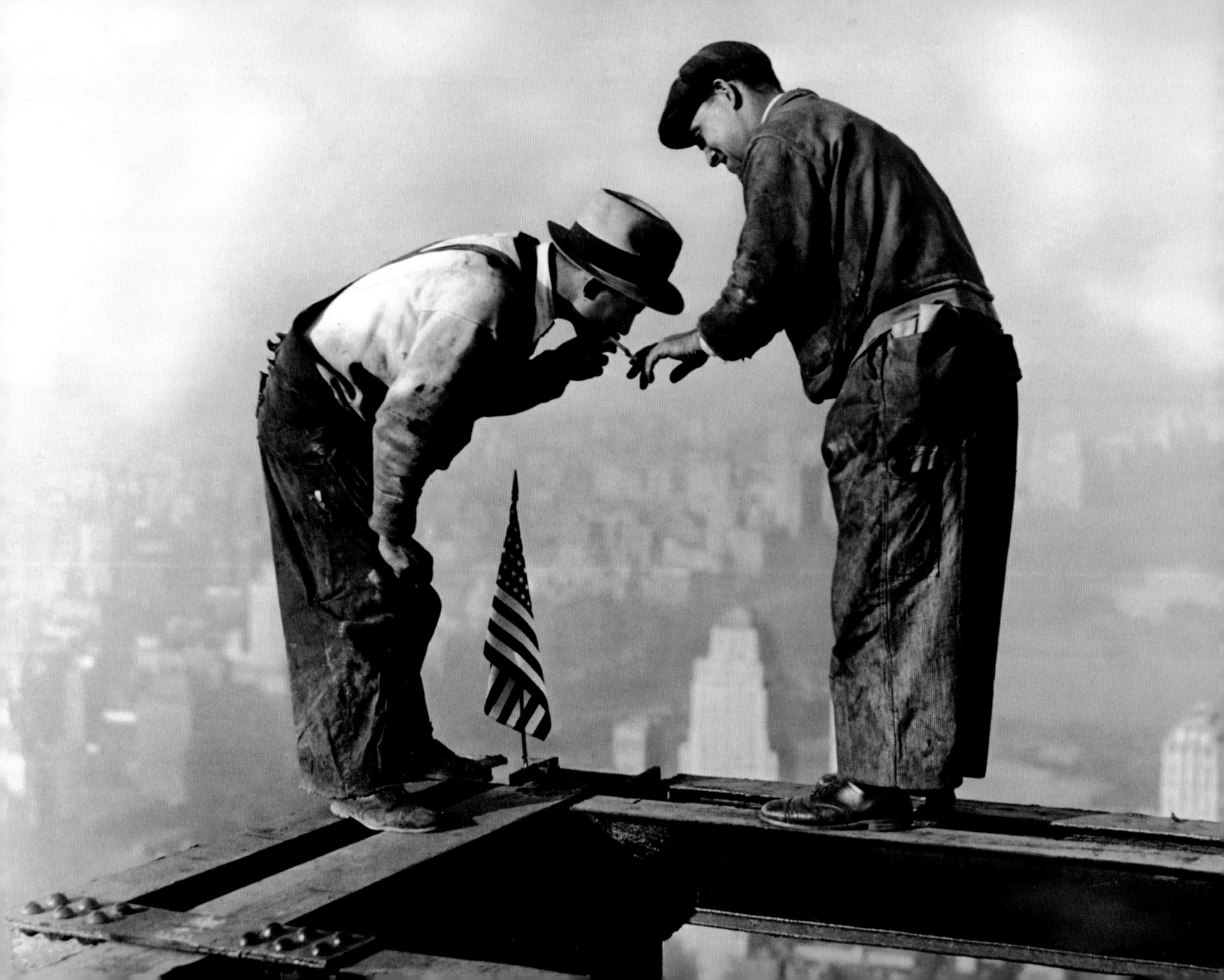

Neither Anderson nor Poole appears to match anyone in "Lunch on a Beam." Interestingly, this photo was dated August 10, 1932, more than a month before the topping-out ceremony. The caption writer not only included addresses for the ironworkers (standard newspaper practice at the time), but also noted Rockefeller Center's former name, "Radio City"—a nod to the recent change. Wide World, a news agency, distributed the photo.

During the 1930s, the hoist ball, a weight that keeps an unloaded crane line under tension, was a quick and easy ride to the work site. Properly known as an overhaul hook ball, it also had another name: the headache ball. I asked Wild Bill Sears why.

"Unfortunate encounters," he said. Still, he added, "Everybody did it."

Today, most states ban riding the ball, which is still used in single-line wire-rope hoisting to keep an unloaded line from whipping around. Sears assured me it's safe, and some states still allow the practice.

In 2004, the son of an ironworker reached out to the Rockefeller Center Archive with unusually strong evidence that his father was one of the men on the beam.[7]

The Urbanneck family had kept a publicity-size 8 by 10-inch photograph of two ironworkers riding a beam. Handwritten across the front was "62nd-floor R.C.A. Radio City, New York 9/15/32." Stamped on the back was "Hamilton Wright," who worked both as a photographer and as an agent for other photographers. >

The family identified the man on the left as their father, George Urbanneck Sr., and said the handwriting on the photo was his. His large face, youthful and handsome beneath a mop of swept-back hair, is unmistakably the fifth man in "Lunch on a Beam." The other young man in the photo resembles the eighth man on the beam, identified in other photos as William Birgir.

Urbanneck appears in several other photos taken at Rockefeller Center in September 1932, often alongside Birgir. Urbanneck wears the same overalls and collared shirt, sleeves rolled up. In most photos, he looks directly at the camera.

The Urbannecks' story is striking for the evidence behind it—evidence so frustratingly absent from so many other contenders for a place on the beam. The family kept another document: a yellowed newspaper clipping of the eleven men on the beam, published October 5, 1932, in the *New York Journal*. Interestingly, the photograph was not "Lunch on a Beam," but the lesser-known variation known as "Breakfast Break" (figure 6.7). We will return to Urbanneck's story in chapter 8.

7.7 Joseph McClosky (left) and Edward Smith light a cigarette. (Rockefeller Group photo 297)

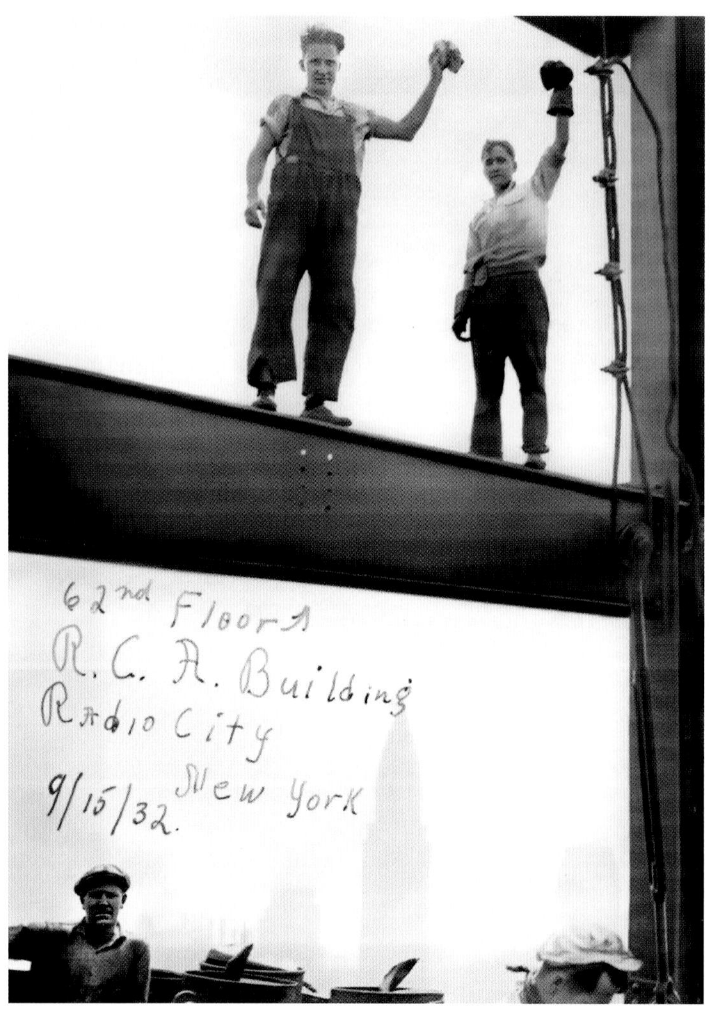

7.8 George Urbanneck and William Birger. (Rockefeller Group photo)

A careful reader may ask: How tall *is* the R.C.A. Building? It seems Merle Crowell couldn't make up his mind. Some releases said sixty-nine stories, others seventy. Consider this caption, released with another photo taken September 15 (figure 3.2): "Daring workmen swinging high over New York on the new R.C.A. Building in Rockefeller Center. A veritable forest of steelwork. The R.C.A. Building in Rockefeller Center, which will tower 70 stories and contain more office space than any other building in the world, greets New York's famous skyline. This building will contain two million square feet of office space, twenty-six electrically shielded broadcasting studios, six audition rooms, equipment powerful enough to broadcast to practically every human on earth, a studio whose ceiling is three stories high, and the roof of which will be beautified by landscaping. There will be more than six acres of landscaped roofs and setbacks in the development. More than 56,000 people are now being employed in all phases of its development."

Crowell almost certainly wrote this caption. It hits all the publicity highs: exaggerated numbers, thousands employed, acres of gardens, and a broadcast studio powerful enough to reach practically every human on Earth. And like most—but not all—of his releases, it puts the height of the R.C.A. Building at seventy stories. This is still being debated: Is it sixty-nine or seventy stories high? Do all, some, or no terraces count? The question persists today even within the architects' offices at Rockefeller Center. But who's counting?

The public celebrated ironworkers as independent and fearless. They were just the sort of men needed when the nation was in the throes of the Great Depression. Crowell and the photographers had discovered willing participants who would strut and swagger for the camera and were proud to be constructing one of the world's tallest skyscrapers. Even today, ironworkers like to point to a skyscraper and brag, "I built that."

None of the photos taken that day reflect the fear and fatigue that came with the job, intensified by "the Great Depression [that] was settling like a shroud over the country."[8] Instead, most images chronicled audacity and pride in the hazardous work. Ironworkers seem to focus on the job and brush off any thought of going into the hole every time they step onto an I-beam.

These images also reflect the camaraderie between the photographers and the ironworkers. Skyscrapers and high-speed cameras were exciting modern technologies that created new jobs and breeds of audacious men. The ironworkers respected the photographers' willingness to join them in dicey maneuvers at spine-chilling heights.

Both were risk-takers. Ironworkers, and perhaps the photographers, lived by the trope: There is no dress rehearsal.

These staged scenes, taken in the fall of 1932, of ironworkers on different beams in various places on top of the R.C.A. steel structure may have led to confusion and contributed to some families' belief that their man is one of the eleven in the iconic photo. At least three photographers and perhaps as many as twenty construction workers participated in a series of photo shoots, most famously—but not only—on September 20, 1932. Some dated images suggest that the photographers returned on different days, shooting groups of ironworkers in various places. Perhaps some ironworkers told their families about posing on a beam, even eating lunch. It could be that this number of photos, with this theme, and hurried and muddled identification by photographers in a hazardous setting created confusion for future generations. Not to mention the sloppy recording of names within the public relations department.

There is another possible explanation: subterfuge. At a moment when a union card was a ticket off the bread lines, some desperate workers would borrow the card of a friend or relative to qualify for work. "Card lending," or "buddy-carding," was prohibited by unions and employers, and both men risked being kicked off the job, out of the union, and blackballed if caught. I found no evidence of card sharing by the ironworkers of Rockefeller Center, but also no way to prove the negative. And the scenario could explain why the photographers got one story, and a worker's family another. But that is only speculation.

I seemed to have reached the limit of what I could learn from the archive. I would have to look further for the three missing names and to confirm my findings. I would have to keep an open mind.

Identification has eluded most searchers. There are many opinions—most on the internet—about who the men were. Sifting through the possibilities took time, but it also narrowed the search. Most of the names put forth needed evidence. Much of the information was simply copied from previous misinformation. I contacted many people who had claimed to have a relative on the beam and got no response. I wondered, was it just satisfying to say? Reassuring? Powerful?

I reached out to the unions and hit a wall. Officials with Local 40 in New York City answered questions about the history of ironwork and offered to find membership lists from the 1930s, but I came back empty-handed. I had even less luck at 440 in upstate New York, Local 361 on Long Island or Local 764 in Nova Scotia. A typical response was, "Our records from that time are difficult or impossible to access." I felt new sympathy for all the people who approached me with a story about a man on the beam and left disappointed.

Or perhaps the wall of silence from the union halls was, itself, a clue that helped explain why so few ironworkers came forward in their lifetime to claim a place on the beam. It was certainly a tradition. Arnold Manoff, the WPA writer who interviewed Chris Thorsten in 1939, returned to the union hall on East Eighty-Fourth Street to collect more stories, only to discover that his first visit was the exception to the rule. An ironworker named Sam laid it out for him:

Ya lookin fer Chris? He's workin. Yeh. He's on the Sixth Ave. El job. I remember you. You were aroun here talkin to Chris. I was there too. I ain't got nothin to tell ya. We don like to talk aroun here. We got our own worries. Ask Mike over there. He'll tell ya lotsa stories. Hey Mike! Here's a feller wants ya to tell him stories. Ya see? He ain't interested.

Anything they know they keep to themselves. Does a prisoner talk? Well, it's the same way. The men don't feel like tellin no stories. It's just like a prisoner, y'unnerstan?

Listen. Whaddya wan me ta tellya? I worked in 42 states, Cuba, Alaska, Honolulu. I worked in the steel mills and the iron foundries, inside and out, Bethlehem Steel and udders. See this leg? Broken three times. I got three ribs broken. Ya ain't an iron worker if ya ain't had bones broken, fingers chopped off. Ya see whaddya they gonna tell ya? Dey don't feel like talkin. They keep these things ta themselves. I know the kind of stuff ya want. We ain't got any time for that kinda stuff. The men ain't interested.

Listen I been in this racket 24 years. I just got off a job. They laid us off on the Sixth Ave el. The subway people wuz complainin. There was a meetin about it. We're all laid off except fer one gang on 28th St.

I wuz on that airport job. Yeh for the WPA. I got drunk. Didya see a sign up on the bulletin board about John Hennessey. He was the guy that got drunk with me. The whiskey killed him. Ya think I'm lyin. Ask anybody here. I'm not lyin. He died. They wanted ta know how come I'm not dead. We drank a quart and a half in two hours. Each one a quart an a half. Three quarts all together. Henessey [*sic*] died from it. I'm alive.

Monday, I'm goin on a job. Over on 86th St. 12 story buildin. That'll last a mont' and a half about that much. Then they'll be beggin us to come ta work. There's a 12-million-dollar prison job startin up in Greenhaven. Take two and a half years. Not me: A year is enough for me. Work a year and quit. Nice work all inside on the cells. Bethlehem Steel is in on it.

Naa the men don feel like talkin. I know what ya mean. Naa we don do that kinda stuff. Tell stories, naa. That's bullshit. We don go in fer it. We don go in fer braggin. No lyin. That's kid stuff. That's show off stuff. We ain got any time for it. We like to drink but that's all. We don't have those kind of guys aroun here. Look at em. They never talk. They ain't interested in it. They'll laugh at ya.

What ya wanna get is the people that stan around and watch us work. They do all the talkin. They bullshit all the time. We don do it. It don concern us. We do the work up there, rivetin and we ain't got time fer talkin.

There ain't nothin in it fer us, no money, nuthin, so long, OK.[9]

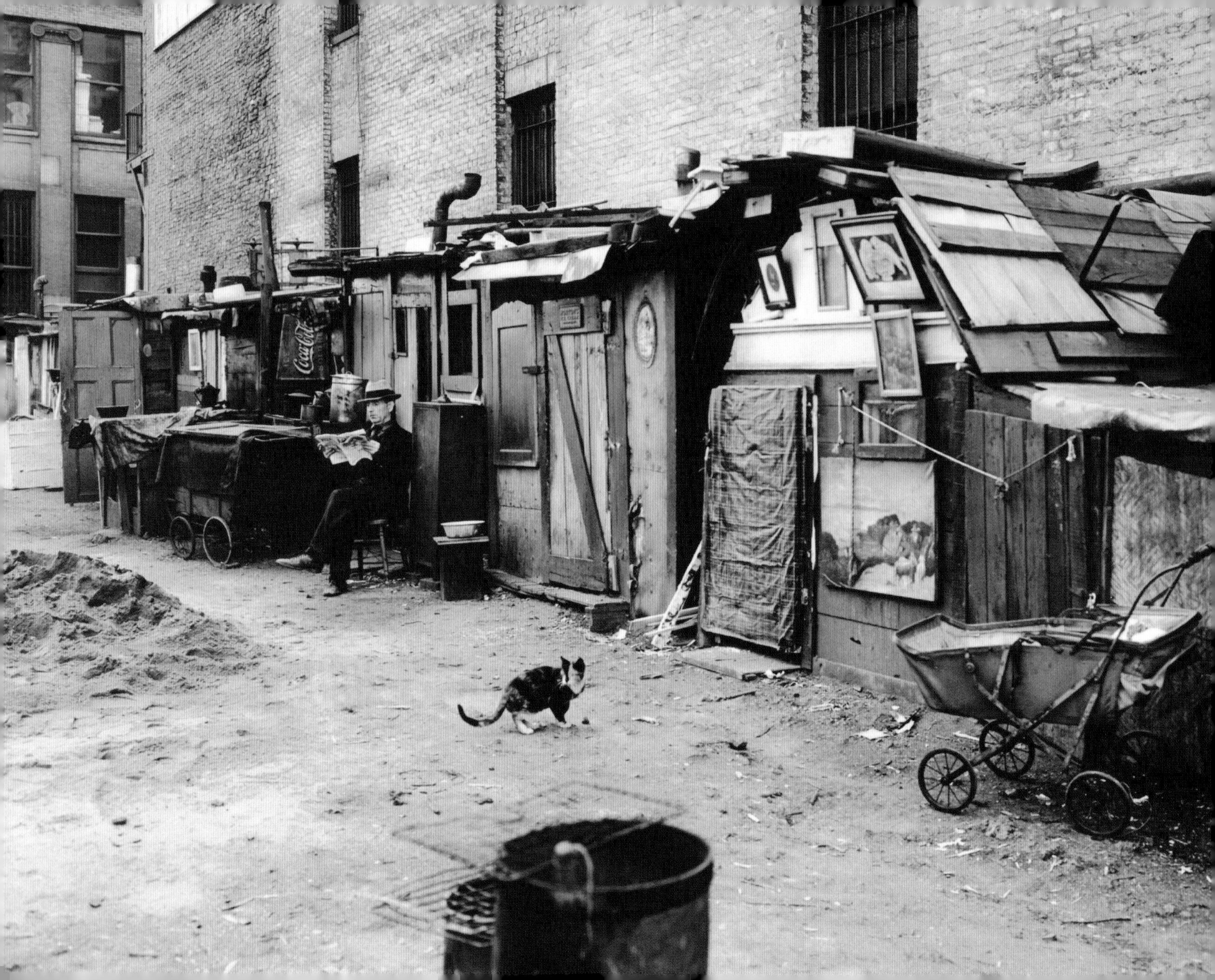

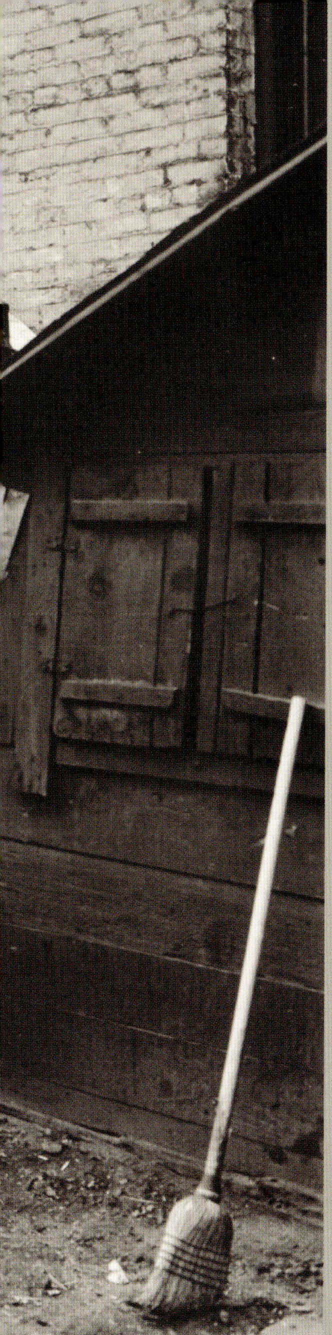

8

IRONWORKERS CAME FROM MANY PLACES

8.1 Shanties on West Houston Street in 1935. (NYPL photo)

L ENIN'S WASN'T THE ONLY FACE chiseled off the lobby of the R.C.A. Building that frigid night in February 1934. Behind the socialites, Diego Rivera had tucked in the teetotaling Junior, with his round spectacles and an improbable martini. And behind Lenin, Rivera had tucked Bernhard Berntsen, an ironworker and amateur artist who liked to pause in the lobby on his way to and from his work on the scaffolds. Capital and labor, balanced as if on a steel beam.

Berntsen was born in a village in Norway in 1900, in a cabin without electricity or running water.[1] When he was ten, his family moved to Oslo, where his father worked as a machinist in the city's booming shipyards. When he was nineteen, he signed onto a ship to earn passage to America, where he lived with an aunt in New York.

He joined the US Army in 1920 and left it a fluent English speaker. He Americanized his first name, from Hilmar to Bernhard.

He moved to Chicago and went to work on a metal press at the Western Electric Company's massive Hawthorne Works, which was cranking out twenty-five thousand new telephones a week. He took art classes at the Norwegian Arts and Crafts Club. At a play sponsored by the club, he met a fellow Norwegian immigrant, Alma Christiansen. They married in December 1922.

In 1924, Berntsen found work as an ironworker—not in a riveting gang, but as a scaffold rigger. The work was dangerous, and he saw more than one compatriot fall to his death. During Chicago's boom years of the 1920s, he worked on the Tribune Tower, the Elks Memorial, and the Edgewater Beach Hotel. He lugged his brushes and an easel onto the scaffolds to paint in his downtime—immortalizing his fellow construction workers.

In 1928, Berntsen followed the skyscraper boom back east. He and Alma settled in Bay Ridge, an immigrant enclave of working-class Scandinavians. He joined Ironworkers Local 361 and remained a member in good standing for fifty years. He found work on the Chrysler and the Empire State buildings. He continued his interest in painting and took classes at the Art Students League with John Steuart Curry, an American painter who, like Berntsen, found his subjects in working-class men.

With the onset of the Great Depression, Berntsen was out of work for a year. Jobs were scarce in the city, but he was eventually hired on through a contractor he knew at the new Coast Guard Academy in New London, Connecticut. After that job wrapped up, steady work was again hard to find. In 1930, Berntsen's fortune changed: He signed on to erect the scaffolding at a major development in midtown Manhattan: Rockefeller Center.

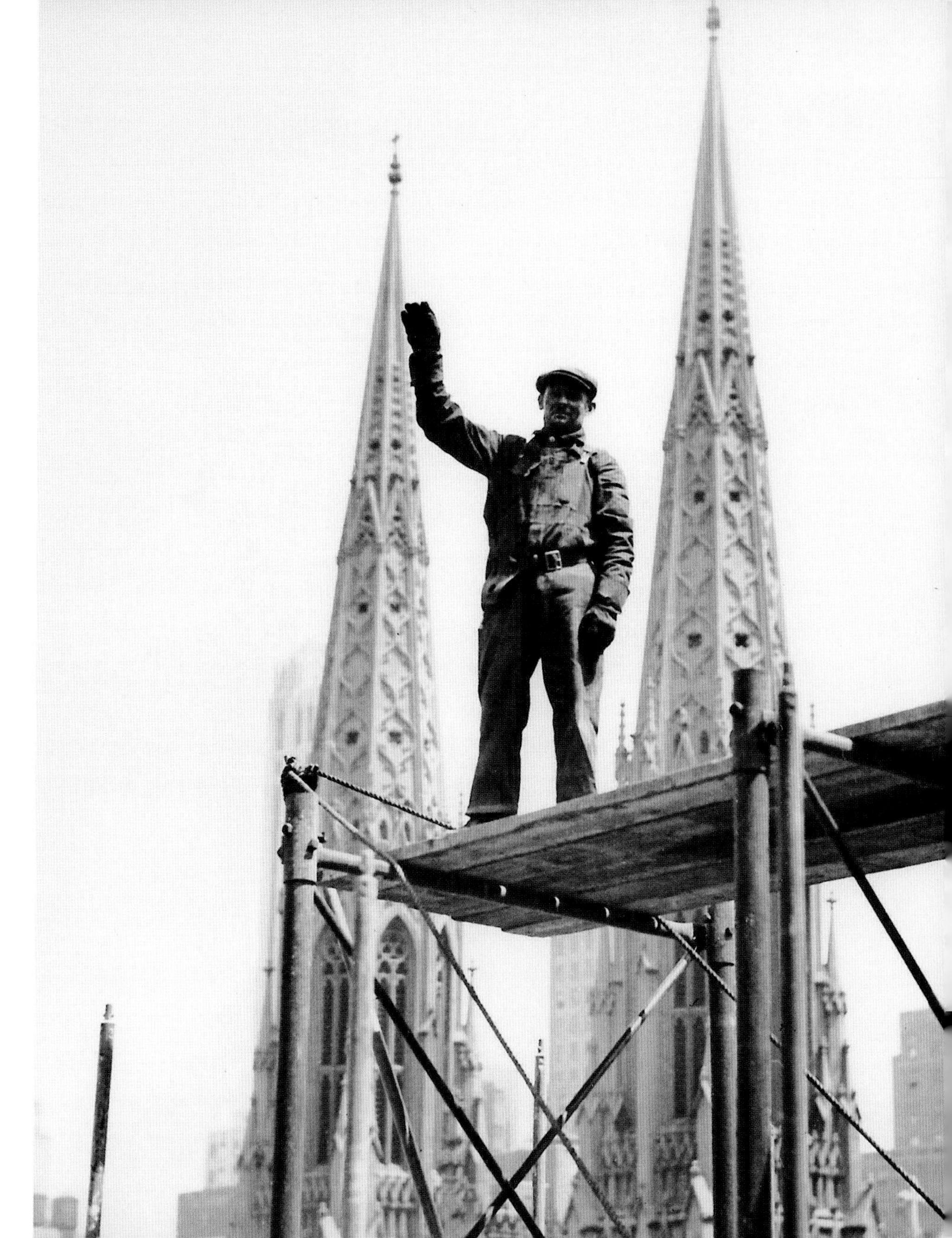

8.2 An ironworker in front of St. Patrick's Cathedral on July 27, 1932. (Rockefeller Group photo)

By the spring of 1933, the structural ironworkers had finished their work on the R.C.A. Building. But the crews finishing the windows, facade, and high interior spaces kept scaffolders like Berntsen busy. As an amateur artist, he was drawn to Rivera's emerging mural in the lobby. In his free time, he joined the small crowd of spectators there. And Rivera, who liked to draft actual workers as models, picked Berntsen out of the crowd.[2]

Many of the ironworkers shared Berntsen's immigrant story. They came from Ireland, Germany, and Eastern Europe, or their fathers had, and the sons followed them into the trade.

George Urbanneck was the son of German-speaking immigrants. His father, Otto Hugo Urbanneck, was born in Thuringia—"the green heart of Germany"—on October 13, 1876. Otto immigrated to the United States in 1902 aboard the German steamship *Pennsylvania* and settled in New York, where he found work as a sheet-iron worker and boilermaker. On October 1, 1910, he married Mathilde Streitz, a fellow German speaker who had recently arrived from Bohemia.

They settled on Bradhurst Avenue, in a Scandinavian ethnic enclave south of the Polo Grounds. In August 1914, as the first shots rang out from World War I, the Urbannecks welcomed their first son, George Otto. The following year, as war consumed Europe and anti-German sentiment seized the United States, Otto declared his intention to renounce his German citizenship and become a naturalized US citizen—the first step, at the time, toward American citizenship.

When the United States entered the war, Otto registered for the draft—ready to fight for his new nation against his old. He listed his occupation as an ironworker and his employer as Post & McCord. Fifteen years later, the Urbannecks had moved to New Bergen, New Jersey, and an eighteen-year-old George Urbanneck followed in his father's footsteps, taking one of his first jobs as an ironworker for Post & McCord, erecting the steel spine of Rockefeller Center.

In the first quarter of the twentieth century, steel skyscrapers transformed the skyline of New York. Construction was thriving, and ironworkers were in demand. By the end of 1929, the Great Depression caused construction work to come to nearly a standstill, leaving many families with extraordinary hardships that would continue for years. Men who had defined themselves as the family breadwinner now stood in soup lines. Homeless families gathered in shanty towns called Hoovervilles.

"There was a large barren area west of Riverside Drive that had been cleared to make way for the development of the west side express highway," recalled Harold McClain, the 1930s ironworker. "Shacks and shanties of all sorts began to accumulate there, and soon it had the name Hoovertown: as usual, the American people were blaming all their troubles on the President. It became a vast jungle for the down-and-out, and many of the old ironworkers gravitated to it."[3]

Not until 1936 did the Works Progress Administration, part of President Roosevelt's New Deal, begin to significantly impact employment through the federally funded construction of public buildings, bridges, and roads.

Ironworkers came from diverse ethnic backgrounds, often even in a single gang. The danger demanded teamwork, and the ironworkers I met took pride in their ability to work together. In his own indelicate way, McClain celebrated the diversity of his comrades: "'The Dago,' an Italian foreman named Tio Caffasse," "Big Oak, an Indian riveter," "Little Irish, a rivet jack," "Joe Paxton, a stubborn, hardworking Scotchman," and "Big Frog, a French Canadian bridgeman."[4] They had to get along to keep their jobs, and ironwork was a made-to-order occupation for assimilating into America.

Families I interviewed expressed their pride in ancestors who sought out one of the most dangerous jobs. Often our conversations began, "Those were hard times."

Many of today's ironworkers are second-, third-, or even fourth-generation ironworkers. Their grandfathers, even great-grandfathers, walked iron. Nowhere is this family tradition more celebrated than in the Kahnawake community that straddles the border of New York and Quebec.

Around 1908, "the Kahnawakes became part of a large melting pot within the trade. Scandinavians, Irish, Newfoundlanders, Germans, and migrators from the South all joined the ironworkers at this time. They had various nicknames, from 'fish' and 'goofynoofies' (Newfoundlanders) to 'Squareheads' (Swedes and Norwegians) to 'tar heels' and 'deacons' (Southerners), but they had one thing in common—the brotherhood of being an ironworker and a union man."[5]

Over the years, "Lunch on a Beam" has become an emblem for ironworkers. "There isn't an ironworker in New York City who doesn't see the picture as a badge of his bold tribe."[6] The picture is world renowned. Nobody knows who took it. And for most of its ninety years, no one has known who's in it.

As I talked to ironworkers or their descendants, I saw how powerfully identities were shaped by a relationship to one of the men on the beam. Because questions about evidence—my work as a researcher—put some claimants on shaky ground, many turned defensive or dismissive of the lack of tangible proof.

To solve the enigma of the men's identities, I felt compelled to follow clues with even a hint of veracity.

Some answers were to be found in the Kahnawake Mohawk Reserve. Since the end of the nineteenth century, Kahnawake Mohawks have prospered as ironworkers and maintained a cohesive community in upstate New York. Family networks offered multiple testimonies and heirloom photographs to identify specific ironworkers.

The Kahnawake Mohawks are part of the six nations of the Haudenosaunee (formerly known as Iroquois) Confederacy and have the longest history of any ethnic group of ironworkers in America. By 1932, members of the Mohawk Nation, including the Caughnawaga, Akwesasne, and Kahnawake, already had a tradition of walking steel. They were called "Skywalkers."[7]

Richard Hill defined Skywalkers in his eponymous history of Mohawk ironworkers. "Skywalkers is an idea that was born over one hundred years ago when the first Mohawk walked the iron," Hill wrote. "It has taken us years to appreciate the importance of ironwork as a modern tradition among our own people. For generations, ironwork has been a fact of life for many of our families. It is time to honor those who have worked the iron. Ironwork will continue to be a family tradition for the Woodland Indians as long as there is another skyscraper to build. Indians will be on top."[8]

The Haudenosaunee Confederacy Reserve straddles northern New York State and southeastern Canada and is on the banks of the Saint Lawrence River. In 1896, the Dominion Bridge Company was constructing a railroad bridge across the Saint Lawrence River. Part of the bridge had to be located on the land of the Mohawk Reserve. The Mohawks demanded jobs in return for agreeing to build there, and the company complied. History has it that they quickly learned bridge construction.

Eight years later, in 1904, Mohawks were hired on as seasoned ironworkers to another bridge over the Saint Lawrence River: the Quebec Bridge. The project was one of the first to cement the reputation of Quebec Mohawks as world-renowned high-steel workers. It was to be the longest cantilever bridge in the world, with more than 1,800 feet between its piers. During construction on August 29, 1907, without warning, the bridge shuddered and collapsed into the river, plunging seventy-six men to their deaths. Thirty-three were from Kahnawake. More than two-thirds of them were married, leaving behind twenty-four widows and dozens of children. Five Kahnawake family names went down with the bridge: Leaf, Lee, Blue,

Bruce, and Mitchell. The bridge's weight far exceeded its carrying capacity. The engineers had made serious errors.

Nevertheless, the surviving Mohawk ironworkers resolved to continue in the trade and "boomed out," traveling in small groups across Canada and the United States to find work. A history of New York's ironworker unions records that "Mohawk ironworker John Diabo came to the city to work on the Hell Gate Bridge in 1915. Others of his tribe followed, eventually forming a settlement during the 1920s of about 400 men, women, and children in the North Gowanus neighborhood of Brooklyn."[9] Since then, they have worked construction on almost every building and bridge in skyscraper city.

Mohawk ironworkers commuted from the Reserve to New York City. On Sunday nights, the men packed into cars and, for eleven or twelve hours, rocketed down two-lane Route 9, making the weekly four-hundred-mile trip from Kahnawake to Brooklyn, where they shared lodgings before returning on Friday to the reservation. In 1927, to ease their border crossing, a federal court judge ruled that Mohawks could pass freely between Canada and the US since their territory included parts of both nations.

In the 1980s, by some estimates, 60 percent of employed men in Kahnawake were ironworkers. "Ironwork has brought respect to Indians," notes anthropologist Sandra Busatta, "not only because Indian ironworkers are competing with the white man, but also because they are at the top of their profession."[10]

Scott Berwick, the film archivist of the Kahnawake Cultural Center, assisted me in the search for the men's identities with introductions to families of Mohawk ironworkers. Although they do not have documentary evidence (like paystubs or work records) of their relatives being on the beam, they have added to the search by describing life in an ironworker's family on the Reserve, the long drives to Brooklyn where the men shared rooms, and the long periods the men were away booming out to jobs. The families who followed them created new roots while retaining ties to their ancestral homes on the Reserve. Families schooled their children in Brooklyn, but they returned to Kahnawake each summer, perpetuating their cultural heritage. The Reserve anchored their lives.

In my research, I found a unique community whose strong, multigenerational ties to ironworkers could substantiate stories and events.

Berwick introduced me to Reaghan Tarbell, who was then the executive director of the Kanien'keha:ka Onkwawén:na Raotitióhkwa Language and Cultural Center in Kahnawake. "There are not as many ironworkers today," Tarbell said. "But it's a way of life. Some carry on the tradition."[11]

"Ironworking has become the fabric of our identity,"[12] she told me.

Hers was one of the many Mohawk families that passed ironworking from generation to generation—whose storied surnames include Diabo, Rice, Phillips, McComber, Beauvais, Montour, Goodleaf, Jocks, Cook, and Collin. Several of these families have long claimed they have relatives who are among the men in "Lunch on a Beam."

When I asked about acrophobia, Tarbell said, "It's not so much about being fearless—for some ironworkers, it's damn scary—but they have pride in the fact that they are part of a tradition that's been passed down over generations." Plus, she added, "Ironworking has always paid better than anything else available to them on the reserve."[13]

In our final interview, I asked Reaghan if "Lunch on a Beam" still had significance with the Mohawks. She answered, "Yes, it is an image frequently used in social media, and you can find it hanging in many homes. It is about pride."[14]

Amanda Diabo told me that ironworking has been passed down in her family since 1907, when her great-grandfather, Peter Stacey, missed work the day the Quebec Bridge fell. Her grandfather, father, and now her husband have carried on the tradition.

Diabo places her great-grandfather Peter Stacey as the third man in "Lunch on a Beam." Peter Stacey would have been forty-nine years old when the photo was taken in 1932 and most likely worked as a bolter-up or riveter. "He wasn't very tall," said Diabo, who never met Stacey but heard he was "stout," with big hands."[15] However, her identification conflicts with the caption of archive photograph #120, which names the third man on the beam as Joseph Eckner.

Lynn Beauvais told me her family goes back four generations of Mohawk ironworkers. Her grandfather, father, partner, and brothers have all been ironworkers. "Grandfather Joe Jocks worked on the R.C.A. Building and was a member of Local 40," she told me. "He was part of a raising gang—a riveter. It was hard work. He operated the Hell-dog."[16]

From my point of view as a researcher, it was exciting to me that Beauvais knew her grandfather, albeit as a child. Her memories of him are vivid, perhaps because she and her sister were her grandfather's "favorites" and routinely spent time with him. Lynn was among the few people I interviewed who claimed firsthand knowledge of a man on the beam. She identified him as the fourth from the left, *and* he had told her stories about his time as an ironworker.

In *High Steel*, Jim Rasenberger repeats the claim that Joe Jocks was fourth on the beam. "It's what everyone believes," Bill Sears, the Kahnawake ironworker-slash-historian, told me. Sears said he had no proof—only the scuttlebutt around the reservation.

Beauvais said her grandfather worked on many buildings in New York. She recounted a dramatic, if unsubstantiated, story he told her: "During the Great Depression, men were desperate for jobs, and men would wait in the street for someone to fall off so they could take their job."[17] (Though not at Rockefeller Center, where union contracts prevented builders from hiring off the street. Workers had to come from the union hall.)

Beauvais talked to me about the role women traditionally took in the family. "They were strong and responsible for everything: the children, where they lived, paying the bills, even carpentry," she said. "My grandmother bought a small two-room house and added rooms herself. There were no shared responsibilities at home. The men ventured out as they traditionally did and brought home the food or, in this case, the money. Sometimes they would be gone for months to far-off places like Alaska."

Lynn continued: "In the old days there were no safety lines, and they didn't wear helmets. It was hard work, but they never talked about the danger. Our men have always really enjoyed their work. They have pride. You can tell an ironworker by the way he walks. They have a noticeable walking gait—a swagger. You can almost imagine them in moccasins hunting in the woods."[18]

I asked Lynn if her great-grandfather had been the first ironworker in her family. "No," she answered. "He worked in the law field. Not all the men in the family walk iron. My cousin is a professor."[19]

I confirmed Lynn's reminiscences about her grandfather with her cousin Chris Jocks, who is the chair of the Indigenous Studies Department at Northern Arizona University in Flagstaff. His side of the family had taken a different route, mostly away from the Reserve and ironwork. His father—Joe Jocks's son—was a cartographer for the US Air Force. Chris grew up on military bases and spent summers with his extended family in Kahnawake. He was in awe of his Mohawk grandfather, whom he and his brothers knew as "Big Daddy." He said, "Boda [as his cousins called him] was funny, intelligent, big and strong, and protective of us children."

One summer, Chris recalled, he and his cousins attended a ballgame. When two white men began making snide comments about the "Indian children," Big Daddy silenced them with a look.

And the photograph? "It was taken for granted," Chris said, "that he was the fourth man from the left on the beam."[20]

Bill Sears was a proud ironworker, the historian of New York's Ironworkers Local Union 440, and a fourth-generation Kahnawake ironworker who loved to relate stories about his years working steel construction. "These men were significant in helping to build the skyline of New York City," he said. "They were also famous for drinking, fornicating, and fighting."[21]

Looking at the famous photo, Sears reminisced: "The lunch boxes were ordered from the nearby Blarney Stone Bar, a favorite watering hole, and brought up on a load of steel." He points to the lettering "VO" and "VOS" stenciled on the boxes. "This indicated the boxes originally came from Bronson, a Canadian whiskey distiller, and were reused." Prohibition was the law when the picture was published on October 2, 1932. Bill sarcastically added: "Perhaps the eleventh man on the beam felt the law wasn't relevant eight hundred and forty feet above the ground."[22] Or, were the Bronson boxes a not-too-subtle message about the successful smuggling of Moonshine across the US and Canadian border during Prohibition?

Today, ironwork remains a prestigious job in the Reserve. The pay and benefits are good. The Mohawks are proud of this tradition and flaunt it—as Sears said: "They are effing good at it!"

Sears was confident that two of the men on the beam were Mohawk ironworkers: the fourth man, Joe Jocks, and the sixth, John Cook. But Tarbell identifies the sixth man as Peter Rice. With solid endorsements but no paper trail, the aura of mystery remains.

A 2002 museum exhibition about Mohawk ironworkers identified three of these men on the beam: Stacey as the third man from the left, Jocks as the fourth, and Rice as the sixth.[23] The traveling exhibition, created by the National Museum of the American Indian in New York, was organized in the wake of the destruction of the World Trade Center, only a few blocks from the museum. One of the exhibit's creators, Devorah Romanek, said the identifications came from the ironworkers' relatives, including Beauvais. Like me, she found the evidence for Joe Jocks—including multiple photographs from Rockefeller Center and other jobs—to be the strongest.[24]

Asked why it matters who is on the beam, Romanek grew thoughtful. "We have this ongoing conversation in the larger culture about America as a nation of immigrants," she said. "But we are a nation of immigrants and indigenous people and descendants of slaves. As long as that image continues to be an important part of the American psyche, the American myth, it's important to get it right."

As bad as the Great Depression was in the United States, it was worse in many parts of Europe. Twenty percent of the population was unemployed, and the situation was spreading. Families migrated to America in record numbers, especially to New York. The hope was that men would find work. The reality was grim.

Gusti Popovic was a lumberjack and carpenter born in eastern Slovakia. Many accounts credit him as the eleventh man on the beam, notable for the liquor bottle in his hand. He was identified by his grandson, Ivan Popovic, who said he made the connection in 1989, on his first visit to the West after the fall of the Iron Curtain. In interviews with Slovak media, the artist and filmmaker said he saw "Lunch on a Beam" in a Vienna department store, then realized his family had the same photo in an old album. "When we unglued it from the black hard paper on which it was stuck, I could read: 'My dearest Mariska, Here I write to you from New York, where we are building America. Don't you worry about me. As you can see, everybody is eating but me, who is holding the little flask.[25] Yours, Gusti.'"[26]

After several years working as an ironworker in America and Canada, his grandson said, Popovic returned to his native village, Vyšný Slavkov, in the Levoča District of Slovakia. He bought fields and forest land with the money he had earned walking iron. During World War II, he was killed by shrapnel, and in 1948, his land was nationalized by the Communist government. In his village today, Gusti Popovic is remembered with a stone memorial. It is decorated with a copy of "Lunch on a Beam."[27]

It was an enticing story, but there are reasons to doubt it. No contemporary accounts confirm it, or even suggest that Gusti Popovic worked as an ironworker or at Rockefeller Center. His grandson has declined to show the note to curious reporters, and has produced no photos of Popovic for comparison. (He did not respond to me.) And Gusti's wife, Maria Popovic, died in 1930—two years before the photo was taken and purportedly mailed to her.[28]

In 2012, another claimant came forward. June Bjorndahl White self-published *The Last Man on the Beam*, which put the famous bottle in the hand of her father, John Paul Nathaniel Bjorndahl. White said Bjorndahl, who died in 1955, was an ironworker on the R.C.A. Building, as well as the Empire State and Chrysler buildings. White said she recognized her father in "Lunch on a Beam," and that her late elder brother "said on many occasions he regretted not having a copy of the famous picture of Dad and the other guys on the girder." Once again, however, no contemporary records or accounts confirm this story. And family photographs bear, at best, a passing resemblance to the eleventh man on the beam.

Rudy Silla was born in Austria. Orphaned, he signed on at thirteen to a sailing vessel as a mess attendant. By 1914, he graduated to larger ships in the Cunard Line and was crisscrossing the oceans. After a series of torpedo attacks in World War I, he settled in New York seeking a "safer" trade, as he later told an interviewer: structural ironwork.[29]

Today, his family claims Rudy is the first ironworker on the left in the famous photo. "My late husband Harry was the oldest son of Rudy," Christina Silla told me. "Harry always said his father talked about this moment and how he was one of the guys on the beam, which became the 'Lunch atop a Skyscraper' photo."[30]

The family used facial recognition software to compare a photo of Rudy Silla with the first man on the beam, which found a "high probability" of a match. The family provided several photos showing Rudy at different ages and in various situations, including his wedding picture. Several members of Rudy's family say he told them he was on the beam.

The photos bear a strong likeness, but once again, the evidence is not conclusive. Other photos in the Rockefeller Center Archive that were taken that day[31] identify the first man on the beam as John O'Rielly (figure 7.3). Silla's union magazine, *Topping Out*, profiled him upon his retirement in 1962. Although his family says Silla talked often about the photo, the article notes highlights of his career without mentioning Rockefeller Center or "Lunch on a Beam." Of course, these details don't rule him out, either.

Other families have written to the Rockefeller Center Archive to share the stories of their ironworkers. Darlene Pearson Castillo reached out about an ancestor, fatally injured soon after the famous photo: "Our family is claiming the second man from the left as Viktor Pierson from Sweden," she wrote. "He came over in 1922. He changed his name to Victor Pearson. Unfortunately, a few months after the picture was taken, he lost his arm on the job and died because of it."[32]

Scott Jandovitz approached me in 2023 with his story about his great, great grand-uncle, Rudy Knott. "Grandma June had an old print of 'Lunch atop a Skyscraper' in the porch of her house in Queens," Jandovitz told me. "A few years before she passed, I asked her about it on one of the days I was visiting for dinner and she told me that her Uncle Rudy was one of the men on the beam. When asked which one he was, she pointed to the man fourth from the right."[33] Scott included a picture of Uncle Rudy at a family event. There was nothing that could substantiate their story, and it conflicts with other evidence identifying William Birgir as the seventh man on the beam.

Michael Brehenny was born in Ireland in 1905. "He is the man fourth from the left in the 'Lunch atop a Skyscraper' photograph," his grandson Gene Breheny[34] told me. "He was a bricklayer and did work on the R.C.A. Building." Gene also pointed out that the fourth man has "cement on the side of his shoes and the white socks he always wore."[35] He sent photos of his grandfather for comparison.

"He was from Galway. Ireland closed his village and forced him and his father to leave for Roscommon when he was around 17," his grandson said. "When he was 13, until he left Ireland, he would farm and follow his father to England to work the coal mines. He came to America with his aunt in 1927, not coming through Ellis Island, but through Manhattan."[36] His aunt's husband was a foreman at the Rockefeller Center construction site and got him a job as a bricklayer. He eventually met another Irish immigrant at a dance in Yorkville where many Irish maids went on Saturday evenings. They married and moved to the Bronx, and had six children. He left construction for a railroad job in 1935, retiring as a motorman in 1970.

But his grandson's story raised questions. Why was a bricklayer working on the sixty-ninth floor that day? The masons who clad the building in brick and Indiana limestone followed the ironworkers up the building, working several floors below. If he was there, why would a bricklayer be asked to join the ironworkers on the beam? There were plenty of ironworkers available and photographed that day. And the claim conflicts with another: Members of the Mohawk community are unanimous in the belief that the fourth man is Joe Jocks.

The brothers Magnus and John Pedersen immigrated from Norway, where they had worked as shipbuilders. Magnus Pedersen lived in Queens, his daughter, Ruth Pedersen Smith, told me. She claimed they were the third and fourth men from the left. He and his brother John would go daily to "the corner," where ironworkers assembled to get work assignments. "It is called a 'shape up,' where union members go for jobs," she said.[37]

Once again, these identifications conflict with others. Archival notes on photos (figures 7.1 and 7.4) identify the third man as Joseph Eckner, and family sources identify the fourth man as Joe Jocks.

Nevertheless, Magnus's grandson provided an interesting bit of family lore. "The photographers bought the men those lunchboxes to get their cooperation," said David Pedersen, who heard the story from his father. "Who would turn down a free meal in the midst of the Depression?"[38] The six identical lunchboxes in "Lunch on a Beam" could support that idea, but if anyone bought the ironworkers lunch that day, my money is on Crowell.

Harold and Jerome McClain were another pair of ironworking brothers. Jerome's grandson, Brian McClain, reached out to me in 2021. He shared his family photo album, showing Jerome working on several steel skyscrapers and bridges.[39] One photo places Jerome McClain on the grillage at Rockefeller Center. Another shows him in a group of ironworkers building a bridge.

The McClain brothers grew up on a farm in Indiana. Jerome was born in 1900 and died in 1941, three days before Pearl Harbor, in a bridge collapse in Hartford, Connecticut. A ninety-eight-ton girder slipped and struck the nearly completed span, which plunged into the icy Connecticut River, killing fourteen men. According to his obituary, Jerome McClain was a foreman on the site. He left a wife and two children.

Brian never knew his grandfather. What he knows he learned from family, their photo album, and a remarkable 240-page memoir by his Uncle Harold. In a nod to the oxidized color of structural steelwork, Harold titled his unpublished manuscript *Red Iron*.

Harold's journal fulfilled his lifelong urge to write about his experiences during the three decades he and Jerome crisscrossed America, raising steel bridges and buildings. Set mainly in the 1930s, the journal chronicles injuries, death, and ruination, remembered stoically as part of the job. Despite the hardships, his journal reveals more pride than pity.

On the Depression: "Some of my friends, however, were already destitute," he wrote. "The Salvation Army was helping some, but they couldn't carry much of the load. The churches were doing what they could but naturally took care of their own first, and very few ironworkers could establish convincing ties. By the nature of their work, they are mostly nomadic. 1931 was a rough year. The Great Depression was settling like a shroud over the country."[40]

The McClain family photo album also contains the photograph "Hats Off." The family believes Jerome McClain is the seventh man from the left. Indeed, in family photos, he looks remarkably like the seventh man. But photos in the Rockefeller Center Archive appear to identify the seventh man as Howard Kilgore (figure 7.3) or James Kovan (figure 7.4).

I returned to Saunders, the photography professor, and asked him to compare McClain with the seventh man. "These men definitely look like they could be the same guy," said Saunders, who enlarged their faces. "If you look closely at the ears, they look identical, and he has very distinctive ears."[41]

I had to agree.

The more detailed photos of Jerome McClain I saw, the stronger his resemblance grew to the seventh man. There were telltale features: the ears were spot-on, the nose and

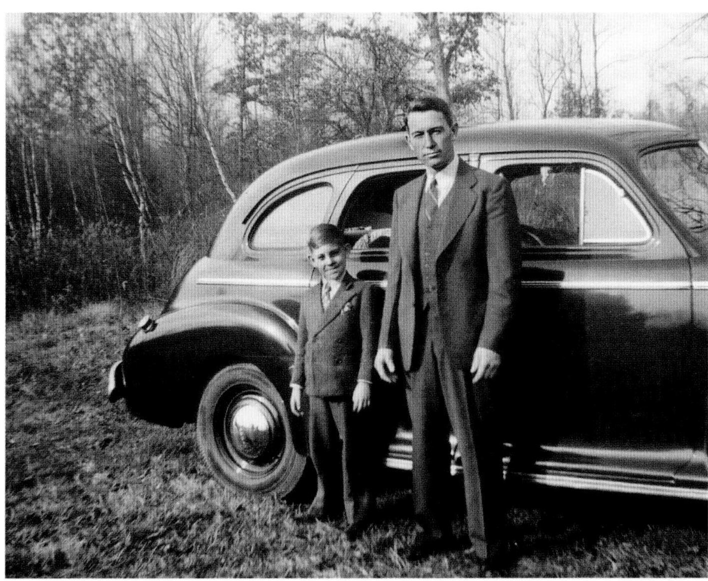

8.3 Jerome McClain and his son around 1940. (Family photo courtesy of Brian McClain)

hairline were identical, and the lips were a match. And Brian McClain noted one more distinctive feature: Both his grandfather and the seventh man have a slight concavity in their lower rib cage. The condition, known as "sunken chest," "funnel chest," or "pectus excavatum," is benign unless the concavity is pronounced, and it affects one in about four hundred children.

McClain is a strong contender for the seventh place. After reviewing all the evidence, perhaps Kilgore had been misnamed in the caption of the archive photo. We are left to wonder if he is Howard Kilgore, James Kovan, or Jerome McClain. And, as Saunders wrote, "Does that cast doubt on the names in other captions?"

Ironworkers from Newfoundland were dubbed "Newfies" or "fish." Bob Walsh of Iron Workers Local 40 says they are still called fish. A gang of ironworkers from Nova Scotia was also called "a guppy gang."

I turned to the phone book to find a contact in Newfoundland who could connect me with ironworker families. I dialed the general store in Avondale, Newfoundland, and from there, I found Harold Flynn.

Flynn's uncles were ironworkers in New York City from the 1930s to the 1960s. They worked on the Verrazzano-Narrows Bridge in 1964. He told me, "A great number of men left Newfoundland looking for work in New York." He said the work suited them because many had worked the rigging on fishing schooners "and were not afraid of heights."

"Many," he said, "did not come back."[42]

Harold put me in touch with Carol Ann Lake, also of Avondale.[43] She comes from a family of ironworkers and boilermakers. Carol said many men left the area around Conception Bay during the 1930s to work construction in New York. "It was the only place they could make a living," she said. She also noted that most of the men did not return to Newfoundland.

"These men were called fish because they had originally climbed the rigging of fishing schooners. The schooners had sailed the northeast coast, delivering their hauls of cod, halibut, and haddock to cities like Boston, New York, and Philadelphia. They were accustomed to risky work and adept at climbing the masts and adjusting the rigging in all kinds of weather, so climbing girders on land seemed natural to the men, and the pay and conditions were better on land than at sea."[44]

Flynn and Lake were proud of Newfoundland's history of ironworkers. They recited the names of local ironworking families: O'Rielly, Costello, Doyle, Lewis, and Wade. Indeed, Rockefeller Center's archives identify John O'Rielly (Photo #123) as the first man on the left in "Lunch on a Beam."[45]

Both trades were nomadic and took the men away from their families for months. Families would eventually leave Newfoundland to follow their ironworkers. Like the Mohawk ironworkers, many Nova Scotian ironworkers settled in Brooklyn. "Most married Americans and stayed," Lawrence Hawco, president of Local 764 in Nova Scotia, told me.[46]

I understood from both Harold Flynn and Carol Ann Lake that the story of Newfoundland ironworkers is important to the region's economic and social history. Over years of booming out, the men became known for their skill in high-steel ironwork. Many settled in places like Boston and New York, creating Newfoundland enclaves like the Mohawks did in Brooklyn. However, Carol told me, "There is no one left to verify or even relate family lore about the ironworkers."[47]

Over the years, internet sleuths have suggested possible Newfoundlanders in "Lunch on a Beam." Suggestions include Austin Lawton of King's Cove as the third man from the left and Claude Stagg of Catalina as the fifth. Without documentation, they add to the growing list of men-who-might-have-been-on-the-beam.

In 2023, a Michigan man, Quinn Newton, contacted me to say he knew of three Nova Scotia brothers on the beam: The fifth, sixth, and seventh men were Angus, Allan, and Thomas Campbell, he said. Allan Campbell was Newton's great grandfather, and he had heard the story from his grandmother—Campbell's daughter.[48]

I spoke with Newton's grandmother, Jean "Chickie" Salemi, then ninety. She said her father, Allan Campbell, had pointed himself out to her in the photo. She said her parents were married in New Brunswick in 1920 but left the Maritimes because it was so remote and work was scarce. Allan and Regina Campbell settled in New Jersey and had twenty-two children. Salemi added that her father had also worked on the Empire State Building and both the Lincoln and Holland tunnels.

Three union books kept by Quinn's uncle, from 1924, 1937, and 1940, show that Campbell belonged to carpenters unions. Other documents provided by Quinn variously listed Campbell's occupation as blacksmith, carpenter, and—critically, in the 1930 US census—an ironworker living in Jersey City, New Jersey. And family photos do bear a passing resemblance to the sixth man. ("Man, that nose doesn't lie," Newton said. "That's him!") But this claim conflicts with others that identify the sixth man as Peter Rice, and suffers by its overreach: Campbell's "brothers" have been positively identified as other men.

Another Canadian proposed to be on the beam is William Culp, born in 1896 on his parents' Ontario farm. At sixteen, Culp found work as a carpenter; at eighteen, he found a wife. They immigrated to New York, settled in Queens, and had eight children—four girls, four boys. By 1932, he was an ironworker.[49] His great-great grandson, Glenn LaPaitra, told me that his family believes Culp is the third man from the left. Photos of a grandfatherly Culp, taken many years after "Lunch on a Beam," bear a slight resemblance. But other photos taken that day identify the stout third man as Joseph Eckner.

In 2022, a fact checker contacted me from a Spanish quiz show. The show was building a question around "Lunch on a Beam," she said. Is it true, she asked, that the second man came from Spain? This was a new question, but a familiar situation.[50]

Several countries claim their own man on the beam: Canada, Ireland, even Slovakia.

Spanish media was reporting that the second man on the beam was a Basque emigrant, Ignacio Ibargüen, who moved to the United States by way of Argentina and worked his way into the construction of Rockefeller Center.

These reports stemmed from a series of articles on the news site "Editorial Harresi." The author, tipped by a retiring colleague, learned the story from Ibargüen's Spanish relatives. They told him that Ibargüen's American son had visited them in the 1980s, and that they gave him, coincidentally, a framed photo of "Lunch on a Beam." The son unwrapped it and told them, in tears, that the second man was his father, Ignacio.[51]

In a series of eight articles, the author laid out his case. Immigration and residence documents established that in 1932 Ibargüen was thirty-two years old and living in New York with his wife, a toddler, and a baby. His family had been bricklayers in the Basque town of Balmaseda, so perhaps he had taken up the construction trade. And, critically, a family photo of Ignacio with his pregnant wife and elder child—taken, presumably, in early 1932—strongly resembled the second man on the beam.[52] All on top of the son's tearful avowal.

But there is no evidence that Ibargüen worked at Rockefeller Center or was even an ironworker. And there is strong evidence that he wasn't. He told the 1930 US census that he worked as a "fireman," or coal stoker, at a school. A decade later, he still worked at a school, but now as an elevator operator. And once again, other photos taken on top of the R.C.A. Building identify the second man as someone else: George Covan.

I had to give the quiz show the *malas noticias*: Ignacio Ibargüen was likely not on the beam.

In 2015, *Time* magazine counted "Lunch on a Beam" among the one hundred "most influential images of all time."[53] *Time* featured the photo on the book's cover and, in 2016, produced a short video.[54] As of 2025, the video had been viewed more than eleven million times on YouTube, and more than fifteen thousand viewers commented, many on the heroism of the anonymous ironworkers.

"No one unequivocally knows the identities of all the men on the beam or which of the photographers took the iconic picture," Paul Moakley, an editor at *Time*, told me. "However, because the lesser-known second image 'Hats Off' does give a frontal view of most of the faces, it should help clear up the mystery of their identities."[55] Like most researchers, Moakley was unaware of the third photo.

In 2004, the journalist Jim Rasenberger told the story of New York's ironworkers in *High Steel* (HarperCollins). Rasenberger's storyline alternates between the lives of modern ironworkers and the dangerous, often-violent history of the trade. Based on his research here at the Rockefeller Center Archives and elsewhere, Rasenberger suggested ten possible names for the men on the beam:

> As for the identity of the ironworkers, many Mohawks are convinced that the fourth from the left is Joe Jocks of Kahnawake, while Newfoundlanders insist that the shirtless man in the middle is Ray Costello of Conception Harbour. Captions on other photographs taken that same day identify the three men on the far left as John O'Rielly [*sic*], George Covan, and Joseph Eckner. The shirtless man whom Newfoundlanders believe to be Ray Costello is identified elsewhere as Howard Kilgore (though people who knew Costello swear it's he) and the next three are identified as William Birger [*sic*], Joe Curtis, and John Portla. The name of the man on the far right, drinking from a flask during Prohibition, is not recorded.[56]

Fifteen years after he wrote *High Steel,* I asked Rasenberger why he thought so many people claim to have relatives in the picture. "It has a kind of iconic power," he said.[57]

In 2012, Irish brothers Éamonn and Seán Ó Cualáin sought to identify two ironworkers—Irish, of course—in their documentary film, *Men at Lunch.*

The filmmakers discovered "Lunch on a Beam" in 2009, hanging in a pub in County Galway. The pub regulars celebrated two men on the beam as famous locals who had achieved something remarkable in America. This claim and the pub banter surrounding the legend intrigued the Ó Cualáin brothers, who set out to investigate whether the two men in the famous photo were Galwaymen Sonny Glynn and Patty O'Shaughnessy. Their search took them from Ireland to New York and Boston. They premiered the documentary film *Men at Lunch* in Toronto three years later.

During their research, the filmmakers interviewed the sons of Sonny Glynn and Patty O'Shaughnessy, who maintain their fathers were in the photo: Glynn at the far right and Patty O'Shaughnessy at the far left. Patty O'Shaughnessy's son was adamant. "You don't grow up to the age I am now," he told the filmmakers, "without knowing who you are and who your father is."

Although the project began as a tribute to Irish immigrants, the Ó Cualáin brothers went on to examine other possibilities. They analyzed news clips and photos archived at Rockefeller Center and Corbis. They compared "Hats Off" with other photos taken that day and concluded that the first man from the left is Joe Curtis, and the third man is Joseph Eckner.

Éamonn told me that while visiting New York to research their film, the brothers bumped into a family at P. J. Clarke's, a well-known Irish bar, who were confident that they had a man on the beam.

The visitors from Texas were insistent and provided the brothers with a photo of their ironworker. Facial recognition software declared a match "unlikely." The brothers had stumbled into the hardest part of my job: researching the truth sometimes means telling people no. It invariably disappoints, and many reject the findings. At least a verdict of "Unlikely" leaves some room. In their hearts, it is not "No," but "Maybe."

Éamonn emphasized the importance of "Lunch on a Beam" in Ireland as an emblem of America. "For them to place themselves, or their family, on this beam, it goes to the DNA of America," Éamonn said. "To have a family member seated on that beam proves they had a part in building this city, and the building of America. It's the superpower of the world, it came from humble beginnings, and a lot of good people stay humble." Éamonn remarked on the sense of pride and the work ethic that people conveyed to him as they told family stories about their man on the beam. "We came from a hardworking family. We came from the bottom and worked our way up and now we're here."

In Ireland, Éamonn said, young adults will hang a print of "Lunch on a Beam" when they move into their first apartment, or college dorm. "That's who I see in the photograph," Éamonn said. "It inspires them." In his estimation, the only American photo hanging in more homes is the portrait of John F. Kennedy.[58]

The brothers came away skeptical from their search for the men's identities. "Deep down, I hope that the identities of all eleven men are not found," Seán told me. "The mystery adds to the magic of the photo."[59]

Over the years, many publications have returned to the mystery of the men's identities. Each article adds new claims, most of them family lore almost impossible to verify.

In 2003, the *New York Post* invited readers to submit their family stories about the men on the beam.[60] "Callers to the *Post*, citing photographs, union records, and family stories, provided 41 names for the 11 men," the *Post* reported. The paper featured a few pictures provided by people who are certain that their relatives are in the photograph. Many of the forty-one names in the *New York Post*

article appear nowhere else in my research. Still, some could be true. Maybe.

Smithsonian magazine interviewed Seán Ó Cualáin the year his documentary came out. "We can all place ourselves on that beam," he said. "I think that is why the photograph works." Merle Crowell would agree.

And I share the frustration of the people who know their uncle, their grandfather, is one of those men. There is no single piece of hard evidence—no list of names, no contemporary, published claim—just a few old photos and family lore. It was almost a hundred years ago, and that generation has died and taken many stories with it. As an archivist, I understand how easily old pictures can get lost or destroyed, and there weren't many on-the-job photos taken by family members in the 1930s. Cameras were used to record family events: birthdays, weddings, or a new baby—not a working man in dirty clothes on the grillage. The snapshot camera was yet to arrive: It wasn't until 1936 that the inexpensive Argus Model A-1936 transformed amateur photography. It was the first low-cost, easy-to-use 35-millimeter film camera in the world. Thirty thousand were sold the first week at $12.50.

Saunders, the photography professor, compared the ironworkers' faces, body types, clothing—any detail that would help confirm identity. We worked on the pictures for over two years—our opinions and questions flew between New York and Bottineau, North Dakota. As we compared the men, we frequently encountered frustrating conversations about details: "This one is tough. The shirt is similar, but the sleeves are not rolled up in one. I'm also not sure if the sleeves would roll up that far."[61] Nearing the end of my research, Saunders expressed his admiration for the men and the fortunate preservation of the iconic photo. "It is very sad that they are unknown. Not merely for the amazing and dangerous work they did, but also for the power and scope this image has had on our nation and even the world."[62]

The ironworkers came from many places, but in the 1930s, one place they did not come from was the African American community.

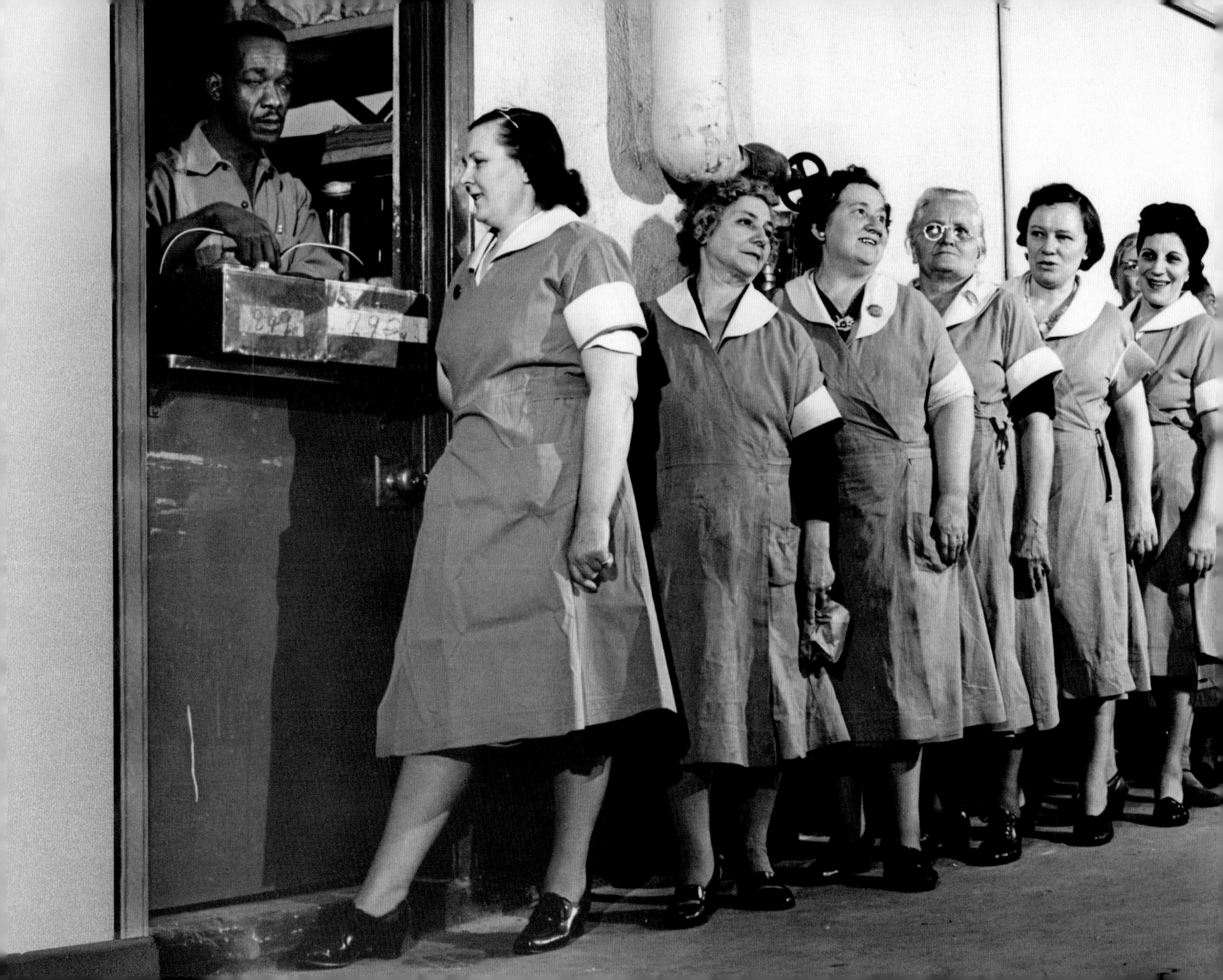

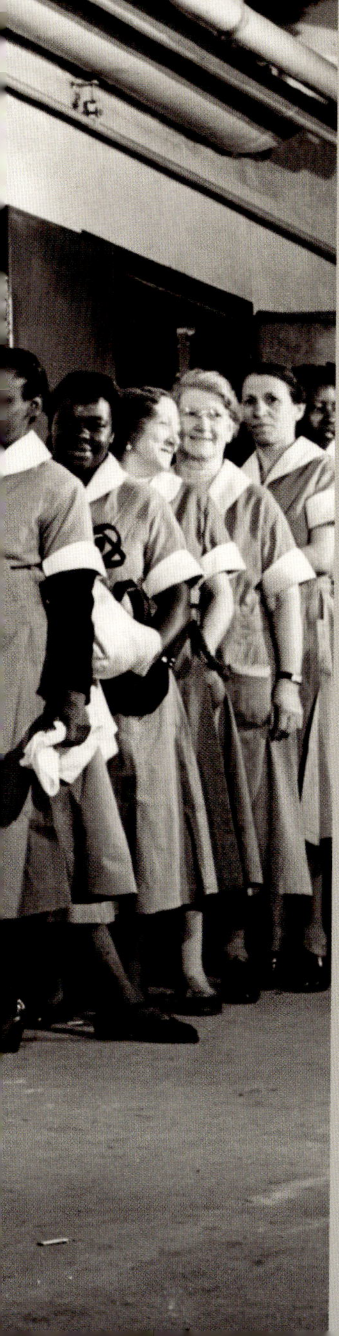

9

NOT PICTURED

9.1 Cleaners line up in the sub-basement of the R.C.A. Building to receive cleaning equipment. "The cleaners, responsible for the maintenance of the Center's 5,734,209 square feet of rented area, face the task each evening which may be compared with cleaning 3,750 six-room houses." (Rockefeller Group photo 1204 by Roy Stephens)

A T FIRST GLANCE, "Lunch on a Beam" evokes the American Dream—immigrant and Mohawk iron-workers sitting shoulder to shoulder, joined in courage, purpose, and toil as they build the world's greatest city. But a more complicated American story emerges from the photograph's negative space—from who isn't there.

The builders of Rockefeller Center, the largest construction project in New York, employed no Black construction workers. In May 1931, The Cooperative Committee on Employment, a group based in Harlem, approached Joe Brown of Todd and Brown. What, asked the Committee, was Rockefeller going to do about it?

Brown acknowledged that there were no Black construction workers but said Rockefeller Center contractors did not discriminate and "will not bar a colored person who applies" if he meets "the contractor's requirements"—which, he pointed out, "included union membership." With the major construction unions, including the ironworkers, closed to Black workers, this amounted to a policy of total exclusion.[1]

While the American Federation of Labor officially opposed racial discrimination, the national leadership could not or did not enforce that policy upon local unions, which actually controlled membership and hiring decisions.

Civil rights leaders pressed the AFL to do more, but they could do little more than document the inequities. In 1930, the National Urban League released a 284-page report, identifying twenty-two unions that excluded Black workers as a matter of policy.[2]

During the period prior to the World War the repeated efforts of Negro spokesmen and interested white persons to entrench Negro workers in industrial positions, with such increments as might accrue to them from these positions, were futile. For one hundred years, America had relied almost entirely upon the European immigrants who had come to their shores for its industrial labor and the adjustment of this immigrant group was considered more satisfactory than could be expected of the Negro worker. The World War, however, exerted profound changes. This immigration was suddenly checked. New recruits for industry were necessary and the Black American was the most available supply. The activities of labor agents were bringing Black workers into northern industries in great numbers. They went into those industries needing masses of unskilled workers—the steel and iron industries, construction, stockyards, railroads, road maintenance and construction. In many instances they entered as strikebreakers. These new industrial opportunities were in no small way responsible for the migration of 1,200,000 Black Americans who moved from South to North between 1915 and 1928.[3]

T. Arnold Hill, the director of industrial relations for the National Urban League, pressed the AFL to keep its pledge to end discrimination in its member unions. "There can be no peace in the hearts of white workers if black workers take their jobs when they are on strike," he wrote to the president of the AFL in 1925, "and there can be no peace in the hearts of black workers if they are denied not only the privilege to organize but also the right to labor because white workers object."[4]

Ironworker union halls in the 1930s and for decades thereafter excluded Black workers through a variety of schemes, from the thinly veiled (family preference, endorsement of a current member) to the transparently racist (convoluted applications, reserved for Black applicants, in the style of Jim Crow poll tests).[5]

Ironworker unions had also developed a reputation for insularity and violence after a twenty-five-year labor conflict with an equally recalcitrant employers association.[6] Even in an era when strikers routinely attacked replacement workers, and employers' private security forces frequently attacked striking union members, the ironworkers stood out. Across the country, officials with the ironworker unions were implicated not only in violence against replacement workers—so-called "strikebreakers" or "scabs"—but also in acts of sabotage against non-union construction projects and other perceived enemies.

The most infamous of these was the bombing of the *Los Angeles Times* building. The paper was stridently anti-union, at a time when California was divided between the employer-friendly, open-shop model of Los Angeles and the labor-friendly, highly unionized model of San Francisco. On the evening of September 30, 1910, a militant young labor activist planted a suitcase full of dynamite in an alley beside the building. Hours later it detonated, creating an inferno that destroyed the building and killed twenty-one people.

An alarm clock and other evidence linked the bombing to others around the country, and investigators zeroed in on James McNamara, a labor activist, and his brother John McNamara, the head of the Bridge and Structural Iron Workers Union in Indianapolis and a charter member of the national ironworkers union. Their case became a cause célèbre for labor leaders, certain of persecution by anti-union employers and their government lackeys until the brothers confessed. The case set back the labor movement in southern California for decades and cemented the ironworkers unions' reputation for violence.[7]

Discrimination on job sites was the same across the nation. Between 1931 and 1936, the Hoover Dam project employed over twenty-one thousand men. Only twenty-four of them were Black construction workers.[8] New York's Ironworkers Local 40 did not accept a Black member until 1963. The following year, that ironworker was the subject of a *New York Times* profile by the writer Gay Talese, who followed one understatement—"Negros have never gotten into ironwork"—with another, calling Local 40 "a union, which like many other construction unions, never sought Negro members."[9]

The article appeared thirty years after the famed photo "Lunch on a Beam" thrilled the nation. For a writer famed for scrupulous, telling detail, Talese presents a shadow of his subject, Michael Stewart. The headline focuses on Stewart's account that he was treated "fair." What is fair? The question was not answered.

Nor did the writer peer too closely at why Stewart was "the first Negro in this type of construction work."

When pressed on the exclusion of Black construction workers, Rockefeller and his construction managers, Todd and Brown, may have been able to blame racist union practices. But they had no such excuse for the hiring practices of Rockefeller Center Operations, which followed a clear racial hierarchy.

As buildings were completed, Todd and Brown hired hundreds of maintenance workers. Jobs in the public eye—doormen, greeters, and guides—went to whites. So did hundreds of positions for elevator operators and window washers. The R.C.A. Building alone featured seventy elevators and 5,285 windows.[10]

Image was paramount.

The first uniformed cadres were organized under Samuel L. "Roxy" Rothafel,[11] the unofficial "Mayor of Radio City." In September 1931, the impresario joined Web Todd on a five-week tour of Europe, with an entourage of architects, engineers, and two theater experts from NBC, to study innovations in the theater, opera, ballet, architecture, acoustics, and traffic planning. The press was alerted to the trip undertaken "in interest of New York's Gigantic Building and Amusement Center." The three-page release continued: "Pretentious plans are being made for the entertainment of the master showman and his entourage. Formal and informal receptions will be held in Berlin, Moscow, London and Paris." High on Roxy's list was the Buckingham Palace guard. He considered their uniforms the smartest in the world. He envisioned his theatrical "Service Troops" with the style and discipline of the British. That would include uniformed pages, ushers, messengers, ticket-takers, guards, and other employees.[12]

Management, equally eager to impress potential tenants and the public, followed suit. Uniforms created the

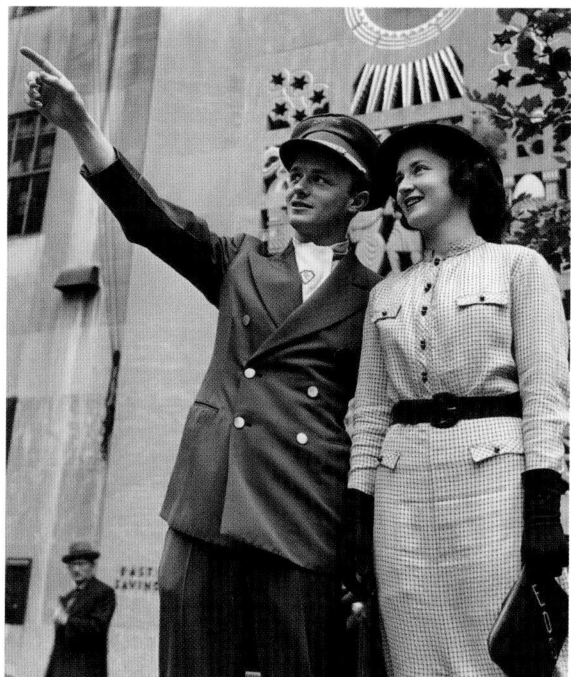

9.2 At its completion in 1939, Rockefeller Center employed 39 tour guides, all white men. (Rockefeller Group photo 771)

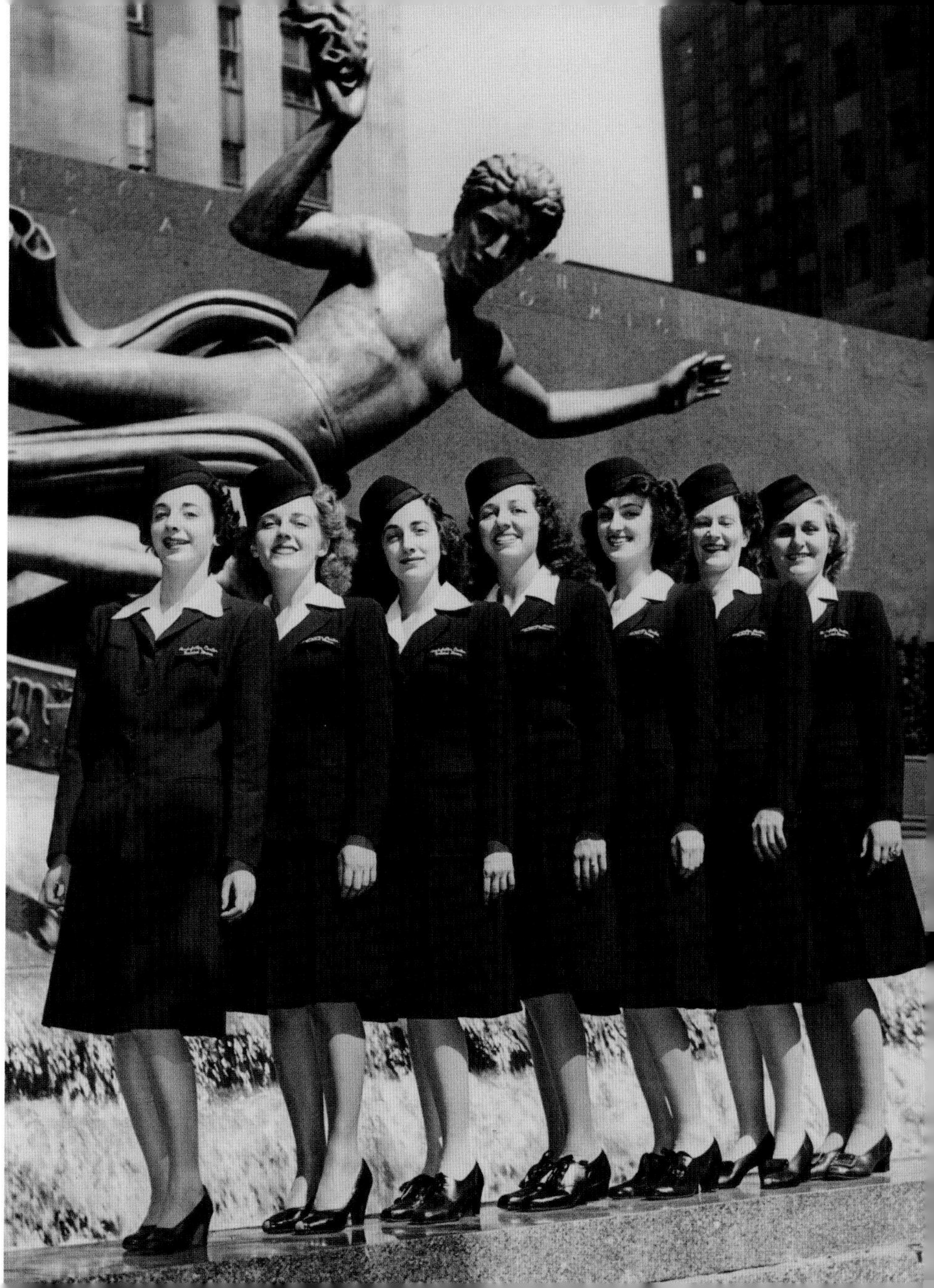

9.3 During World War Two, women replaced men as tour guides. "A well-informed Centerette will guide you through Rockefeller Center and show you all the amazing wonders of this 'city within a city,'" promised a 1943 brochure. (Rockefeller Group photo 961)

appearance of official, efficient teams, from window washers to elevator operators. These workers played an important role in the image of the Center by creating an "orderly and congenial atmosphere, and thereby added to the superiority of the space."[13]

Among the elite were twelve young, white tour guides, easily identifiable by their "Ask Me" badges. They sported white silk ascots above their double-breasted light-gray uniforms embroidered with "RC." They roamed the Plaza and the Observation Deck. They were versed in the history, architecture, art, and entertainment of the Center and ready to answer questions and impress visitors from the Corn Belt. The role of tour guide paid $27.50 a week, not bad for the aspiring actor Gregory Peck.

Black workers filled jobs done at night, behind the scenes, or both: painting, cleaning, hauling trash, and polishing trim and floors. This racial job ceiling limited both hiring and advancement opportunities for Black workers.[14]

At Rockefeller Center, the racial job ceiling was enforced from the top. In the summer of 1932, Junior's real estate advisor, Charles Heydt, wrote to Joseph Brown: "Do you know whether anything has been decided as to whether we will have colored elevator operators, or whether we will have colored porters? I have a number of applications from colored people living in our

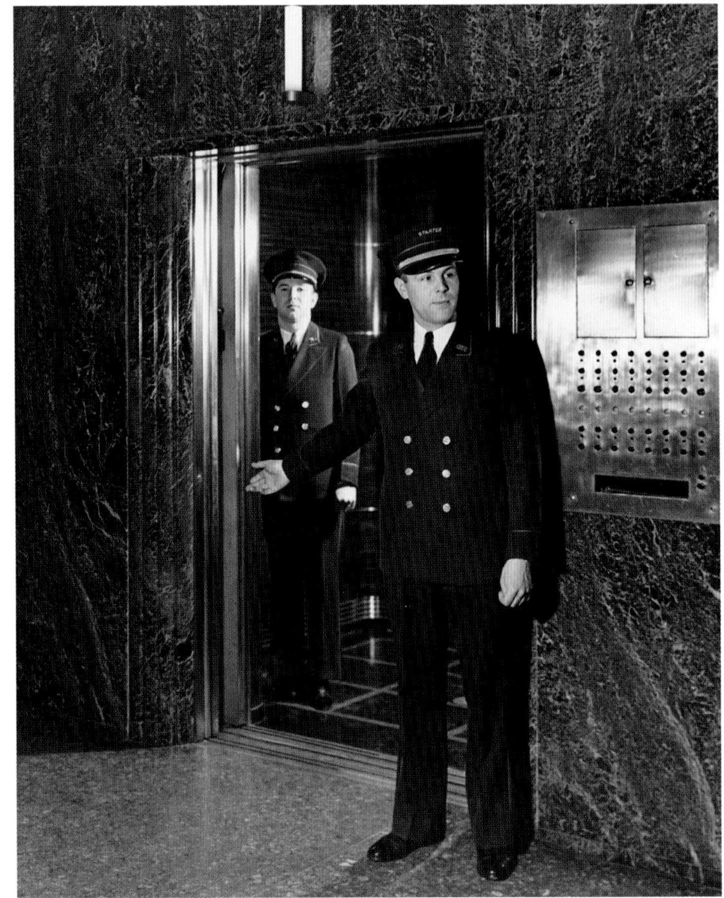

9.4 Elevator operators at the R.C.A. Building. "I am quite sure," wrote developer Joseph Brown, "that a canvass of the Managers would result in a unanimous recommendation for white help." (Rockefeller Group photo 600 by Wendell McRae)

apartments,[15] who are looking for jobs and if there are to be any openings, I will file their names."[16]

The response came in a week: "Nothing has yet been decided, insofar as I know, with reference to the elevator operators and porters for the Rockefeller Center buildings.

"In view of our experience in the past, I am quite sure that a canvass of the Managers would result in a unanimous recommendation for white help."[17]

The letter was signed "Todd & Brown Inc.," above Brown's initials. An unsigned copy of the letter, presumably a draft, bearing the same date and initials, contained a third paragraph, more explicitly racist:

> As you know, the elevator cabs have gotten to be pretty close, tight-fitting boxes, and I do not believe the public would react very favorably to riding in such a cab for the length of time it would take to travel into the upper stories of our tall building.[18]

The third paragraph and its disappearance invite questions: Did Brown reconsider saying the quiet part out loud? Did Heydt ask him to tone it down? And what was Junior's role in this exchange between his adviser and top developer? The outcome was decided. It would be almost two decades before Rockefeller Center hired its first Black elevator operator.

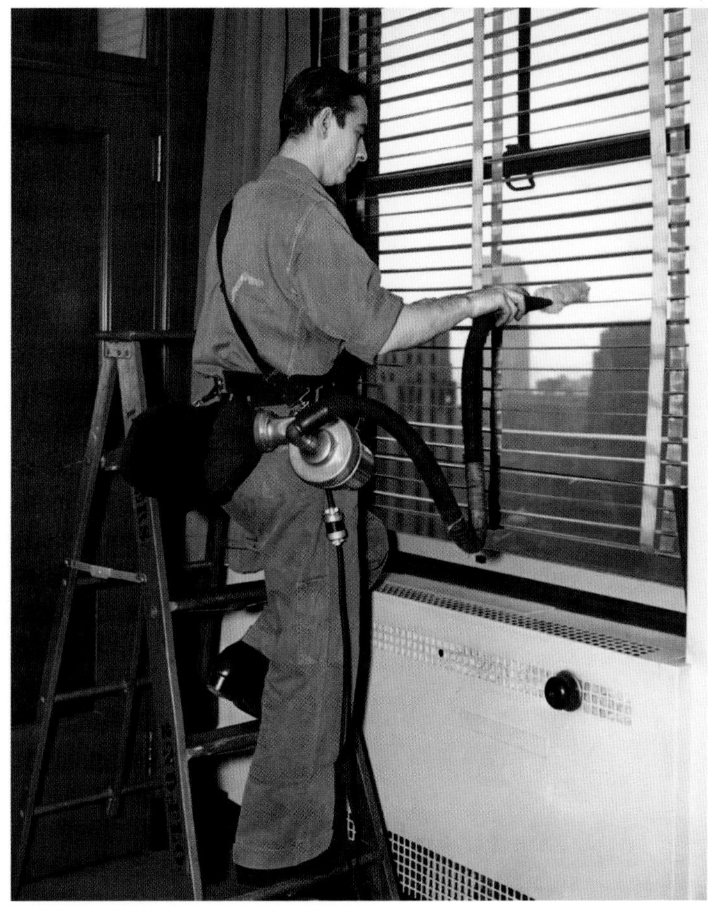

9.5 A high duster cleans venetian blinds in the R.C.A. Building. (Rockefeller Group photo 687)

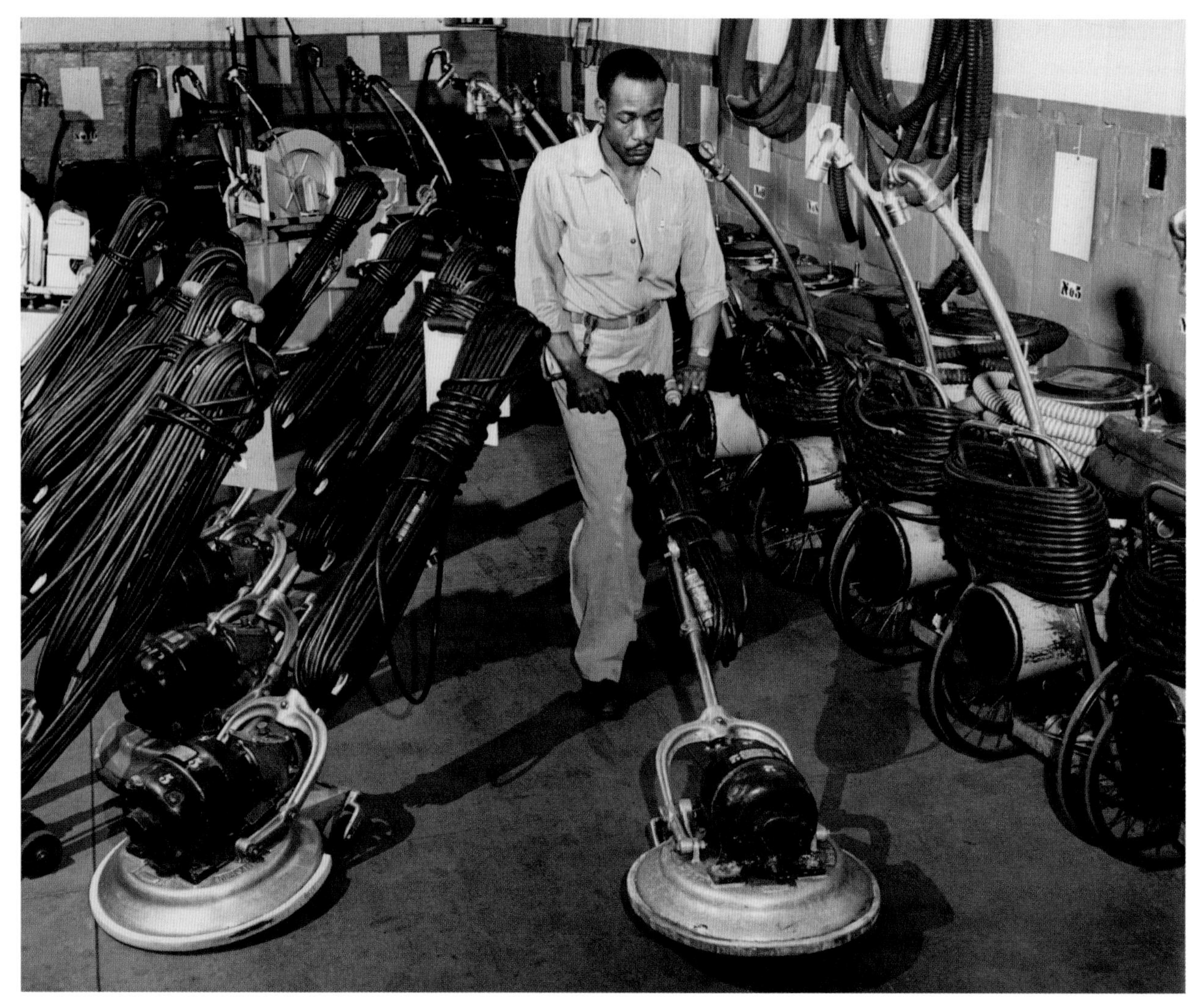

9.6 More than 600 employees worked in Rockefeller Center's Cleaning Division. The most visible jobs were reserved for white workers. (Rockefeller Group photo 1205 by Roy Stephens)

The archive's photos tell the story of Rockefeller Center's racial job ceiling. Until after World War II, there were no images of African Americans in Rockefeller jobs seen by the public. They were the invisible workers who polished the gleaming stone floors, and the women, called "low dusters," who cleaned the offices and toilets. Men did the "high dusting," changing light bulbs and cleaning high areas on lifts and ladders. Their workday began at dusk after the office workers went home.

And even those jobs, though not barred to Black workers, went mostly to low-skill white workers. In Photo #1204, a few Black women stand in a line of mostly white cleaners, awaiting their assignment from a Black quartermaster.

This racial job ceiling began to crack following World War II. Among Rockefeller Center's first Black elevator operators was Eugene Bullard—a decorated veteran of both world wars whose exploits as a French fighter pilot and spy earned him the nom de guerre "The Black Swallow of Death." At Rockefeller Center, he worked in relative anonymity until a 1959 interview with Dave Garroway, founding host of the *Today Show*. Radio City Music Hall didn't hire a Black Rockette for sixty-two years, until Jennifer Jones joined the troupe in 1987.

A bitter irony was that racial discrimination had pervaded the founding of Rockefeller Center, despite the declared commitment of John D. Rockefeller Jr. and his sons to address America's racial injustices. In 1932, the Rockefeller family was the single largest donor to the civil rights movement, as well as the largest funder of schools and colleges for Black students. (Though even those efforts were limited by a deference to Jim Crow policies. "Despite good intentions and the resources supplied by the vast Rockefeller fortune, work done in acceptance of the framework of segregation fell short of creating true racial equity.")[19]

Evidence of the Rockefellers' aspirations and their limits can be found throughout the R.C.A. Building, where the gray-tone murals of Spanish painter José María Sert adorn the elevator banks.

After the embarrassing public spat with Diego Rivera, the Rockefellers were pleased to find an artist they could work with. "Artists are very cooperative," John Todd telegrammed from Paris. Sert showed Todd a series of sketches, agreeing each time to Todd's changes.[20]

The result was four murals celebrating human progress. The most prominent, *American Progress*, centers Abraham Lincoln—a hero not only of abolitionists, but of Republicans like Todd and the Rockefellers. This was the mural that replaced Diego Rivera's *Man at the Crossroads*. Lenin was out. Lincoln was in. Sert understood the assignment.

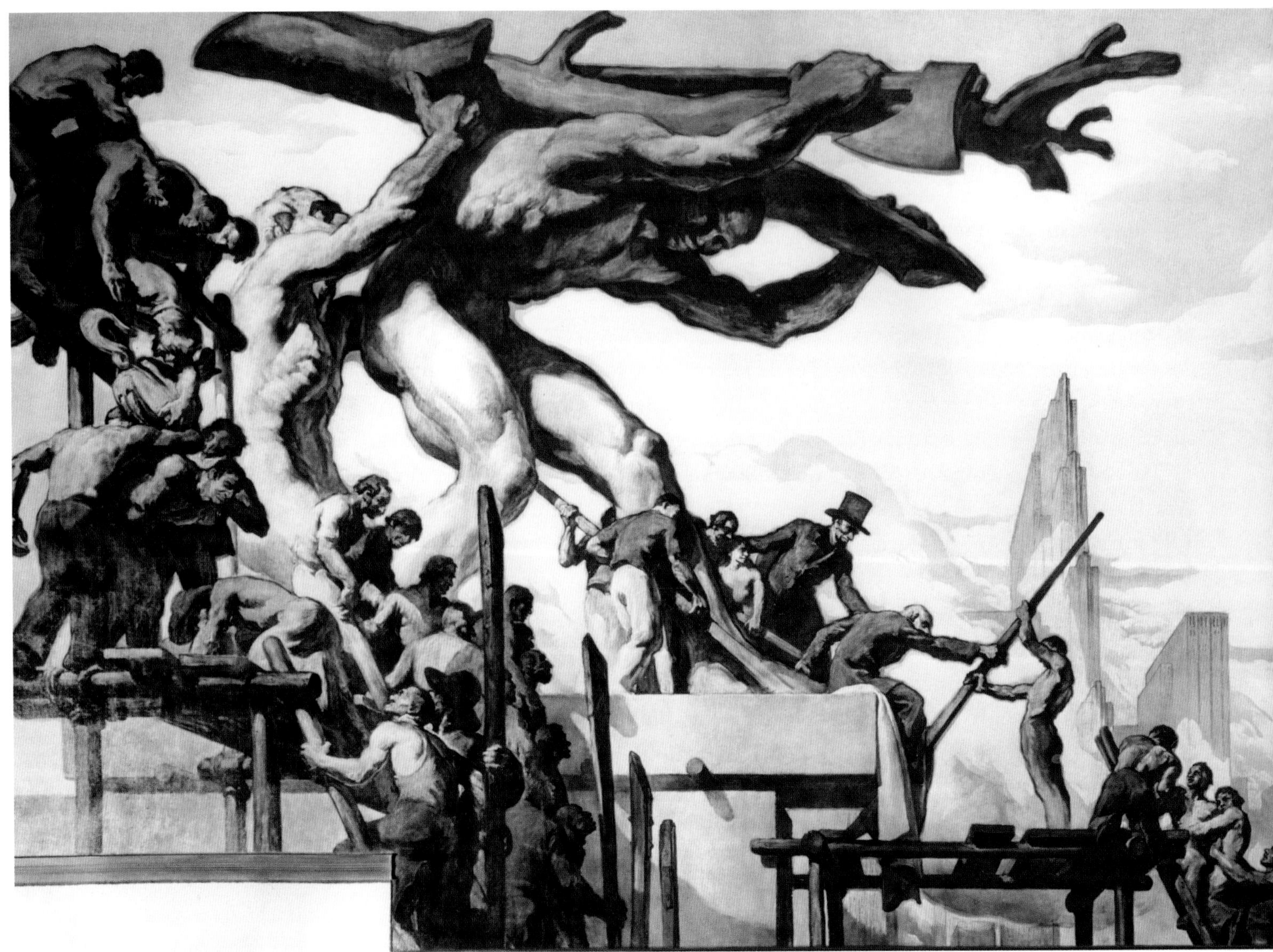

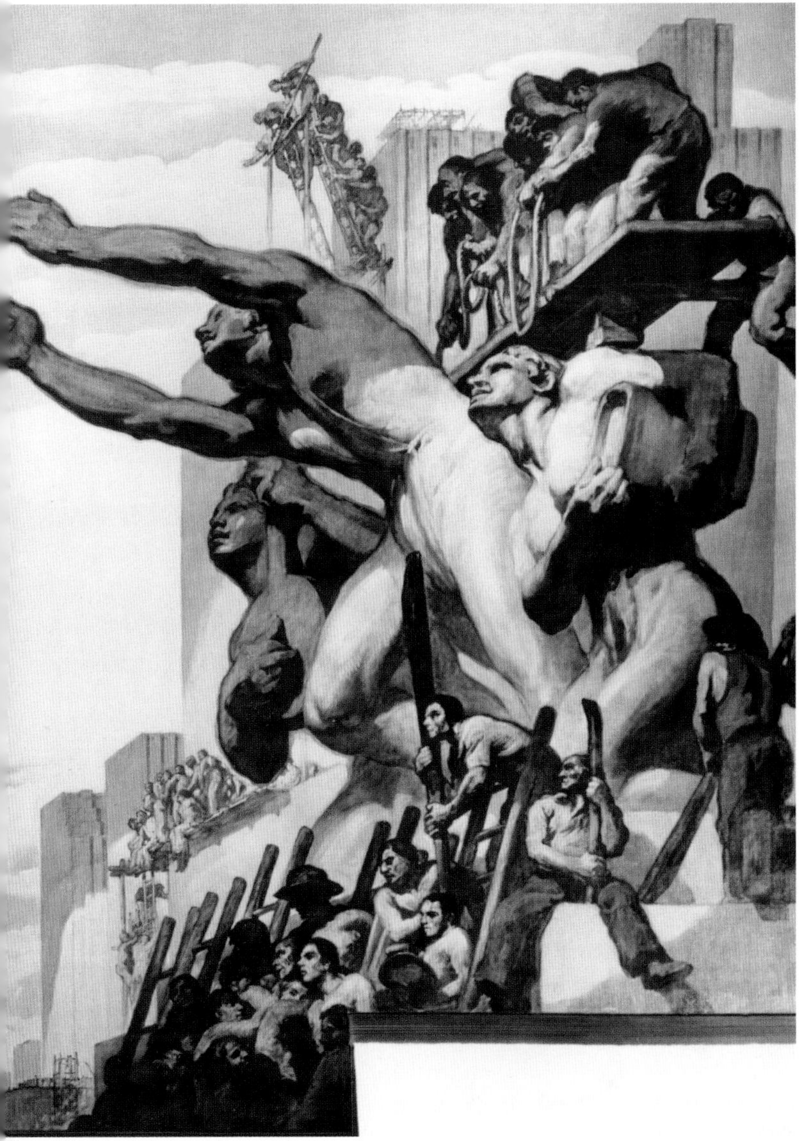

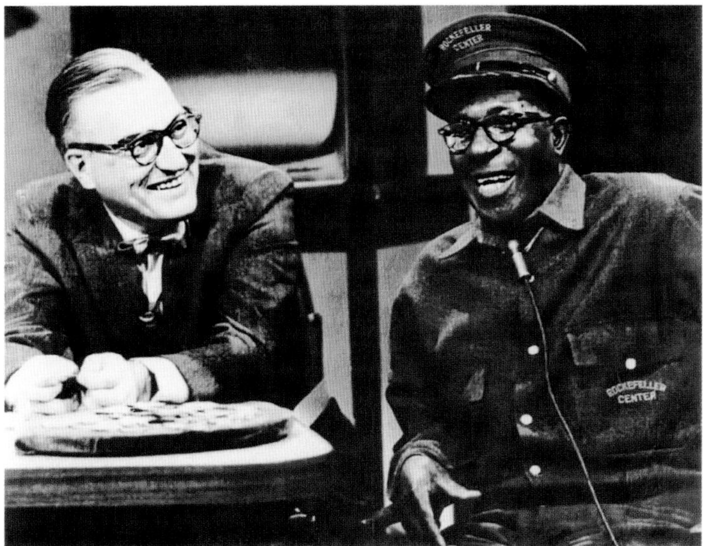

9.8 Eugene Bullard, one of Rockefeller Center's first Black elevator operators, was interviewed by Dave Garroway for the *Today* show in 1959. (Rockefeller Group photo)

9.7 American Progress by Jose Maria Sert. (Rockefeller Group photo 699)

Down the hall, Sert's mural *Abolition of Slavery* depicts white-coded liberators freeing enslaved Black men. The lone slave driver wears a billowy vest and Mediterranean features as he whips a fallen Black man. White people were liberators, Black people victims, and slavery a foreign institution—was the backdrop, as white greeters whisked visitors past Sert's murals to a white elevator man.

Abolition of Slavery invites us to reconsider Crowell's prescription for the perfect image, "a group photography of all the readers, so that each reader could have the fun of finding himself in the picture," and what it tells us about "Lunch on a Beam." Each picture invites the audience to identify with its subject. When we ask who has fun finding himself in the picture, we know whom the picture is for.

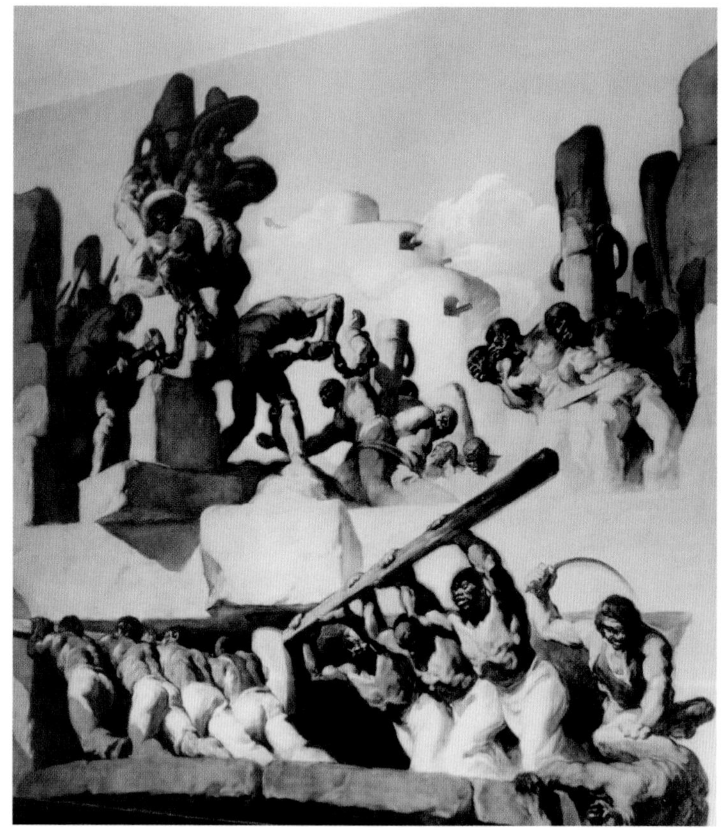

9.9 *Abolition of Slavery* by Jose Maria Sert. (Rockefeller Group photo 380A)

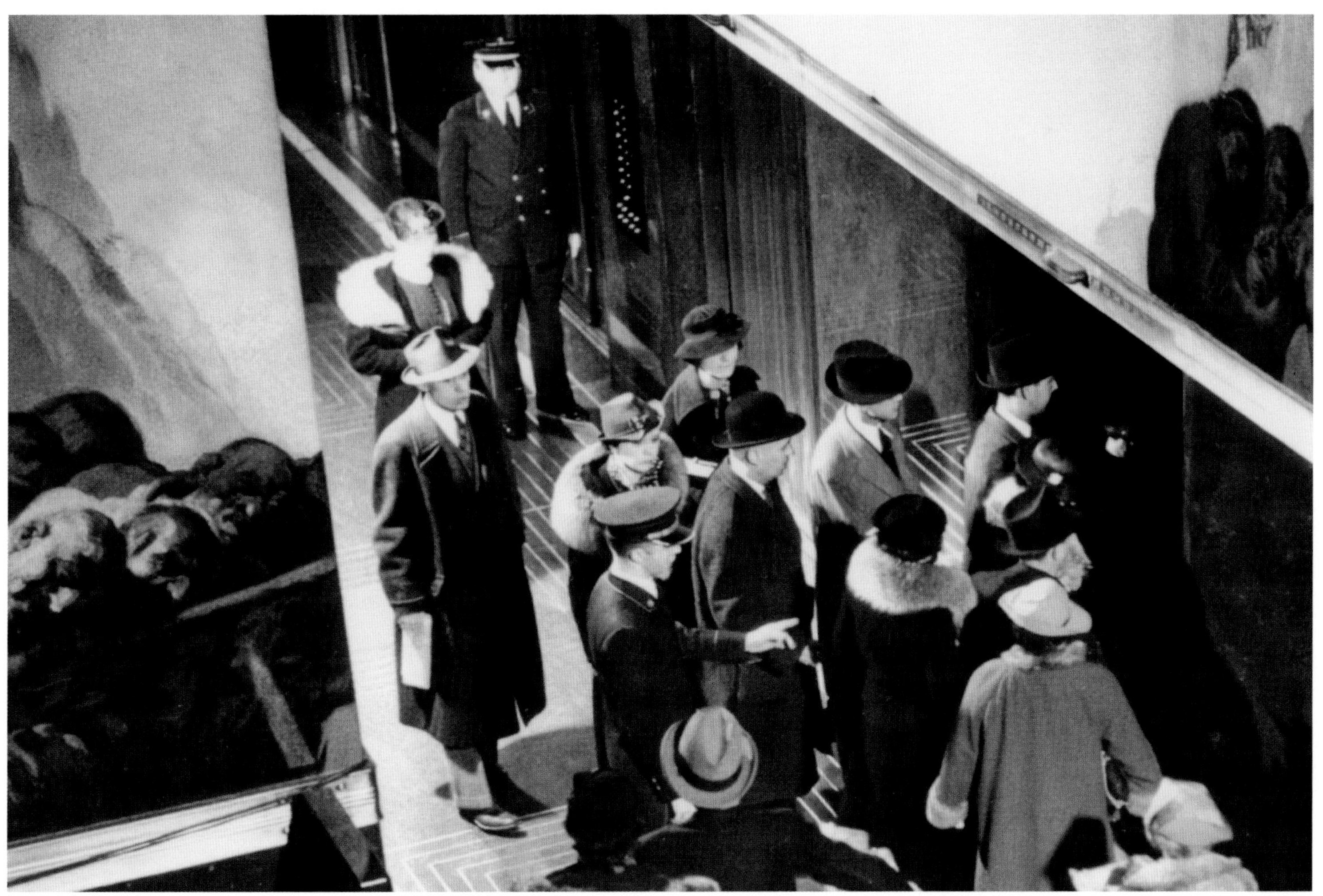

9.10 Visitors pass beneath the murals of Jose Maria Sert as they board elevators in the R.C.A. Building. (Rockefeller Group photo 602)

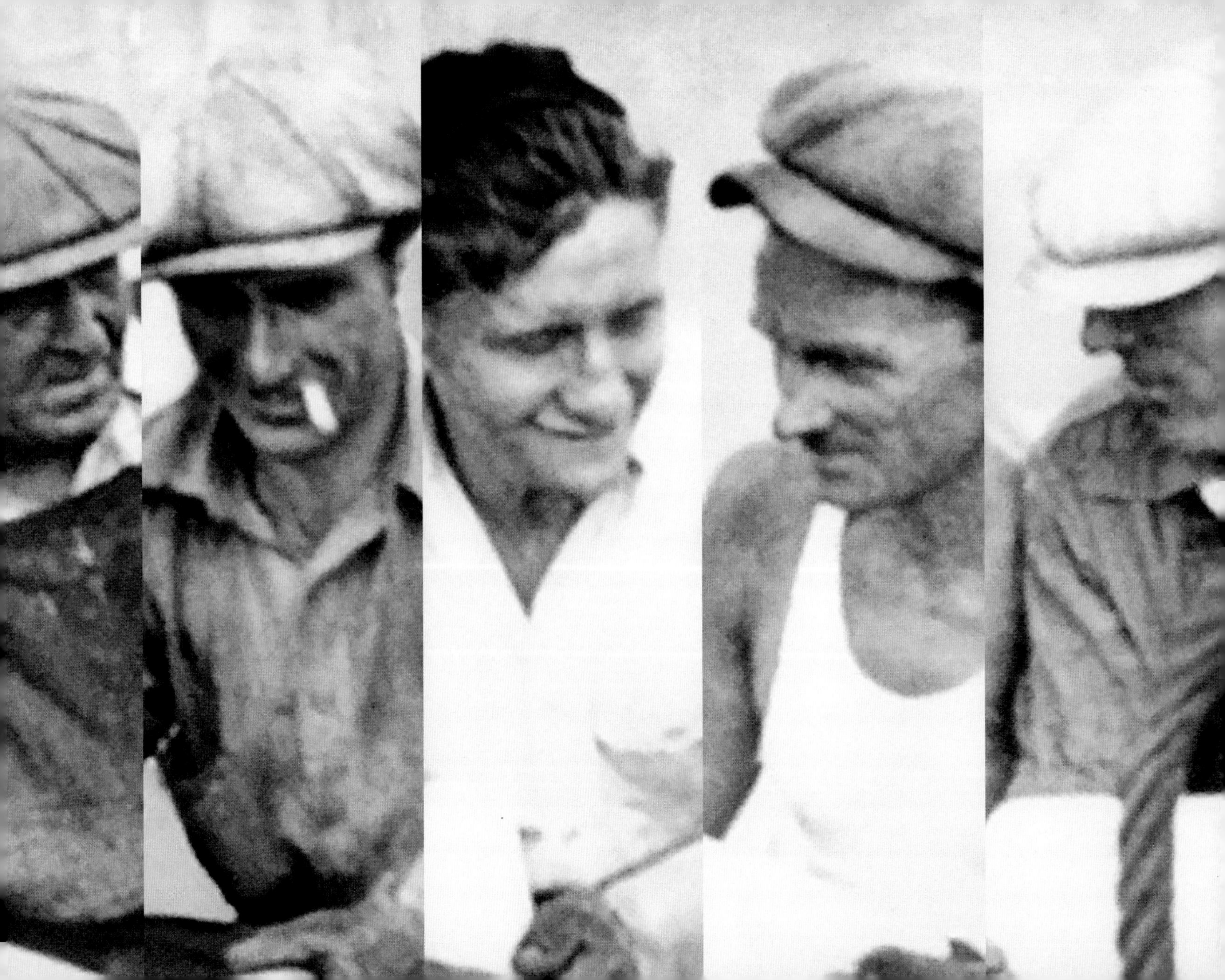

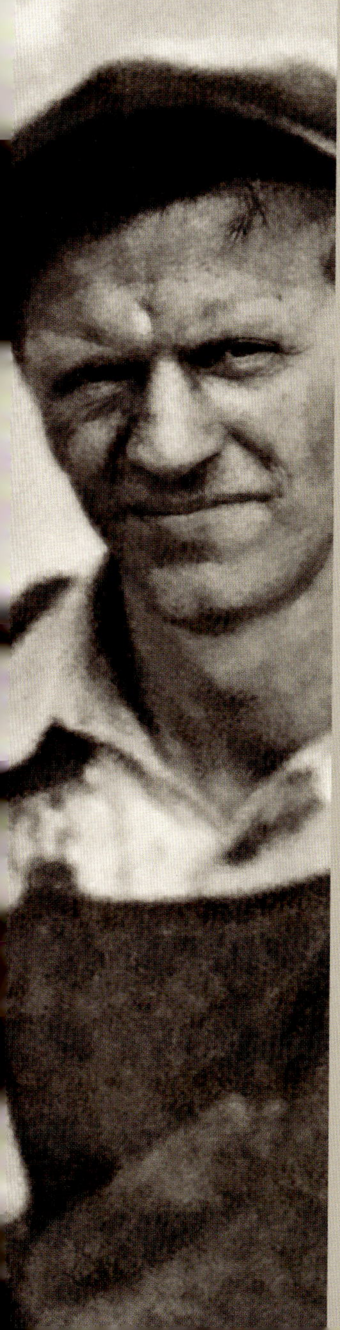

WHO WERE THE MEN ON THE BEAM?

Many who have searched for the names of the men on the beam have come away disappointed. Some, like the Ó Cualáin brothers, console themselves with the thought that the search is what matters or that the mystery is the meaning. The picture is powerful enough without naming the intrepid men. The document captures a moment in history, carries a message, and immortalizes the unnamed men.

I'm reminded again of Merle Crowell's dictum:

Every human being likes to see himself in reading matter—just as he likes to see himself in a mirror. The ideal article for any publication (so far as "reader interest" is concerned) would be one in which every reader could find his own name. The ideal illustration would be a group photography of all the readers, so that each reader could have the fun of finding himself in the picture.

For ninety years, readers have had the fun of finding themselves or their fathers or grandfathers in the photo. But names have power. Real people built Rockefeller Center. Built New York. Built our world. Their stories are our foundation, pylons of struggle and triumph sunk deep in the Manhattan bedrock.

The ironworkers' names have been a mystery with few clues but many tantalizing hints. I was surprised, at first, by the number of people eager to share their family stories but unable or hesitant to answer follow-up questions. Eventually, I understood the urge to protect treasured memories, like old photos, from harsh light.

Many have been satisfied to hang a name on an ironworker and call their search complete, especially if that name is a relative, a local hero, or both. The result is scores of names for the eleven men, often based on some version of Matt O'Shaughnessy's admonition, "You don't grow up to the age I am now without knowing who you are and who your father is." Memory is unreliable. Certainty does not make it true.

Occasionally, I thought: Why am I doing this? Would the mystery be better left unresolved? Anonymity offers everyone a bond with all men who ever walked iron, a place for their family story in an exalted alliance. Would finding the names diminish that bond?

I say no. That universal connection can exist alongside personal recognition. Even draw strength from it.

Now, after seven years, I am coming to the end of my search. The identifications I have made are gratifying, yet my lust for answers is still with me. I hope that this book leads to more questions and more answers. There will always be another story, but for now, it is time to build with what we have. Based on the available evidence from the archive and beyond, the most likely identification for the eleven men, from left to right, is:

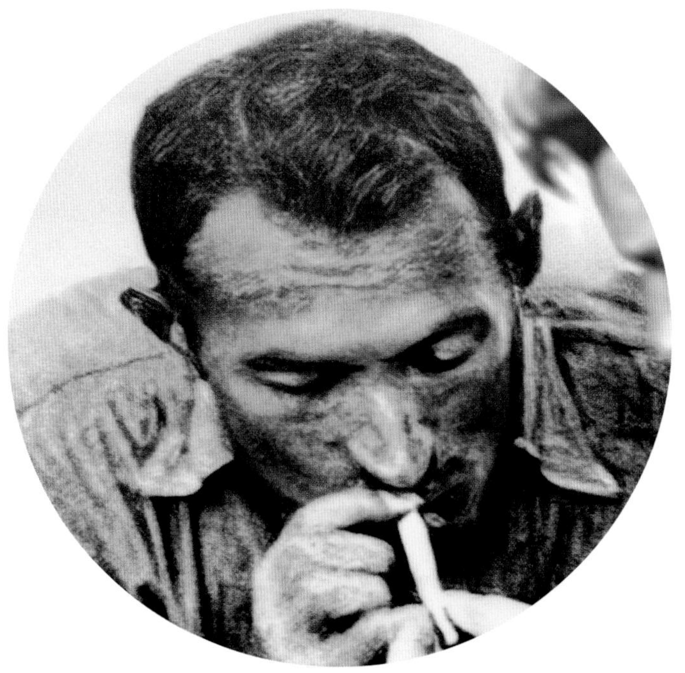

1. John O'Rielly, identified in the Rockefeller Center Archive. Other names proposed for this man, with less evidence, are Rudy Silla, Matty O'Shaughnessy, and Bill Melendy.

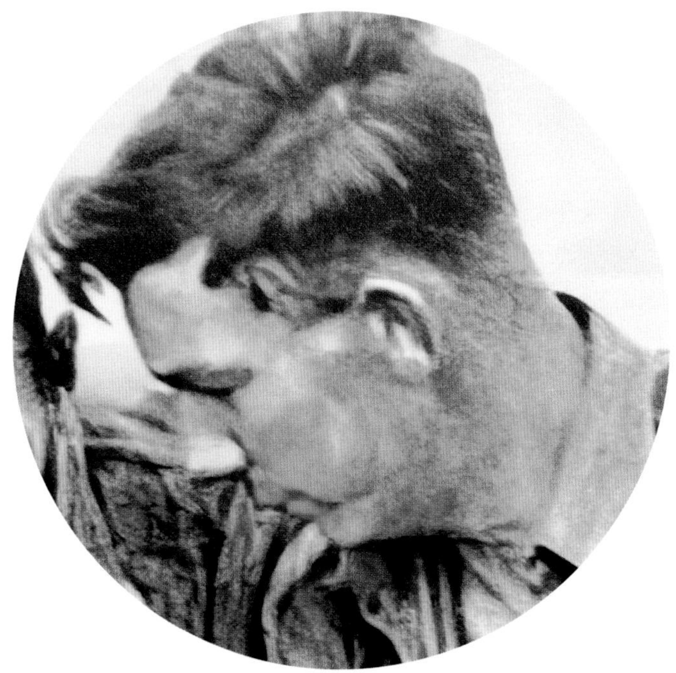

2. George Covan (or Kovan), identified in the Rockefeller Center Archive. Other names proposed for this man, with less evidence, include James Joy, James Owen McGlynn, and Victor Pearson.

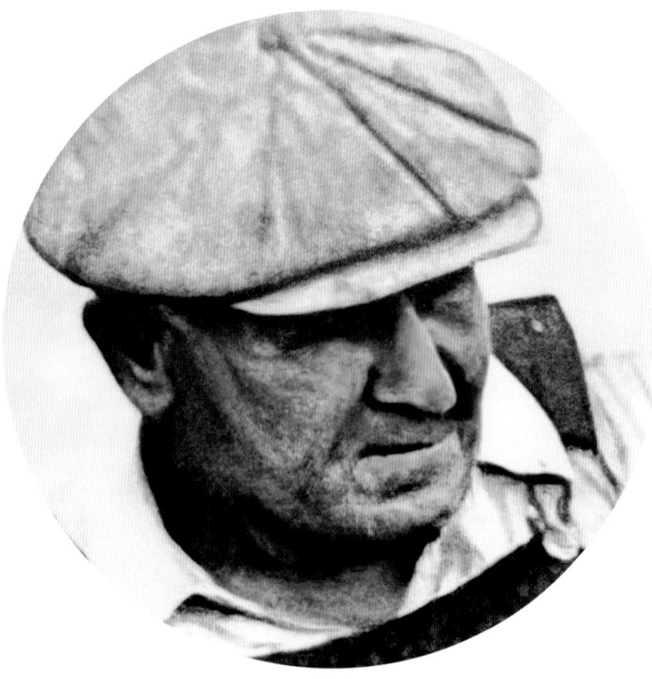

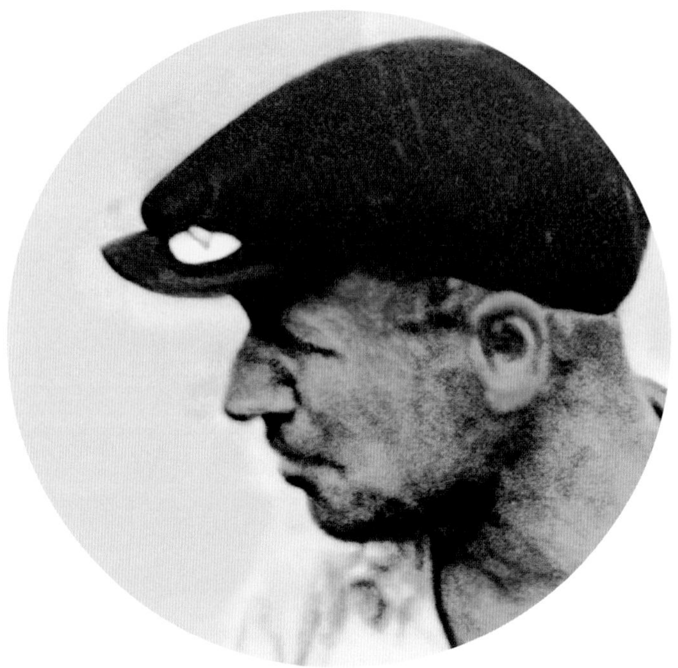

3. Joseph Eckner, identified in the Rockefeller Center Archive. Other names proposed for this man, with less evidence, include Michael Baresich, Martin Dolan, Thomas Enright, Richard Fennell, Steven Foley, Edwin Stone Goodbred, James Grosso, Frank Harazim, Howard Kilgore, Robert Kimmel, Frank Pascale, Magnus Pedersen, Mike Penny, Ralph Rawding (or Redwing), Michael Sabatino, John Joseph Smith (or Smit), Peter Stacy, Claude Stagg, Mike Wade, and John Wood.

4. Joseph Jocks, identified by family members. Other names proposed for this man, with less evidence, include Michael Brehenny, George Brooks, John Cook, William Lyons, and John Pedersen.

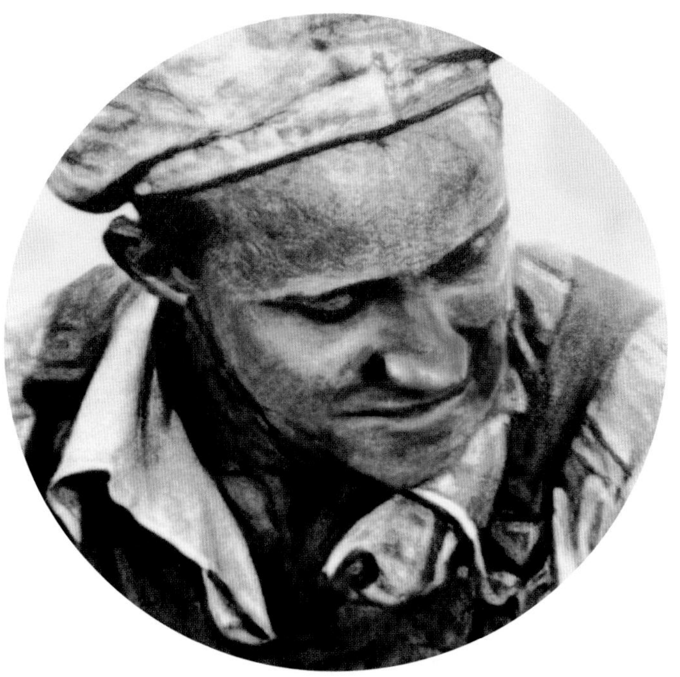
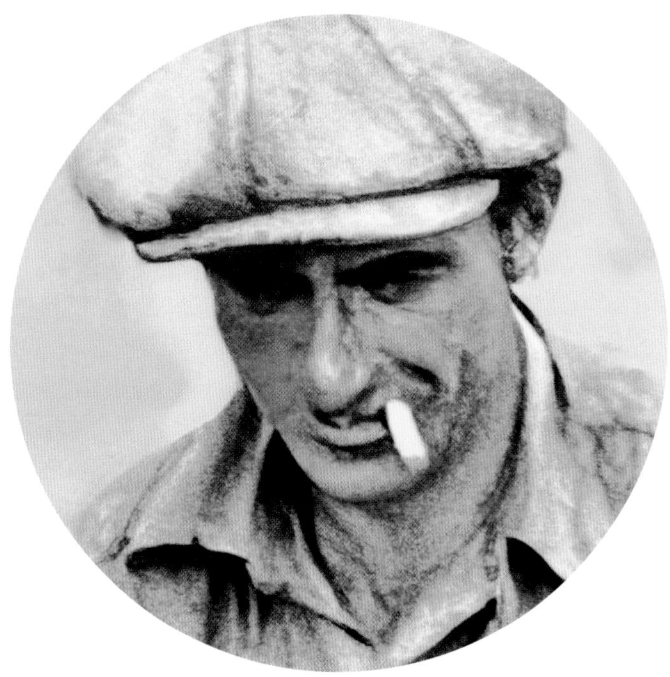

5. George Urbanneck, identified by family members with contemporary evidence. Other names proposed for this man, with less evidence, include Peter Rice, Claude Stagg, and Albin Svensson.

6. Peter Rice, identified by family members. Other names proposed for this man, with less evidence, include Joseph Buenti, Edward Allen Campbell, Ray Costello, John Daley, Patrick Dugan, Martin Higgins, Phil Keating, Arthur Macintosh, Frank Pelligrino, and Brian Rice.

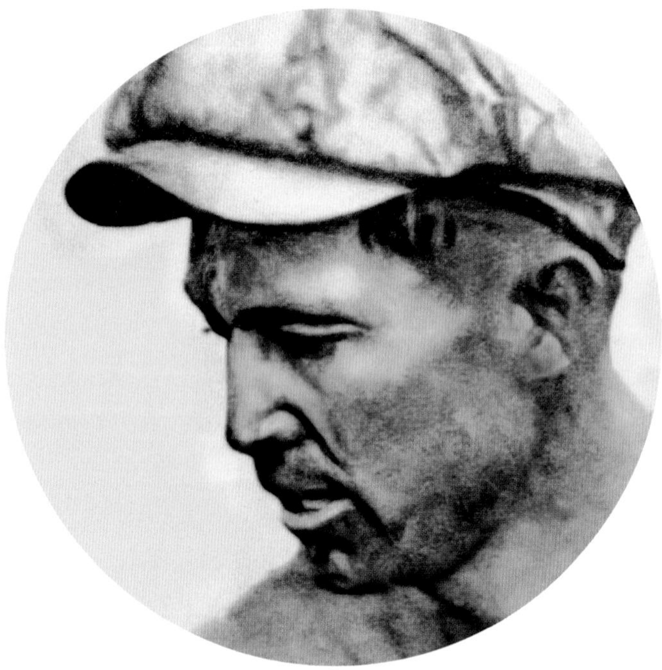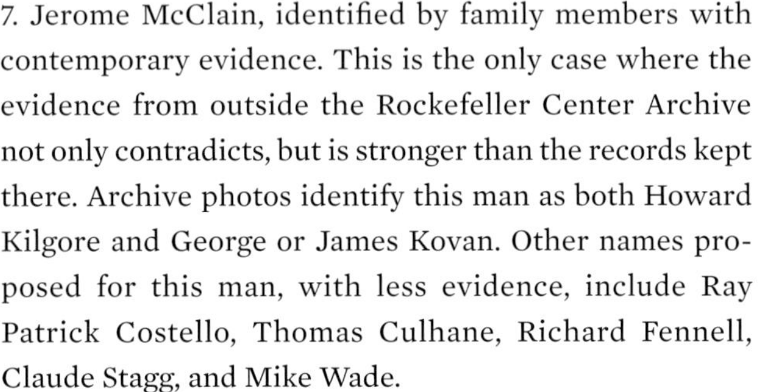

7. Jerome McClain, identified by family members with contemporary evidence. This is the only case where the evidence from outside the Rockefeller Center Archive not only contradicts, but is stronger than the records kept there. Archive photos identify this man as both Howard Kilgore and George or James Kovan. Other names proposed for this man, with less evidence, include Ray Patrick Costello, Thomas Culhane, Richard Fennell, Claude Stagg, and Mike Wade.

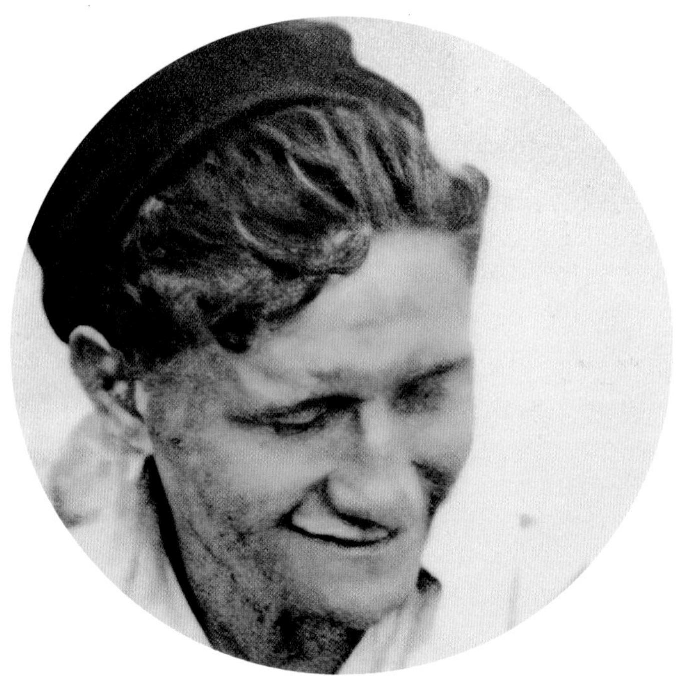

8. William Birgir, identified in the Rockefeller Center Archive. Other names proposed for this man, with less evidence, include William Lyons and Joe Curtis.

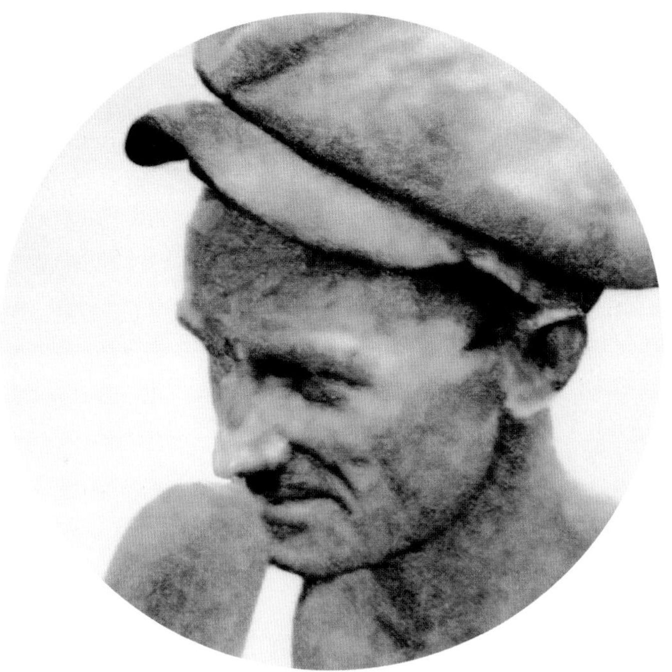

9. Joe Curtis, identified in the Rockefeller Center Archive. Other names proposed for this man, with less evidence, include Harry Brender, Angus Sears, Alan Billings, Vincent Hughes, Berger Holton, Charles Kent, and William Moss.

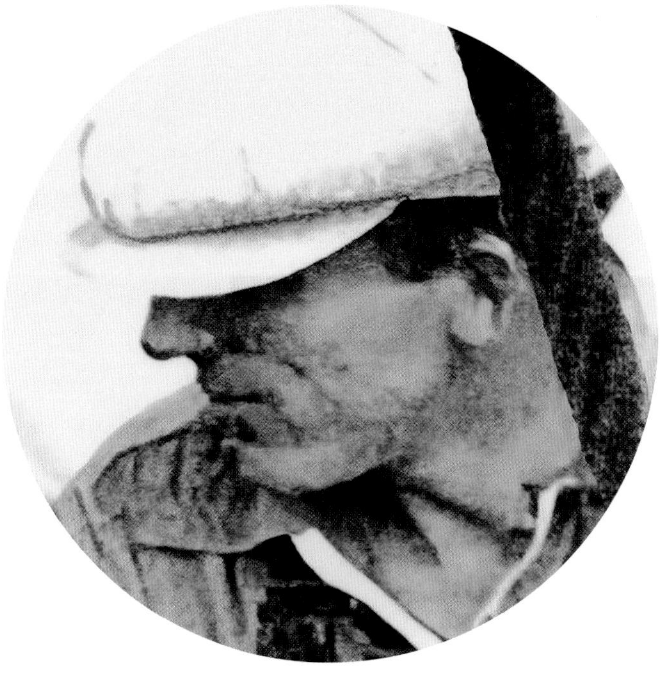

10. John Portla, identified in the Rockefeller Center Archive. Other names proposed for this man, with less evidence, include Edwin Johnson.

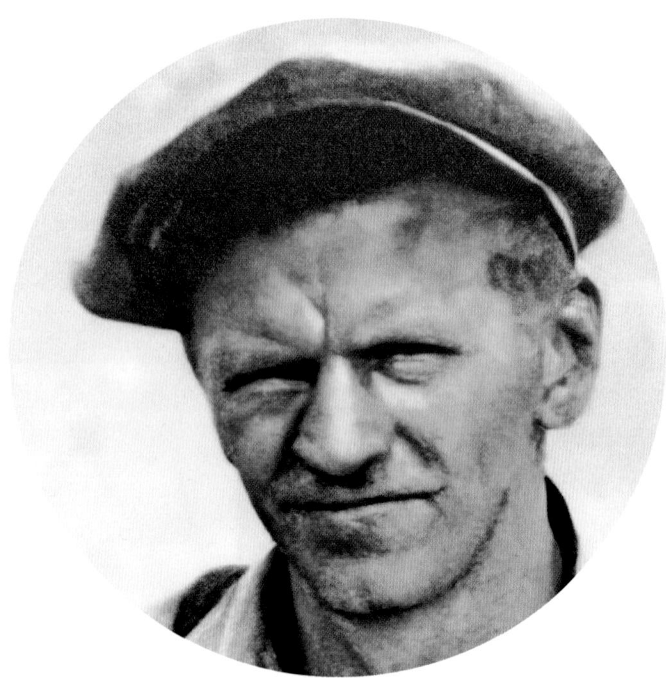

11. The eleventh man remains unidentified with any confi-
dence. Names proposed without much evidence include
John Paul Nathaniel Bjorndahl, David Cherry, Patty Flynn,
Sonny Glynn, Gusti Popovic, and Axel Uddgren.

Many times, as I drove out to meet ironworkers or their families, I wondered if this would be just another meeting of wishful families and optimistic thinking on my part. Despite those worries, I hoped to find provable material concerning the identity of a man on the beam. I continually honed my list of questions, limiting them to basic questions to see if the family had a story I hadn't prompted. I wanted memories as undistorted by time as possible.

Often, the "proof" was a mélange of family lore and old wedding portraits showing a man who had some resemblance—sometimes striking—to one on the beam. Perhaps it was a treasured story about the 1930s ironworker in their family, passed down through generations. Perhaps it was magical thinking. Legends. Yarns. Anecdotes. Sometimes, the evidence was solid: photos, news clips, dates, places, and multiple sources.

Was I also guilty of magical thinking?

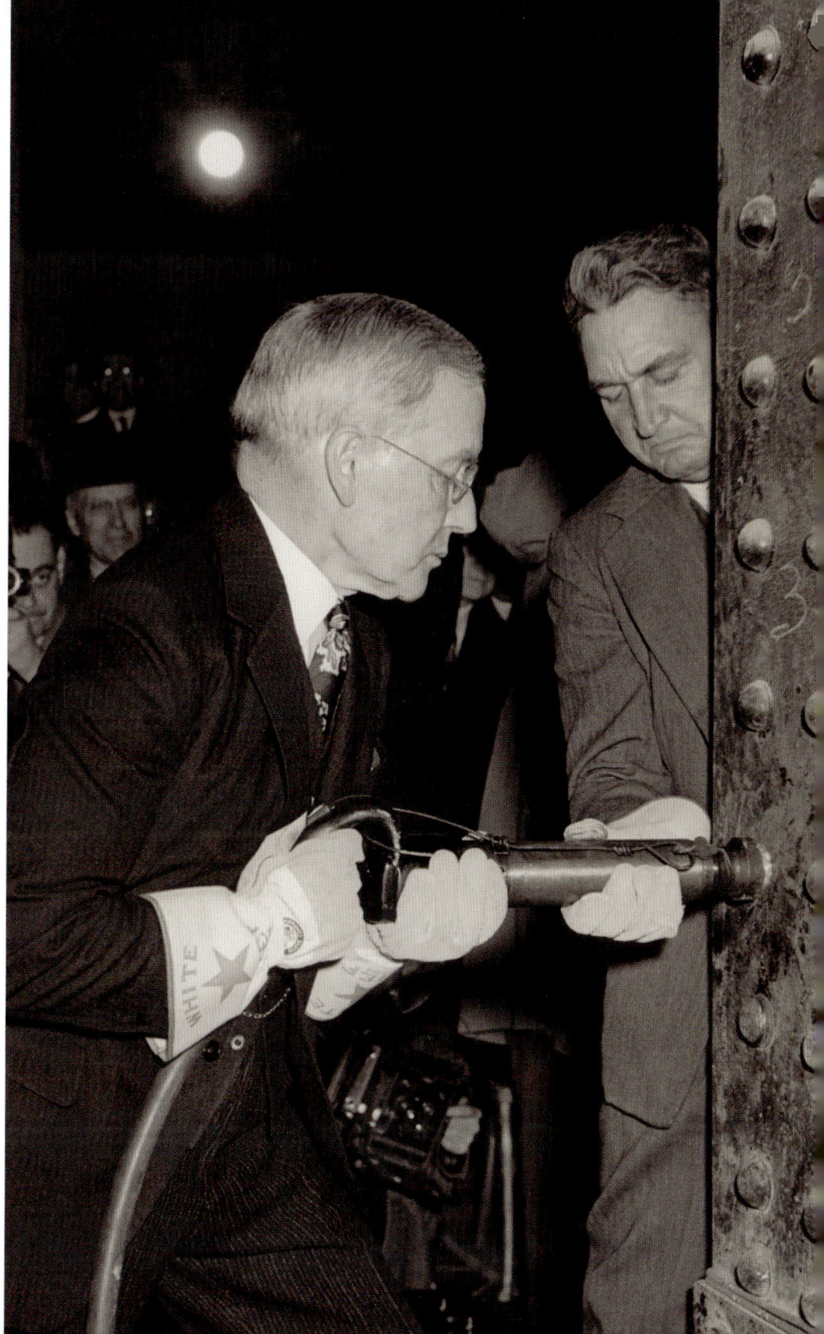

11.1 At a ceremony on Nov. 1, 1939, John D. Rockefeller Jr. drives the final, ceremonial, silver rivet of Rockefeller Center's last original building, 1230 Avenue of the Americas. "He has always had a suppressed desire to drive a rivet," said his son Nelson. "The Center is now complete — the Center really begins." (Rockefeller Group photo)

If I worked hard enough, could I solve long unanswered questions, like—who were the men? What were their names? Where did they come from? How did they get jobs in the middle of the Great Depression? Was I arrogant to think I could find answers when so many had only guesses?

When I did arrive at a place where stories are preserved, like the Iroquois Indian Museum, I expected to find a treasure trove of information. I naively referenced my decade at the Metropolitan Museum, with its warehouses of material and legion of curators, supported by a multibillion-dollar endowment and unquestioned cultural authority. Instead, I found a few devoted people working with few objects and little funding to fight a history of erasure. The dearth of information reinforced my realization that there are many people still struggling for a place in America.

Naively, I thought that, as a nation, we had progressed toward a unified and more equal society. I hoped to write that these eleven men—an amalgam of immigrants and native people working side by side—helped lay the groundwork for a more inclusive society. In my perfect narrative, those Slovaks, Irish, Germans, Nova Scotians, and Native Americans working shoulder to shoulder to build the city of the future were also building the society of the future.

Research is replete with the unexpected. When Covid struck, and face-to-face interviews became impossible for a time, I relied on the phone and the internet. This changed the nature of my research. I was unable to go to meetings, libraries, and union halls. I couldn't read facial expressions or body language. Conversations are deeper in person, and pauses for reflection are more meaningful. I scribbled furiously while listening to people on the phone search their memories. I couldn't easily prompt them. It was remote and isolating. Reams of notes piled up. Frustrated, I spent hours scrolling online collections, looking for clues. When something turned up like the photo "Breakfast Break," I was elated, certain there was more out there if I just kept digging.

It was an arduous task because I was ninety years late.

I cursed the 1930s publicity department, which hadn't bothered to identify the men, and the photographers, who also made a botch of recording names. But I was also thankful for the documents and photos preserved in an archive created by the Rockefeller Group—even if their custodians had been more concerned about the facade than the nuts and bolts.

The Last Rivet by Merle Crowell is a slim book published to commemorate the completion of Rockefeller Center in 1939. Of the hundreds of men who drove more than ten million rivets into the steel skeleton of Rockefeller Center, the book names exactly one: John Davison Rockefeller Jr.

NOTES

*1 — They Were Better Off
Than Most*

1. The stock market crash of October 1929 unfolded across several days that began with a large sell-off on "Black Thursday," October 24, and reached its most devastating plummet on "Black Tuesday," October 29. Economists still debate how the crash related to the decade of economic depression that followed.
2. Michael Breheny interview, July 29, 2015.

*2 — The Genesis of
Rockefeller Center*

1. Weisman, *The Architectural Significance of Rockefeller Center*, 8.
2. The "Old" Metropolitan Opera House was among the first structures to be considered by the New York City Landmarks Preservation Commission for landmark status in 1965. The opera house was destroyed with the Commission's consent in 1967 and replaced by a new opera house at Lincoln Center.
3. Balfour, *Rockefeller Center: Architecture as Theater*, 16.4. "Billions Lost in Wall Street

Panic," *New York Daily News*, Oct. 25, 1929, 16.
5. Karp, *The Center: A History and Guide*, 16.
6. Balfour, *Rockefeller Center: Architecture as Theater*, 12.
7. Okrent, *Great Fortune*, 198.
8. Balfour, *Rockefeller Center: Architecture as Theater*, 12.9. "John D. Rockefeller, Jr., 1874–1960," Rockefeller Archive Center, rock-arch.org/resources/about-the-rockefellers/john-d-rockefeller-jr/.
10. Letter, Heydt to John D. Rockefeller Jr., Aug. 19, 1929.
11. Letter, Heydt to Junior, Aug. 15, 1929.
12. Okrent, *Great Fortune*, 248.
13. Hellman, "The Man Behind Prometheus—I," 35.14. Newhouse, *Wallace K. Harrison, Architect*, 28.
15. Nelson Rockefeller introduced us in 1978. Afterward, Rockefeller said wryly that Harrison considered himself "the creator of the Center."
16. Balfour, *Rockefeller Center: Architecture as Theater*, 29.
17. Christy, *The Story of Rockefeller Center*, 48.
18. Okrent, *Great Fortune*, 109.
19. *RCA Minutes*, Dec. 6, 1929.
20. Weisman, *The Architectural Significance of Rockefeller

Center*, 46.
21. Weisman, *The Architectural Significance of Rockefeller Center*, 47.
22. Weisman, *The Architectural Significance of Rockefeller Center*, 47–48.
23. Weisman, *The Architectural Significance of Rockefeller Center*, 48.
24. Kilham, *Raymond Hood Architect*, 185.
25. Okrent, *Great Fortune*, 183.
26. Mumford, "Sky Line: Mr. Rockefeller's Center," 29.
27. Post's father was the Gilded Age architect Bruce Price (1845–1903).28. Post, "Radio City 'Ugliness,'" *New York Herald Tribune*, March 26, 1931.
29. Goldberger, "Rockefeller Center at 50," *New York Times*, June 17, 1982.
30. Okrent, *Great Fortune*.
31. Kilham, *Raymond Hood Architect*, 158.
32. Trotta, *Fighting for Air*, 47.
33. Safire, "On Closing Hurley's Bar," *New York Times*, Oct. 16, 1975, 39.
34. Steve Elling email, Aug. 9, 2012.
35. Robert Walsh interview, May 12, 2022.
36. McClain, *Red Iron*, 158.
37. Fosdick, *John D. Rockefeller, Jr.: A Portrait*, 266.

38. Balfour, *Rockefeller Center: Architecture as Theater*, 19.
39. Balfour, *Rockefeller Center: Architecture as Theater*, 19.
40. *Taylorville Breeze*, March 20, 1931, 1.
41. "Radio City Steel Enough to Build Twelve Warships," *Youngstown Vindicator*, March 20, 1931.
42. Bean, Arthur J. "Prosperity Sign Posts," *Boston Post*, March 22, 1931.
43. The number of stories of the R.C.A. Building has always been something of a debate, even within Rockefeller Center. The building's certificate of occupancy counts seventy stories, which includes the "pent houses." (Weisman, *The Architectural Significance of Rockefeller Center*, 118.)
44. Lippmann, "Today and Tomorrow," *New York Herald Tribune*, Dec. 30, 1932.
45. Rockefeller Center, Inc., *The Story of Rockefeller Center: From Facts to Fine Arts*, 22.
46. Okrent, *Great Fortune*, 157.
47. Unsigned memo, Rockefeller Center Archive, June 14, 1936.
48. Weisman, *The Architectural Significance of Rockefeller Center*, 115.
49. RCA press release 337, Dec. 17, 1933.

50. RCA press release 337, Dec. 17, 1933.

3 — Making the Image

1. "Pickets to Haunt J.D. Rockefeller, Jr." *New York Times*, April 29, 1914, 5.
2. Fosdick, *John D. Rockefeller Jr.: A Portrait*, 153. (See also Chernow, *Titan*, and Okrent, *Great Fortune*.)
3. Mackenzie's political career in Canada's Liberal Party led him to the prime minister's office in 1921.
4. Collier and Horowitz, *The Rockefellers*, 130.
5. Chernow, *Titan*.
6. Sinclair, *The Brass Check*, 311.
7. "Joins in Fete," *Circleville Herald*, Oct. 22, 1929, 2.
8. McNamee et al., "Light's Golden Jubilee," NBC Radio Broadcast, Oct. 21, 1929.
9. Erdman, "Edward Bernays and the 'Golden Jubilee of Light'" *Theatre Annual*, 1996, 49–64.
10. *History of the Personnel System*, 454–56.
11. Crowell, "John M. Siddall," *The Youth's Companion*, 1926, 878.
12. "John M. Siddall, Doomed, Worked On," *New York Times*, July 17, 1923, 1.
13. For more, see Pendergast, *Creating the Modern Man*. Pendergast explores how the changes at *The American* and other magazines reflected, and propelled, a transformation in American values and perceptions of masculinity from the Victorian era to the twentieth century.
14. *Vanity Fair*, Sept. 1926, 67.
15. Reilly, "Editors You Want to Know," *The Author and Journalist*, Oct. 1929.
16. "Crowells Have Largest Magazine Audience," *Springfield News-Sun*, Nov. 1937, 5.
17. Fosdick, *John D. Rockefeller Jr.: A Portrait*, 259.
18. RCA press release 50, April 27, 1932.
19. "Roxy's Name May Be Transported to Radio City," *Variety*, Oct. 27, 1931, 7.
20. RCA press release 1, July 25, 1931.
21. RCA press release 4, Aug. 22, 1931.
22. RCA press release 77, Aug. 10, 1932.
23. Smith, *On His Own Terms*, 117.
24. Morris, *Those Rockefeller Brothers*, 66.
25. "Cowboys of the Sky" advertisement, *Los Angeles Times*, May 8, 1924.
26. Ayn Rand worked as a script reader on *Skyscraper*. DeMille rejected her proposed rewrite, and some accounts credit the rejection as inspiration for her own skyscraper melodrama, *The Fountainhead*. Other accounts chalk the story up to Rand's habit of self-invention. See Scott Eyman, *Empire of Dreams: The Epic Life of Cecil B. DeMille*.
27. RCA press release 72, July 20, 1932.
28. "Workmen Top Off Tallest Building in Rockefeller Center," *New York Sun*, Sept. 27, 1932.
29. Ebbets, *Body of Evidence*, 22.
30. Tami Ebbets interview, 2021.
31. Bill Leftwich Jr. interview, 2021.
32. Bill Leftwich Jr. interview, 2021.
33. Newspictures, Inc. and Acme-Newspictures were separate New York photo agencies.
34. No evidence suggests the radio was connected to power. It was likely a silent prop.

4 — Men at the Crossroads

1. Hailey, "John D. Rockefeller Jr.'s Creed," *New York Times*, July 17, 1962, 17.
2. Rockefeller Jr., "We believe . . ." *Rockefeller Center Magazine*, Dec. 1939, 30–31.
3. Chernow, *Titan*, xix–xxii.
4. "Themes for Decorative Work," Rockefeller Center Archive, May 1932.
5. Alexander, as quoted in Bleecker, *The Politics of Architecture*, 33.
6. Balfour, *Rockefeller Center: Architecture as Theater*, 138.
7. Okrent, *Great Fortune*, 183.
8. Bleecker, *The Politics of Architecture*, 334.
9. George Vincent had been president of the Rockefeller Foundation since 1917.
10. Letter from John D. Rockefeller Jr. to Arthur Woods, May 5, 1932.
11. Buxton, "Imagining Rockefeller Center."
12. Christy, *The Story of Rockefeller Center*.
13. Roussel, *The Art of Rockefeller Center*, 12.
14. Crowell, "New Frontiers."
15. Buxton, "Imagining Rockefeller Center."
16. Alexander et al., *Millard Sheets*.
17. Crowell, "New Frontiers."
18. Okrent, *Great Fortune*, 218.
19. Roussel, *The Art of Rockefeller Center*.
20. "The Largest Mural Painting Ever Done," *Los Angeles Times*, Apr. 24, 1930, 30.
21. EverGreene Architectural Arts, "Empire State Building Ceiling Murals."
22. Roussel, *The Art of Rockefeller Center*, 230.
23. Greek mythology, the "Titanomachy," the Titans' war against the Olympians, was a generational battle for supremacy over the universe.

The younger Olympians, led by Zeus, vanquished and punished the elder Titans.

24. RCA press release 82, Aug. 28, 1932.

25. Letter, Hood to John D. Rockefeller Jr., Oct. 7, 1932, quoted in Balfour, 150.

26. Balfour, *Rockefeller Center: Architecture as Theater*, 151.

27. Letter, Nelson Rockefeller to Clifford Wright, Sept. 23, 1932.

28. Letter, John D. Rockefeller Jr. to Raymond Hood, Oct. 12, 1932.

29. "Oral History Interview with Lucienne Bloch," Aug. 11, 1964.

30. Keyes, "Destroyed by Rockefellers, Mural Trespassed," National Public Radio Weekend Edition, March 9, 2014.

31. Rivera, "I, who had become inured to storms, only painted on with greater speed," from *My Art, My Life: An Autobiography*.

32. Letter, Nelson Rockefeller to Rivera, May 4, 1933.

33. Letter, Rivera to Nelson Rockefeller, May 6, 1933.

34. Some accounts put Robertson at the head of the phalanx in the R.C.A. lobby; others have Rivera summoned to Robertson's office for his final check and marching orders.

35. Okrent, *Great Fortune*, 319.

36. A crucial metal framework, designed to leave space between the original wall so that the mural could be removed if required, had been omitted.

5 — *"All We Got Is Hard Luck"*

1. Manoff, *Chris Thorsten, New York City*, 1938.

2. McClain, *Red Iron*, 158.

3. McClain, *Red Iron*, 158.

4. "Fire Sweeps Tower of New Skyscraper," *New York Times*, June 30, 1931, 27.

5. *Graziano v. Post & McCord, Inc.*, 1934.

6. Manoff, *International Bridge*, 1939.

7. McClain, *Red Iron*, 166.

8. McClain, *Red Iron*, 167.

9. Rasenberger, *High Steel*, 142.

10. Bill Sears interview, 2016.

11. Manoff, *Chris Thorsten, New York City*, 1938.

12. RCA press release 105, Jan. 3, 1933.

13. US Bureau of Labor Statistics, *Census of Fatal Occupational Injuries Summary*, 2020.

14. The clearance at mean high water is 228 feet. The RMS *Queen Mary 2*, built to Verrazzano-Narrows Bridge specifications, was designed with a shorter funnel to pass under the bridge with almost thirteen feet to spare at high tide. "This Ship Is So Big, The Verrazano Cringes," *New York Times*, April 18, 2004, section 1, 28.

15. Robert Walsh interview, Oct. 13, 2022.

16. Robert Walsh interview, May 2022.

17. Bill Sears interview, 2016.

18. McClain, *Red Iron*, 50.

19. *Graziano v. Post & McCord, Inc.*, 1934.

20. Details of the rivet gang's operation from "Riveters," *Rockefeller Center Weekly*, Jan. 10, 1935, 12.

21. "History," Ironworkers Local 361.

22. Simmons, "'The Continuous Clatter,'" *Journal of the Society for Industrial Archeology* 23, no. 2, 1997, 4–20.

23. *Graziano v. Post & McCord, Inc.*, 1934.

24. RCA press release 102, Dec. 8, 1932.

25. Bob Walsh interview, Sept. 17, 2021.

26. US Census Bureau.

27. McClain, *Red Iron*.

6 — *"Lunch on a Beam" and Variations*

1. The album contained this note, by Carolyn Holton & Associates, Inc., about the firm's preservation work: "Clippings removed from back sheets were attached, washed, deacidified with calcium bicarbonate, supported with lens tissue on one or both sides, attached to acid-free Permalife back sheets. Calligraphy titles. Sheets encapsulated in mylar album leaves. Post binder constructed of sized lines."

2. Bill Sears interview, 2016.

3. Jenish, D'Arcy. "Raising Steel," *Legion Magazine*, Nov. 11, 2009.

4. Jenish, D'Arcy. "Raising Steel," *Legion Magazine*, Nov. 11, 2009.

5. Bill Sears interview, 2016.

6. Rasenberger, *High Steel*.

7. Ken Johnson interview, July 2022.

8. The ironworker was George Urbanneck. See chapter 7: "Into the Archives."

9. *Berliner Illustrirte Zeitung* 42, 1932.

10. Galofré-Vilà et al., "Austerity and the Rise of the Nazi Party," *Journal of Economic History*, 2021, 81–113.

11. Evidence suggests the sequence of the photographs was: First "Lunch on a Beam," then "Breakfast Break," and then "Hats Off."

12. The photograph was first distributed under the title "Hats Doffed," later "Hats Tipped," and finally "Hats Off."

13. Clint Saunders interview, 2021.
14. "Booming Out: Mohawk Ironworkers Build New York," traveling exhibition, 2002.
15. Hine used the Press Graflex camera, produced between 1907 and 1925. He used 5 by 7-inch glass-plate negatives or 4 by 5-inch sheet film.
16. Edom, *Photojournalism: Principles and Practices*, 217.
17. Rosenblum, *America & Lewis Hine*, 17.

7 — Into the Archive

1. I count among my professional successes excising, in 2012, the extra "Center" from the Rockefeller Center Archive.
2. Though the photographer is not identified, Leftwich Jr. suggested the photo is typical of his father's style.
3. Bob Donner email, Jan. 28, 2025.
4. Various captions identify ironworker Kovan as "James," "Joe," "George," and "J."
5. Periodicals of the era were rich with allusion to the classics. *Buffalo Times* published "Lunch on a Beam" on Sept. 30, 1932, under the headline "A Cup of Coffee, a Sandwich and Space," echoing Omar Khayyam's "A jug of wine, a loaf of bread, and thou."
6. Clint Saunders email, Nov. 2020.

7. Letter, George Urbanneck Jr., Nov. 14, 2004.
8. McClain, *Red Iron*, 163.
9. Manoff, *International Bridge*, 1939.

8 — Ironworkers Came from Many Places

1. Details of Berntsen's early life come from Miller, *Steel Girders and Steeplechases*.
2. Berntsen wasn't the first worker Rivera had drafted. His assistant Lucienne Bloch recounted how a handsome young nightwatchman was selected to model the central figure. "When the workmen filed in the next day, and as usual gazed at the latest section of Diego's work, they began to snicker and joke. And a joke it is! They told us, 'That man is Hugh Curry Jr., the grandnephew of John F. Curry of Tammany Hall!!! He has a cushion job.' Diego had us scrape him off at once. Then he chose a great-looking guy right from the workers there and the Union permitted him to pose." Bloch, "On Location with Diego Rivera," *Art in America*, Feb. 1986.
3. McClain, *Red Iron*, 164.
4. McClain, *Red Iron*, 27, 44, 46, 180.
5. "History," Ironworkers Local 361.
6. *Time, 100 Photographs*, 12.

7. Aside from George Lucas's use of the name, Skywalker has its origins in American heritage. An 1856 collection of Native American folklore, *The Myth of Hiawatha*, records an Ottawa story called "Onaiazo, the Sky-Walker."
8. Hill, *Skywalkers*, preface.
9. "History," Ironworkers Local 361.
10. Busatta, "The Native American Entrepreneur," 2005.
11. Reaghan Tarbell interview, May 2022.
12. Reaghan Tarbell interview, July 30, 2017.
13. Reaghan Tarbell interview, 2020.
14. Reaghan Tarbell interview, May 2022.
15. Amanda Diabo interview, 2019.
16. Lynn Beauvais interview, May 30, 2022.
17. Lisa Beauvais interview, May 30, 2022.
18. Lynn Beauvais interview, May 30, 2022.
19. Lynn Beauvais interview, Nov. 28, 2023.
20. Chris Jocks interview, Nov. 30, 2023.
21. Bill Sears interview, 2017.
22. Bill Sears interview, 2017.
23. "Booming Out: Mohawk Ironworkers Build New York," traveling exhibition, 2002.
24. Devorah Romanek interview, Nov. 10, 2022.

25. Hanigovská, "The Grandson of the Slovak from the Legendary Photo" *Dobré Noviny*, May 26, 2021.
26. Šimkovičová, "Popovič Lunching Atop a Skyscraper," Radio Slovak International, Nov. 27, 2017.
27. Hanigovská, "The Grandson of the Slovak from the Legendary Photo," *Dobré Noviny*, May 26, 2021.
28. Vondráček, "How Gusti from Slovakia Fraudulently Rewrote History," info.cz, Jan. 4, 2022.
29. "Rudy, a Sailor who Loved the Sea, Couldn't Wait to Get to the Beach," Ironworkers Local 40, *Topping Out*, Vol. 1, no. 6, Feb. 1962.
30. Christina Silla interview, 2019.
31. "Lunchtime on the World's Tallest Building," Rockefeller Group photo 123.
32. Darlene Pearson Castillo email, Nov. 28, 2015.
33. Scott Jandovitz email, Dec. 18, 2003.
34. The family changed the spelling from Brehenny to Breheny.
35. Gene Breheny interview, July 29, 2015.
36. Gene Breheny email, Nov. 19, 2015.
37. Ruth Pedersen Smith interview, 2016.
38. David Pedersen interview,

Jan. 20, 2016.

39. Brian McClain email, Nov. 6, 2021.

40. McClain, *Red Iron*, 163.

41. Clint Saunders email, Nov. 2021.

42. Harold Flynn interview, Jan. 2020.

43. Avondale is located on the Avalon Peninsula in the province of Newfoundland and Labrador.

44. Carol Lake interview, Jan. 2020.

45. "Lunchtime on the World's Tallest Building," Rockefeller Group photo 123.

46. Lawrence Hawco interview, Oct. 14, 2024.

47. Carol Lake interview, Jan. 2020.

48. Quinn Newton emails, Dec. 2023.

49. 1911 Canadian Census; 1914 Marriage Certificate; 1930 US Census.

50. Estefania Chueca interview and emails, June 29, 2022.

51. Pikizu. "Y Dani nos dijo: El de la foto es mi padre." *Editorial Harresi*, Dec. 8, 2024.

52. Pikizu. "Un Balmasedano En Nueva York." *Editorial Harresi*, April 7, 2024.

53. *Time, 100 Photographs*, 2016.

54. *Time*. "Lunch Atop a Skyscraper: The Story Behind the 1932 Photo," in *100 Photographs: TIME* (video), Nov. 28, 2016.

55. Paul Moakley interview, 2020.

56. Rasenberger, *High Steel*, 208.

57. Rasenberger interview, 2020.

58. Éamonn Ó Cualáin interview, Nov. 8, 2024.

59. Seán Ó Cualáin interview, 2020, and email, Nov. 23, 2021.

60. Cross, "Up in the Air," *New York Post*, Oct. 26, 2003.

61. Clint Saunders email, Oct. 2021.

62. Clint Saunders email, Oct. 2021.

9 — Not Pictured

1. Letter, Joe Brown to Willard S. Richardson, May 7, 1931.

2. Reid, *Negro Membership in American Labor Unions*, 1930.

3. Reid, *Negro Membership in American Labor Unions*, 1930.

4. "Asks Green to Outline A.F. of L. Negro Policy," *New York Times*, Jan. 16, 1925.

5. *United States v. Local No. 8, Int. Ass'n of Bridge, S., O. & RI*, 1970.

6. Haber, *Industrial Relations in the Building Industry*, 1930.

7. "M'Namara, Bomber, Dies in San Quentin," *New York Times*, March 9, 1941, 38.

8. Simonds, *The Boulder Canyon Project*, 1995.

9. "Quiet Negro Pioneer Breaks In on High Steel Construction Job: First of Race in Union Here Says Co-Workers Have 'All Treated Me Fair'," *New York Times*, Sept. 3, 1964.

10. "R.C.A. Building Facts," Rockefeller Center Archive.

11. Rothafel was already a celebrity entertainer when he was recruited to head Radio City Music Hall. When the high-kicking dance troupe from his former theater, the Roxy, followed him to Radio City, the Roxyettes became the Rockettes.

12. RCA press release 12, "'Radio City' Envoys off to Europe," Sept. 22, 1931.

13. Weisman, *The Architectural Significance of Rockefeller Center*, 124.

14. Trotter, *Workers on Arrival*.

15. The Dunbar Apartments in Harlem, funded by Rockefeller and completed in 1928, were the first large cooperative housing complex developed for Black New Yorkers.

16. Letter, Charles O. Heydt to Joe Brown, Aug. 12, 1932.

17. Letter, Brown to Heydt, Aug. 19, 1932.

18. Letter, Brown to Heydt, Aug. 19, 1932.

19. Goldberg, "Black Education and Rockefeller Philanthropy," *REsource*, Oct. 28, 2022.

20. Rockefeller Center, Inc.— Murals—José Sert; 1933–1943; Rockefeller Archive Center.

BIBLIOGRAPHY

Alexander, Hartley Burr, Arthur Milliear, and Merle Armitage. *Millard Sheets*. Los Angeles: Dalzell Hatfield Galleries, 1935.

Balfour, Alan. *Rockefeller Center: Architecture as Theater*. New York: McGraw Hill, 1978.

Bean, Arthur J. "Prosperity Sign Posts." *Boston Post*, March 22, 1931.

Berliner Illustrirte Zeitung 42, 1932.

Bleecker, Samuel E. *The Politics of Architecture: A Perspective on Nelson A. Rockefeller*. New York: The Rutledge Press, 1981.

Bloch, Lucienne. "On Location with Diego Rivera." *Art in America*, February 1986.

Brisbane, Arthur. "Today." *Taylorville Breeze*, March 20, 1931.

Busatta, Sandra. "The Native American Entrepreneur and the Mohawk Civil War." America Haus Munich, 26th American Indian Workshop, April 11–13, 2005.

Buxton, William J. "Imagining Rockefeller Center." *Issue Lab*. Rockefeller Archive Center, 2009.

Census of Fatal Occupational Injuries Summary. US Bureau of Labor Statistics, 2020.

Chernow, Ron. *Titan: The Life of John D. Rockefeller, Sr.* Knopf Doubleday Publishing Group, 2007.

Christy, Francis. *The Story of Rockefeller Center*. New York: Rockefeller Center, Inc., 1950.

Collier, Peter and David Horowitz. *The Rockefellers*. New York: Holt, Reinhart and Winston, 1976.

Cross, Ashley. "Up in the Air." *New York Post*, October 26, 2003.

Crowell, Merle. "New Frontiers." Rockefeller Center, Inc. (RCI); Rockefeller Archive Center. Undated.

Crowell, Merle. "What Was He Like at Work? 2: John M. Siddall." *The Youth's Companion* 99, no. 50 (1925).

Ebbets, Tami. "Body of Evidence in support of Charles C. Ebbets's authorship of the iconic photograph 'Men on a Beam' Rockefeller Center, 1932." Unpublished article.

Editors of *Time. 100 Photographs: The Most Influential Images of All Time. Time*, 2016.

Edom, Clifton C. *Photojournalism: Principles and Practices*. Dubuque, Iowa: W.C. Brown Co., 1980.

Erdman, Andrew. "Edward Bernays and the 'Golden Jubilee of Light': Culture, Performance, Publicity." *Theatre Annual* 49 (1996).

EverGreene Architectural Arts. "Empire State Building Ceiling Murals." October 1, 2024. evergreene.com/projects/empire-state-building-ceiling/.

Eyman, Scott. *Empire of Dreams: The Epic Life of Cecil B. DeMille*. New York: Simon & Schuster, 2013.

Fosdick, Raymond B. *John D. Rockefeller, Jr. A Portrait*. New York: Harper & Brothers, 1956.

Galofré-Vilà, Gregori, et al. "Austerity and the Rise of the Nazi Party." *Journal of Economic History* 81, no. 1 (2021): 81–113.

George Gustav Heye Center, National Museum of the American Indian. "Booming Out: Mohawk Ironworkers Build New York." Traveling exhibition, 2002.

Goldberg, Barry. "Black Education and Rockefeller Philanthropy from the Jim Crow South to the Civil Rights Era" *REsource*. Rockefeller Archive Center, October 28, 2022.

Goldberger, Paul. "Rockefeller Center at 50: A Model of Urban Design." *New York Times*, June 17, 1982.

Graziano v. Post & McCord, Inc., 241 A.D. 682 (1934).

Haber, William. *Industrial Relations in the Building Industry*. Harvard University Press, 1930.

Hailey, Foster. "John D. Rockefeller Jr.'s Creed Is Unveiled in a Memorial Here." *New York Times*, July 17, 1962.

Hanigovská, Monika. "The Grandson of the Slovak from the Legendary Photo: We Found Out by Chance During a Trip to Vienna That Grandpa Is Famous." *Dobré Noviny*, May 26, 2021.

Hellman, Geoffrey. "Profiles: The Man Behind Prometheus—I." *New Yorker*, November 14, 1936.

Hill, Richard. *Skywalkers: A History of Indian Ironworkers*. Woodland Indian Cultural Educational Centre, 1987.

History of the Personnel System: Developed by the Committee on Classification of Personnel in the Army, C.C.P. 399. Washington, DC, 1919.

Ironworkers Local 40. "Rudy, a Sailor who Loved the Sea, Couldn't Wait to Get to the Beach." *Topping Out* 1, no. 6. (February 1962).

Ironworkers Local 361. "History." https://ironworkers361.com/history/.

Jenish, D'Arcy. "Raising Steel." *Legion Magazine*, November 11, 2009.

Karp, Walter. *The Center: A History and Guide to Rockefeller Center*. Distributed by Van Nostrand Reinhold Co., 1982.

Keyes, Allison. "Destroyed By Rockefellers, Mural Trespassed on Political Vision." *NPR Weekend Edition*, National Public Radio, March 9, 2014.

Kilham Jr., Walter H. *Raymond Hood Architect*. New York: Architectural Book Publishing Co., 1973.

Manoff, Arnold. *Chris Thorsten, New York City*. New York, 1938. Manuscript/Mixed Material. Retrieved from the Library of Congress, www.loc.gov/item/wpalh001462/.

Manoff, Arnold. *International Bridge, New York City*. New York, 1939. Manuscript/Mixed Material. Retrieved from the Library of Congress, www.loc.gov/item/wpalh001463/.

McClain, Harold. *Red Iron*. Unpublished manuscript.

McNamee, Graham et al. "Light's Golden Jubilee." NBC Radio Broadcast, October 21, 1929. Accessed via The Internet Archive.

Miller, Clifford. *Steel Girders and Steeplechases: The Life and Art of Bernhard H. Berntsen*. Lone Oak Press, 2001.

Morris, Joe Alex. *Those Rockefeller Brothers: An Informal Biography of Five Extraordinary Young Men*. Harper, 1953.

Mumford, Lewis. "Sky Line: Mr. Rockefeller's Center." *New Yorker*, December 23, 1933.

Newhouse, Victoria. *Wallace K. Harrison, Architect*. New York: Rizzoli, 1989.

Okrent, Daniel. *Great Fortune: The Epic of Rockefeller Center*. Penguin Publishing Group, 2004.

Pendergast, Tom. *Creating the Modern Man: American Magazines and Consumer Culture, 1900–1950*. University of Missouri Press, 2000.

Rasenberger, Jim. *High Steel: The Daring Men Who Built the World's Greatest Skyline*. New York: HarperCollins, 2004.

Reid, Ira De A. *Negro Membership in American Labor Unions*. New York: The National Urban League, 1930.

Reilly, Rosa Strider. "Editors You Want to Know." *The Author and Journalist* 14, no. 10 (October 1929).

Rivera, Diego, and Gladys March. *My Art, My Life: An Autobiography*. New York: Citadel Press, 1960. Republished by Dover Publications, Inc., 1991.

Rockefeller, John D. Jr. "We believe . . ." *Rockefeller Center Magazine* 2, no. 12 (December 1939).

Rockefeller Archive Center. "John D. Rockefeller, Jr., 1874–1960," n.d. https://rockarch.org/resources/about-the-rockefellers/john-d-rockefeller-jr/.

Rockefeller Center Archive. "R.C.A. Building Facts." Undated.

Rockefeller Center Archive. "Themes for Decorative Work." May 1932.

Rockefeller Center, Inc., *The Story of Rockefeller Center: From Facts to Fine Arts*. 1987.

Rockefeller Center, Inc., "Murals – Jose Sert, 1933–1943." Rockefeller Archive Center.

Rosenblum, Walter et al. *America & Lewis Hine: Photographs 1904–1940*. New York: Aperture, Inc., 1977.

Roussel, Christine. *The Art of Rockefeller Center*. New York: Norton, 2006.

Safire, William. "On Closing Hurley's Bar." *New York Times*, October 16, 1975.

Schoolcraft, Henry Rowe. *The Myth of Hiawatha, and Other Oral Legends, Mythologic and Allegoric, of the North American Indians*. J. B. Lippincott & Company, 1856.

Šimkovičová, Martina. "Popovič Lunching Atop a Skyscraper." Radio Slovak International, November 27, 2017.

Simmons, David A. "'The Continuous Clatter': Practical Field Riveting." *Journal of the Society for Industrial Archeology* 23, no. 2 (1997): 4–20. www.jstor.org/stable/40968400. Accessed June 6, 2022.

Simonds, William Joe. *The Boulder Canyon Project: Hoover Dam*. Bureau of Reclamation History Program, 1995.

Sinclair, Upton. *The Brass Check: A Study of American Journalism*. Published by the author, 1920.

Smith, Richard Norton. *On His Own Terms: A Life of Nelson Rockefeller*. New York: Random House, 2014.

Trotta, Liz. *Fighting for Air: In the Trenches with Television News*. University of Missouri Press, 1991.

Trotter, Joe William. *Workers on Arrival: Black Labor in the Making of America*. University of California Press, 2019.

United States v. LOCAL NO. 8, INT. ASS'N OF BRIDGE, S., O. & RI, 315 F. Supp. 1202 (Western District of Washington US Federal District Court, 1970).

Vondráček, Pavel. "How Gusti from Slovakia Fraudulently Rewrote History," *info.cz*. January 4, 2022.

Weisman, Winston. *The Architectural Significance of Rockefeller Center*. Ph.D. dissertation. The Ohio State University, 1942.

Periodicals

Archives of American Art, Smithsonian Institution. "Oral History Interview with Lucienne Bloch." August 11, 1964.

Circleville Herald (Ohio). "Joins in Fete." October 22, 1929.

Editorial Harresi. "Un Balmasedano En Nueva York" by Pikizu. April 7, 2024.

Editorial Harresi. "Y Dani nos dijo: El de la foto es mi padre" by Pikizu. December 8, 2024.

Los Angeles Times. "Cowboys of the Sky," advertisement, May 8, 1924.

Los Angeles Times. "The Largest Mural Painting Ever Done." April 24, 1930.

New York Daily News. "Billions Lost in Wall Street Panic." October 25, 1929.

New York Herald Tribune. "Radio City 'Ugliness'" by Emily Post. March 26, 1931.

New York Herald Tribune. "Today and Tomorrow" by Walter Lippman. December 30, 1932.

New York Sun. "Workmen Top Off Tallest Building in Rockefeller Center." September 27, 1932.

New York Times. "Pickets to Haunt J.D. Rockefeller, Jr." April 29, 1914.

New York Times. "John M. Siddall, Doomed, Worked On." July 17, 1923.

New York Times. "Asks Green to Outline A.F. of L. Negro Policy." January 16, 1925.

New York Times. "Fire Sweeps Tower of New Skyscraper." June 30, 1931.

New York Times. "McNamara, Bomber, Dies in San Quentin." March 9, 1941.

New York Times. "Quiet Negro Pioneer Breaks In on High Steel Construction Job: First of Race in Union Here Says Co-Workers Have 'All Treated Me Fair'" by Gay Talese. September 3, 1964.

New York Times. "This Ship Is So Big, The Verrazano Cringes" by James Barron. April 18, 2004.

Rockefeller Center Weekly. "Riveters." January 10, 1935.

Springfield News-Sun (Springfield, Ohio). "Crowells Have Largest Magazine Audience." November 1937.

Time. "Lunch Atop a Skyscraper: The Story Behind the 1932 Photo." Video. Nov. 28, 2016.

Vanity Fair. Vol 27, Issue 1. September 1926.

Variety. "Roxy's Name May Be Transported to Radio City— Ivy Lee In on Publicity." October 27, 1931.

Youngstown Vindicator. "Radio City Steel Enough to Build Twelve Warships." March 20, 1931.

Letters

Letter, Charles O. Heydt to John D. Rockefeller Jr. August 15, 1929. Rockefeller Archive Center.

Letter, Charles O. Heydt to John D. Rockefeller Jr. August 19, 1929. Rockefeller Archive Center.

Letter, Joe Brown to Willard S. Richardson. May 7, 1931. Rockefeller Center Archive.

Letter, Charles O. Heydt to Joe Brown. August 12, 1932. Rockefeller Center Archive.

Letter, Joe Brown to Charles O. Heydt. August 19, 1932. Rockefeller Center Archive.

Letter, Nelson Rockefeller to Diego Rivera. May 4, 1933. Artist file: Rivera. Rockefeller Center Archive.

Letter, John D. Rockefeller Jr. to Arthur Woods. May 5, 1932. Rockefeller Archive Center.

Letter, Nelson Rockefeller to Clifford Wright. September 23, 1932. Rockefeller Archive Center.

Letter, George Urbanneck Jr. to Rockefeller Center Archive, November 14, 2004. Rockefeller Center Archive.

Press Releases

Press release 4. Rockefeller Center Archive. August 22, 1931.

Press release 12. "'Radio City' Envoys off to Europe." Rockefeller Center Archive. September 22, 1931.

Press release 50. Rockefeller Center Archive. April 27, 1932.

Press release 72. Rockefeller Center Archive. July 20, 1932.

Press release 77. Rockefeller Center Archive. August 10, 1932.

Press release 82. Rockefeller Center Archive. August 28, 1932.

Press release 102. Rockefeller Center Archive. December 8, 1932.

Press release 105. Rockefeller Center Archive. January 3, 1933.

Press release 337. Rockefeller Center Archive. December 17, 1933.

Christine Roussel is the archivist of the Rockefeller Center Archive. For many years, she worked at the Metropolitan Museum of Art as director of the reproductions studio and special assistant to the director. Upon leaving the museum, she advised Vice President Nelson Rockefeller on his art collection and founded the monument-restoration company C. Roussel Inc. Her books include *The Art of Rockefeller Center* and *A Guide to the Art of Rockefeller Center*. She lives in New York City.